The Brigade:
A History

Its Organization and Employment in the US Army

John J. McGrath

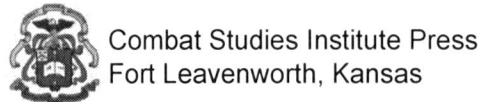
Combat Studies Institute Press
Fort Leavenworth, Kansas

Published by Books Express Publishing
Copyright © Books Express, 2012
ISBN 978-1-78039-673-6

Books Express publications are available from all good retail and online booksellers. For
publishing proposals and direct ordering please contact us at: info@books-express.com

John McGrath

Boston native John McGrath has worked for the US Army in one capacity or another since 1978. A retired Army Reserve officer, Mr. McGrath served in infantry, field artillery and logistics units, both on active duty and as a reservist. Before coming to work at the Combat Studies Institute, he worked for 4 years at the US Army Center of Military History in Washington, DC, as a historian and archivist. Prior to that, Mr. McGrath worked fulltime for the US Army Reserve in Massachusetts for over 15 years, both as an active duty reservist and as a civilian military technician. He also served as a mobilized reservist in 1991 in Saudi Arabia with the 22d Support Command during Operation DESERT STORM as the command historian and in 1992 at the US Army Center of Military History as a researcher/writer. Mr. McGrath is a graduate of Boston College and holds an MA in history from the University of Massachusetts at Boston. He is the author of numerous articles and military history publications and the book *Theater Logistics in the Gulf War*, published by the Army Materiel Command in 1994. Aside from a general interest in things military and historical, his areas of particular interest include modern military operations, the German army in World War II, August 1914, and the Union Army in the Civil War. He also has a keen interest in ancient history, historical linguistics, the city of Boston, and baseball.

FOREWORD

This is a timely work as virtually all current Army transformation initiatives focus in on the maneuver brigade as the key element in future reorganization. New initiatives centered on the Unit of Action (UA) concept utilize variations of the basic brigade design currently fielded in the Army for revamped organizations using projected or recently fielded technology. A study illustrating from where the brigade has come to assume such an important role in Army planning and organization is, therefore, very appropriate. This volume in the Combat Studies Institute Special Studies series additionally fills a void in the historiography of the US Army, illustrating the brigade level of command, both in organizational structure and in battlefield employment.

The brigade has been a key component of American Armies since the establishment of the first brigade of colonial militia volunteers under the command of George Washington in 1758. Brigades were key combined arms organizations in the Continental Army and were basic components of both the Confederate and Union forces in the Civil War, and have been the backbone of Army forces in Vietnam, the winning of the Cold War, DESERT STORM, and in the recent War in Iraq.

The force structure of the US Army has always been a target of tinkering and major readjustments since the short-lived experimentation with the Legion of the United States in 1792-1996. Nowhere is this more apparent than at the level of the brigade. For most of the history of the Army, the brigade was a temporary wartime expedient organization and the first level of command led by a general officer. In the 20th century, it was the basic tactical unit of trench warfare in World War I. However, in World War II it basically disappeared, though organizations such as the armored division's combat command, retained the spirit, if not the name of the organization. Following the late 1950s Pentomic period, the brigade returned in 1963 in a flexible structure very similar to that of the former combat command. As a mission-oriented, task-organized, combat organization, the maneuver brigade has survived the many vicissitudes of Army reorganization.

This work provides an organizational history of the maneuver brigade and case studies of its employment throughout the various wars. Apart from the text, the appendices at the end of the work provide a ready reference to all brigade organizations used in the Army since 1917 and the history of the brigade colors.

Lawyn C. Edwards
COL, AV
Director, Combat Studies

ACKNOWLEDGEMENTS

This work was a work of love. A love for the US Army, its combat organizations, and its organizational and operational history. While I, as the author, take credit for any factual errors, a cast of many are responsible for the completion of this work and its associated research.

Among my colleagues at the Combat Studies Institute (CSI), Kendall Gott stands out as the individual who bird-dogged me onto this project on my very first day on the job. Ken has provided valuable insight and advise on a daily basis ever since. We share a certain insight despite my being an Eastern suburbanite, while he is a Midwestern small-town guy. Robin Kern, the CSI editor and layout wizard, responsible for this project provided its final look and had to deal with the over 66 tables, maps, pictures, and graphics that bring the story of the US Army brigade to life. Robin is now ready to edit for Marvel Comics! Other section colleagues who provided valuable insights, comments, and support include historians Dr. Lawrence Yates and Dr. Gary Bjorge, and editors Phil Davis and Patricia Whitten. Other colleagues in the various sections of CSI were very helpful but are too numerous to cite here.

I must also acknowledge the support of three key members of the CSI team, Lieutenant Colonel Kevin Farrell, former Chief Research and Publication Team; Dr. William G. Robertson, TRADOC Chief of Staff Rides and CAC Command Historian; and Colonel Lawyn C. Edwards, Director Combat Studies, Command and General Staff College, Fort Leavenworth, Kansas. These three not only hired me from halfway across the country, but were instrumental in supporting this project from start to finish. Lieutenant Colonel Farrell nurtured the project, but was transferred before seeing the end product. Dr. Robertson was the thought behind the project in the first place. With the development of the brigade-based Army in 2003-2004, his insight seemed very timely indeed. Colonel Edwards provided valuable insights to the project in various stages of development and provided continual key support which has ensured its completion.

Research and publication assistance was done by many. Among those who stand out include Ed Burgess, Director of the Combined Arms Research Library (CARL), who assisted me either directly or through his subordinates, in the use of his excellent facility, and Alice King, Copyright Clerk, who processed all the copyrights necessary for this work. Retired Colonel Greg Fontenot and his team of researchers assisted greatly by providing materials from his *On Point* project. Off-site support was plentiful. Of those that stand out are many of my former colleagues at the US Army Center of Military History (CMH) at Fort McNair in Washington, DC., including the Chief of Military History, Brigadier General John S. Brown, and the members of the CMH's Force Structure and Unit History Branch, who will probably cringe at some of the unofficial usages of unit organization found in this work. Ned Bedessem and Steve Everett of that branch were particularly helpful on various segments of unit organization research. Finally the guys who invented the Google website need to be mentioned. Without them much research leads on the Internet would be impossible to locate.

Further acknowledgements need to go to several former colleagues: my mentor as an Army historian, Dr. Robert K. Wright, Jr., who is now enjoying a well-deserved retirement in Florida and my oldest friend and colleague in Army history, Dr. Mark Sherry, both of whom advised me and read portions of the work. A third person at CMH who needs mentioning is editor and fellow Bostonian Joanne Brignolo, who has provided constant professional support and advice on this project. My three children faraway in Massachusetts, Andrew, William, and Barbara, will finally know what exactly their father does in Kansas with this publication.

Hopefully this work, in some small way, will help support the soldiers and officers of the US Army worldwide who, as this work goes to press, are still vigorously pursuing victory in the Global War on Terrorism which began on 11 September 2001. This work is dedicated to these soldiers and to all those who will not be coming home.

John J. McGrath
Fort Leavenworth, Kansas
15 June 2004

TABLE OF CONTENTS

FIGURES

TABLES

MAP SYMBOLS KEY

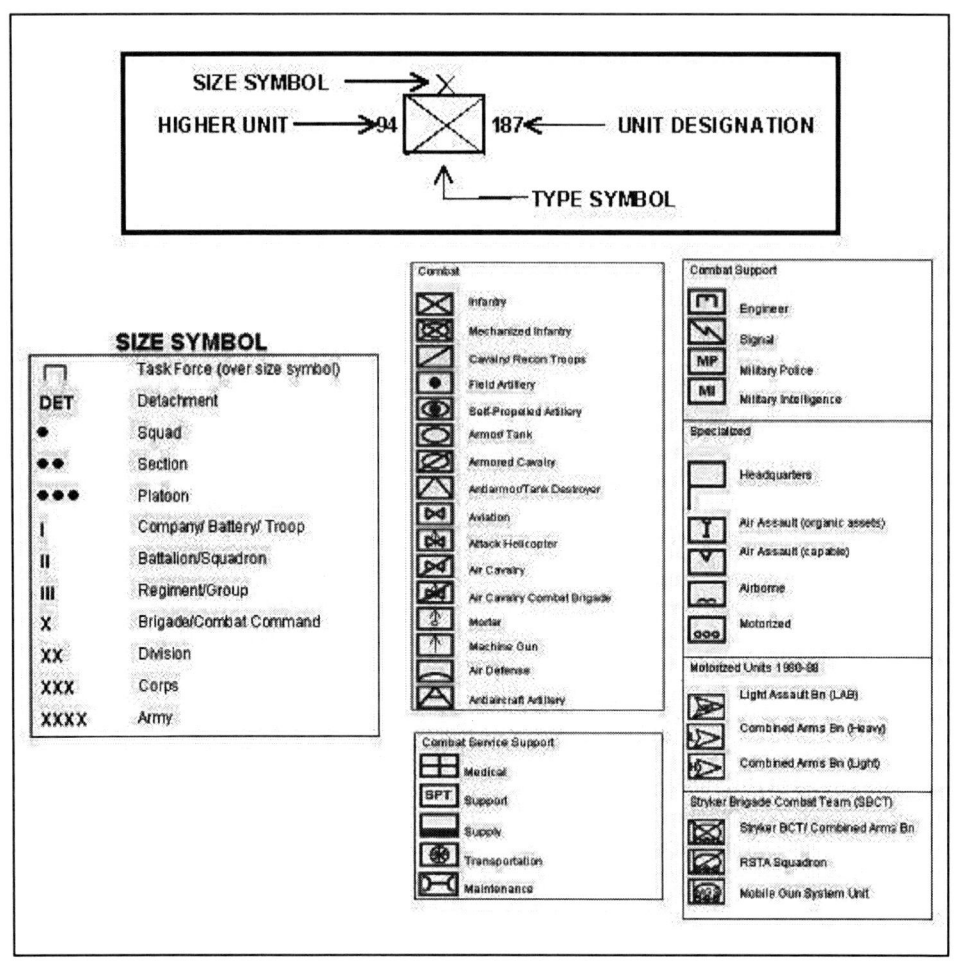

INTRODUCTION

On 12 August 1999, US Army Chief of Staff, General Eric K. Shinseki, announced the commencement of Army force development initiatives designed to transform the Army into a force that would be "more responsive, lethal, agile, versatile, survivable, and sustainable to meet the needs of the nation."[1] Shinseki proposed to effect this transformation by creating two, later six, "technology-enhanced, fast-deployable, and lethal brigades."[2] These brigades, initially coined as Interim Brigade Combat Teams (IBCT), because they would be outfitted with available equipment on an interim basis, showed a subtle shift in US Army force development focus from the division to the brigade. This shift was also reflected in the force structure of the US Army in 2003. In the mid-1990s, the Army, reduced in size after the end of the Cold War, fielded the 10-Division Force structure. After redesignations and unit shifts, there were no nondivisional maneuver brigades in this force structure.[3] However, this lack of separate brigades was deceptive. A closer examination revealed that, while the Army fielded 10 divisional headquarters in 1996, only three divisions had all three of their numbered maneuver brigades collocated with the division headquarters. Two installations, Fort Lewis, Washington, and Fort Riley, Kansas, fielded brigades from different divisions without a division headquarters located on post. In both cases, the respective division headquarters were located overseas. The 1st Brigade, 6th Infantry Division (ID), located in Alaska, was earmarked to act as the third brigade of the two-brigade 10th Mountain Division, Fort Drum, New York. Each divisional brigade located away from its parent division, included the standardized slice of divisional combat support and combat service support units. This complete package, referred to as a brigade combat team (BCT), is essentially a unit able to operate separately from the division, much like the separate brigades were organizationally designed to so operate.[4]

The years after 1996 saw further shifts toward a brigade force when two new separate brigade headquarters were activated, the 172d Infantry in Alaska replacing the 1st Brigade of the previously inactivated 6th Infantry Division, and the 173d Airborne in Italy, and the reactivation of two division headquarters, the 7th Infantry and 24th Infantry (Mechanized), that had no troops of their own, but were responsible for three separate Army National Guard (ARNG) brigades, none of which were located near their respective division headquarters at Fort Carson, Colorado, and Fort Riley. Shinseki's emphasis on the brigade as the level of command to field his new combat teams, in this context, is, therefore, not very surprising.

The brigade, either as part of a division or as an independent or separate entity, is the major tactical headquarters controlling battalions in maneuver combat arms; armor and infantry. The modern maneuver brigade is a flexible organization designed to be task organized for specific combat missions.[5] When operating independently, the brigade is usually the lowest level of command led by a general officer. With organic elements, in the case of the separate brigade, or with attached elements from the division, in the case of the divisional brigade, it is the smallest combined arms unit in the US Amy capable of independent operations.

In current US Army organizational structure, the divisional brigade is the only unit below corps level without a fixed organization.[6] While companies, battalions, and divisions all have organic assigned units, except for a small reconnaissance troop and a headquarters company, the brigade has no assigned troops. Instead it is given a mix of combat battalions from those assigned to the division to complete specific missions. Additionally, in recent years brigades have also received slices of combat support and combat service support units from the division, as well as combat battalions. In this case, the brigade is usually referred to as a BCT.

This work studies the evolution, organizational structure, and employment of the maneuver brigade. In passing, it will also discuss other army brigades, such as those consisting of field artillery, aviation, and engineer units, not usually used in a maneuver role.

As an organization, the brigade has a long history in the US Army going back to the very first organization, the Continental Army. General George Washington established the first brigades on 22 July 1775.[7] The term *brigade* itself first entered the English language, like most military terms, from the French language. The word is first attested in the 15th century as a term for a larger military unit than the squadron or regiment and was first adopted when English armies began to consist of formations larger than a single regiment. The term's origin is found in two French roots, which together meant roughly "those who fight."[8] It is totally fitting that the brigade be designated as "those who fight" because the organization has, throughout most of its existence in the US Army, been a purely tactical, or combat, organization, and currently is where the combat power of the US Army is found.

At the start of the 21st century, debates on the future of warfare and the transformation of the US Army to adjust to this future environment are ongoing. The brigade is usually at the center of transformational organizational structures, either as a replacement for the division as the basic building block for projecting combat power or as the Unit of Action (UA), a flexible organization designed to fight and win battles. While debates and final decisions on this structure are ongoing as of the publication of this work, it is vital that planners understand the history and theory behind the evolution of the US Army maneuver brigade.

This special study outlines and illuminates the history and evolution of the brigade as an organization in the US Army, from the earliest days to the current era. The work follows both the organizational structure and how it was actually employed on the battlefield.

NOTES

1.   Gerry J. Gilmore, "Army TO Develop Future Force, says Shinseki." *Army Link News*, 13 October 1999, <http://www.dtic/mil/armylink/news/Oct1999/a19991013shinvis.html>.

2.   Ibid.

3.   The 10-division force consisted of the 1st, 2d, 3d, 4th, and 25th Infantry Divisions, 10th Mountain Division, 1st Armored Division, 1st Cavalry Division, and the 82d and 101st Airborne Divisions. "Army Announces Divisions to Remain in the 10-Division Force." DOD New Release Reference Number 067-95, 10 February 1995, <http://www.defenselink.mil/news/Feb1995/b021095_bt067-95.html>.

4.   A typical brigade slice included a direct support field artillery battalion, a combat engineer battalion, an air defense artillery battery, a forward support battalion, which was already structured to support the specific brigade, and military intelligence and signal companies.

5.   Aviation brigades, now organic to all types of army divisions, are considered to be maneuver brigades as well. Often such brigades are referred to informally, and incorrectly, as the 4th Brigade of their respective division. This will be discussed in detail later in this work.

6.   See the Conclusion for a discussion of the future projected brigade organization (Unit of Action or UA) in which the brigade would have a modular organization with assets currently found at division assigned directly to the brigade.

7.   John B. Wilson, *Maneuver and Firepower: The Evolution of Divisions and Separate Brigades.* Army Lineage Series (Washington, DC: Government Printing Office, 1998), 3.

8.   The roots are the French verb *brigare*, meaning "to brawl" or "fight," which was in turn from the late Latin word *briga*, which meant "strife" or "contention," and the suffix *–ade*, which was a French adaptation of a suffix found in various other Romance languages, such as Provençal, which came from a form of the Latin past participle. In French the suffix came to have the meaning "the body concerned in an action or process." Therefore, the original meaning of the term brigade would be something like "the body concerned with brawling or fighting." J.A. Simpson and E.S.C. Weiner, *The Oxford English Dictionary*, 2d ed. (Oxford: Clarendon Press, 1989) Vol. I, 148 and Vol. II, 548.

Chapter 1

BRIGADES IN THE CONTINENTAL ARMY

Colonial Background

The brigade as a military organization came about starting in the 15th century when the British army and militia developed a unit to control more than one infantry regiment or cavalry squadron.[1] Brigades were traditionally only temporary units organized when necessary, a status generally maintained in the US armed forces until early in the 20th century. In the New World, where the militia was the only permanent military organization, the separate colonies established different, but similar, systems of organization. In New England, for example, each town had its own militia company or trainband. Above the town level, each county had a militia regiment to control the companies assembled in each of the towns in the county. At the colonial level, there was one general officer who commanded all the colony's militia. This officer was usually called the sergeant major-general, later shortened to major-general.[2] In some colonies, the rank was lieutenant-general or even simply general. In Virginia, the colony was divided into districts. A major-general headed each district, with a major-general of the colony as the ranking officer.[3]

The colonies had little use for brigades. Rarely did a single whole regiment, let alone several, assemble to conduct military operations. When larger expeditions were necessary, special volunteer or militia companies were raised by quota from each town within the colony. On the rare occasions these forces proved to be larger than regimental strength, brigades were not organized. For example, the large expedition against the Narragansett Indians in 1675 consisted of troops from the colonies of Massachusetts Bay, Plymouth, and Connecticut. The forces were organized into specially raised contingents from each colony, each styled a regiment, but the force as a whole was considered an expedition, not a brigade. The command was referred to simply as "the army." The Army's commander, Josiah Winslow, aside from being the governor of Plymouth colony, was also given the title of general and commander in chief of the expedition. No other officer in the expedition ranked higher than major.[4]

The situation was the same 70 years later when the colonials launched their largest expedition ever, the successful attack and seizure of the French fortress of Louisbourg, on Cape Breton Island, off Nova Scotia. Despite the raising of a relatively large army, the senior officer, General William Pepperrell, and his assistant, Major-General Roger Wolcott, were the only generals in an army of over 10 regiments.[5] The force was not subdivided into brigades, though specific missions were often delegated to regimental commanders or to Wolcott.[6]

Brigades and brigadier-generals did not appear in North America until the Seven Years War, when the British government first sent large continents of regular troops to secure its American colonies. The British regular army of the colonial era, like the militia, had no permanent organization larger than regiment, and created brigades only when necessary to control a force of more than three regiments. Pitched battles in Europe had, however, given the British experience with larger units. Brigadier-generals first appear on the continent along with the brigades they commanded.[7] In the British service, brigadier-general was an appointment given to a senior colonel or lieutenant colonel, who was in command of more than one regiment;

in other words, a brigade. The appointment lasted only as long as the officer was in command. Accordingly, the rank of major-general was the first substantive, or permanent, rank of general officer in the British army. The British force sent to take Louisbourg in 1757 consisted of 13 regular regiments. Most regiments had only a single battalion, though two had two battalions. These regiments were divided into three brigades of five battalions each, with each brigade headed by an officer appointed as brigadier-general (for service in North America only). The Army commander designated the brigades by their intended employment as left, centre, and right.[8]

The first brigade of colonial troops also appeared in 1758 in Brigadier-General John Forbes' expedition against Fort Duquesne, Pennsylvania. In his final approach to the French fortress, Forbes organized his command into three brigades. Colonel George Washington, 1st Virginia, commanded one of these, consisting of the 1st and 2d Virginia Regiments. The two Virginia regiments had been raised as special militia units specifically for participating in the Forbes expedition. After the successful seizure of Fort Duquesne, the brigade was discontinued, Washington resigned his commission and the 2d Virginia was disbanded.[9]

Washington and the Brigade

In April and June 1775, after the initial skirmishes between the New England militia and British regular forces near Boston, Massachusetts, and Fort Ticonderoga, New York, the Continental Congress determined to field a force representing all the colonies and run according to its wishes. By unanimous vote, Congress appointed Washington, the only colonial with experience as a brigade commander as general and commander in chief of this new Continental Army on 15 June 1775.

When Washington was appointed, militia forces from the New England colonies had the British garrison in Boston under siege. These forces, organized by state in a very decentralized manner, had just fought the Battle of Bunker Hill. Washington arrived and immediately set out to create order and organization, using his experience of units above regiment level as a guide. He promptly created the first brigades and divisions in US Army history. Initially, the number of brigades was determined by the number of brigadier-generals appointed. An extra brigade was created and temporarily commanded by its senior colonel, as Congress needed to fill one brigadier-general vacancy. Congress had created the first brigadier-generals and major-generals on 22 June. Unlike in the British service, the rank of brigadier-general was a substantive one in the new Army.[10]

Both brigades and divisions were at the start administrative and geographical subdivisions of the Army. Washington divided the siege lines around Boston into divisional and brigade sectors. One division was in reserve. Each of the three divisions consisted of two brigades. Brigades consisted of either six or seven regiments. Only Massachusetts fielded enough total regiments to have brigades formed entirely of troops just from that colony. Regiments from Connecticut, Rhode Island, and New Hampshire, along with small contingents from Virginia and Maryland, were brigaded with Massachusetts units. Brigade strengths fluctuated, with an average size of 2,600 soldiers.[11] Using this organization, Washington successfully completed the siege, which climaxed in the British evacuation of Boston on 17 March 1776.

Following British practice, brigades were initially considered purely tactical units of a temporary nature and accordingly assigned virtually no staff. Originally the regiment was to be the Army's basic administrative and tactical unit. But Washington soon realized the nature of the command precluded this. Troops were recruited from up to 13 different colonies for short-term enlistments. Regiments from different states often had different organizational structures and sizes. Therefore, regiments were often fleeting organizations whose strengths went up and down, mostly down, as time passed. As a result, in practice, the brigade soon replaced the regiment as the Army's basic tactical and administrative unit. Brigades were commanded by brigadier-generals appointed directly by Congress, whose candidacies were usually based on Washington's recommendation. In contrast, regimental colonels were usually appointed by their respective colonial governors or legislatures. By shuffling regiments, Washington and other independent commanders could keep brigade sizes equal, rather than allowing them to wither away, as did some regiments. This allowed for a certain standard flexibility to maneuver forces both on the battlefield and at the operational level. The brigade even assumed a certain standard size. The brigades at Boston had been relatively large. Later in the war at Trenton, New Jersey, in December 1776 and Monmouth, New Jersey, in June 1778, they averaged 1,400 soldiers, while at Yorktown, Virginia, in 1781, brigade strength averaged around 1,000.[12]

The increased importance of the brigade as the unit of stability in the Army led to a gradual increase in its staff and its role in logistics and administration. Initially the brigade staff consisted of a sole junior officer, the brigade major. The brigade major was a position inherited from British tradition. Like the British brigadier-general, the rank was originally only by position being filled by a regimental captain. In the American service, the position became substantive, with the officer being given the rank of major on the staff. The brigade major was a combination adjutant, (i.e., administrator) and aide de camp (messenger and general assistant) to the brigade commander. By 1779, two officers supplanted the brigade major with the titles of aide de camp and brigade inspector. At the same time, two more staff officers were added to the brigade headquarters: a brigade quartermaster, to manage the brigade's supplies, and a brigade conductor of military stores, to manage the brigade's ammunition supply and maintain its weapons.[13]

After the evacuation of Boston, the war became decidedly more mobile. In the New York-New Jersey campaign of 1776, Washington had to be flexible enough to thwart incessant outflanking maneuvers, a favorite tactic of British commander General William Howe, while at the same time having his troops spread out far enough to respond to and assemble on any advancing enemy force. For this type of warfare, Washington depended on the brigade and his corps of brigadier-general brigade commanders as his essential elements. Washington did not command brigades directly, but used his major-generals to command divisions, which controlled the brigades directly. After Boston, most division commanders controlled three brigades, but this could be changed or adjusted based on circumstances. Washington's optimum brigade organization was for a brigade to control three regiments of 700 men each, with three brigades forming a division. Both brigades and divisions would be commanded by general officers and be capable of operating in conjunction with each other or separately. While obtaining the ideal strength and organizational structure was mostly out of his hands, Washington clearly was able to organize his army to fight together or separately. The brigade was the basic unit Washington used to accomplish this.[14]

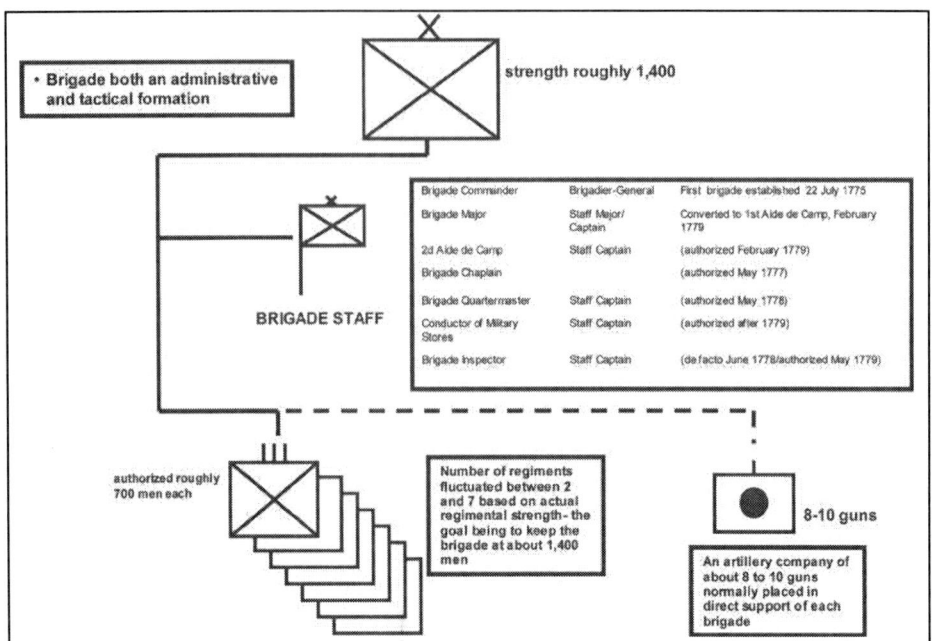

Figure 1. Continental Army Brigade, 1775-1783

Following the setbacks in New York and New Jersey in 1776, Washington decided to strike back at the strung out British forces in central Jersey. Accordingly, on 25 December 1776, he moved to use his whole army in one stroke to destroy the Hessian mercenary forces garrisoning Trenton and threaten the remaining British forces in New Jersey. Minus a diversionary force and a force designated to seal the Hessian route of retreat, Washington had at his direct disposal an attack group consisting of two divisions, each with three brigades, and a separate brigade acting as the advance guard. In a move of great innovation, he had Colonel Henry Knox's artillery distributed among the brigades to provide direct support, thus creating the first combined arms units in US Army history. With these forces, he crossed the Delaware River and advanced on Trenton from the north in two divisional columns, the left commanded by very capable Major-General Nathaniel Greene, the right by the experienced Major-General John Sullivan. Coordination between the columns worked perfectly so that both elements were in position and able to work in unison. The direct support of the artillery and the placement of brigades had the Hessians virtually surrounded before the battle even began. When they tried to attack one of Greene's brigades, commanded by Brigadier-General William Alexander, Lord Stirling, whose attached artillery was pouring fire onto their right flank, they were stopped by massed fire from one of Sullivan's brigades, commanded by Brigadier-General Hugh Mercer, firing into their left flank. After an abortive retreat in which their brigade commander was killed, the Hessians surrendered. The use of combined arms and the maneuvering of brigade-sized forces had won the first battlefield victory in US Army history. A week later, Washington repeated the performance at Princeton, New Jersey, where he outmaneuvered the British relief force. Once again Washington managed to mass his forces at one place by maneuvering and assembling brigades and artillery. The British rear guard was chewed up, resulting in their virtual evacuation of New Jersey for the winter.[15]

After Trenton, Washington formally organized his brigades as combined arms teams and perfected his operational concept for using them in both offensive and defensive operations. An artillery company of between eight and 10 guns was usually placed in direct support of each infantry brigade.[16] On the defensive, brigades were to be deployed within mutually supporting distance of each other. If one were attacked, it was to fix the attackers and then the other brigades in the division, followed by the closest divisions, would advance to mass on the attackers and hopefully double envelope and crush them. Even with this relatively simple doctrine and honed organizational structure, there were teething problems in executing it, especially against the professional soldiers of King George III. This was particularly evident at Brandywine, in September 1777. There Howe, advancing from Chesapeake to Philadelphia, planned to duplicate his flanking maneuver which had been so successful a year before at the Battle of Long Island. Intelligence failures, coupled with a poorly covered right flank, allowed the British to advance deep into the right rear of the American position before they were discovered. Flexibility of organization and Howe's penchant for battlefield pauses allowed Washington to reconfigure his command on the fly and meet Howe's force with seven small brigades under Sullivan, Alexander, and Major-General Adam Stephen. Amid furious fighting, the British overwhelmed the American line, forcing Washington to rush Greene's two brigades from his left flank by forced march 4 miles in 45 minutes to reinforce the position. While this maneuver worked, the force Howe left behind now attacked the weakened left, forcing the Americans to retreat to avoid being crushed between the two British forces.

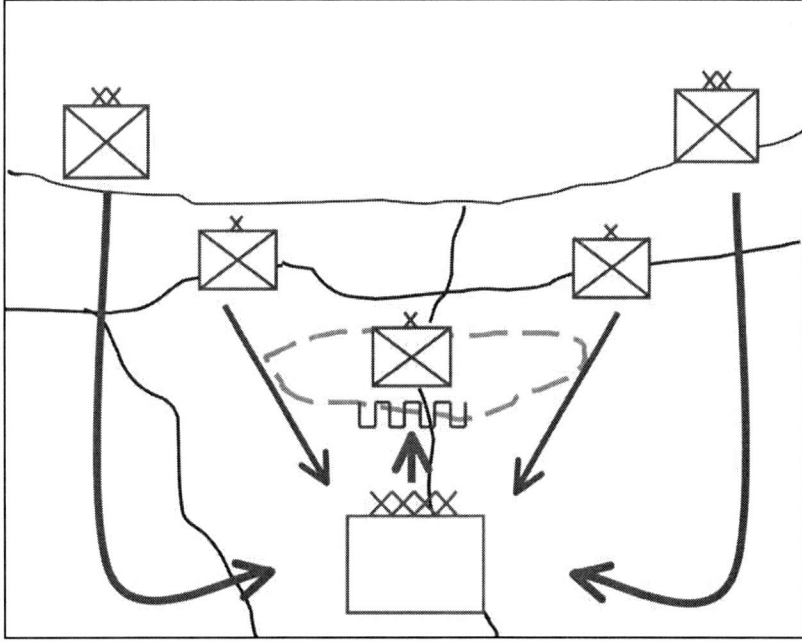

Figure 2. Washington's Defensive Concept for the Employment of the Brigade

Things worked much more effectively in 1780, when the British sortied out of their Manhattan defensive enclave twice near Springfield, New Jersey. Washington's defensive doctrine had reached its apex in the defensive lines covering the British garrison in New York after General Henry Clinton, Howe's replacement, retreated back there from Philadelphia in 1778. Washington encircled the city with brigades posted on high ground with clear observation, out of naval bombardment range and, to provide warning time, about a day's march from the nearest British outposts. Brigades were positioned to be able to easily support each other. Carefully constructed lateral communications allowed for the easy moving of large formations to threatened sectors. The brigade at the focus of the enemy attack was to fix the attackers in place. All other brigades and divisions were to fall in to mass against the attacking force and hopefully double envelope and crush it.[17]

The strength of the American defenses was not lost on Clinton, who chose to pursue campaigns in the southern states, far from Washington, rather than test them.[18] The two exceptions were the twin sorties conducted in June 1780 near Springfield. In both cases, the British forces were soundly beaten and forced to beat hasty retreats to positions where the Royal Navy's guns could protect them. The memory of Springfield so hung with British commander Clinton, that 13 months later when Washington left a skeleton force of 2,500 men behind to watch New York while he marched with the rest of the army to Yorktown, Clinton stayed on the defensive. He did not move to interfere with the American redeployment until it was too late to do anything about it.

Washington's concept was designed to work on the offense, as well as the defense. After Brandywine, the only offensive actions Washington was able to mount were at Germantown, Pennsylvania, in October 1777, and at Monmouth in June 1778. In both cases, the British prevailed after a hard fight, due to American mistakes, simple bad luck, and poor synchronization. At Germantown, Washington attempted to repeat his success at Trenton on a larger scale, with multiple columns massing against the British right flank. Despite ground fog, which limited visibility and the diversion of a brigade to frontally assault the Chew House, an impromptu fortress in the center of the British line, the attack was succeeding. Brigadier-General Anthony Wayne's two brigades were successfully pushing back the British left, when another American division, under Stephen mistakenly came up into Wayne's rear, rather than that of the British, and fired into the backs of their fellow countrymen. In the resulting confusion, the British counterattacked and Washington's right withdrew in confusion. Greene's division, moving to the left of Stephen to encircle the British, was now out on a limb. Greene retreated to avoid encirclement, effectively ending the battle.

The Battle of Monmouth was Washington's last open battle offensive action of the war. In June 1778, British commander in chief Clinton decided to consolidate his forces at New York. Accordingly, he evacuated Philadelphia and proceeded to march across New Jersey for a rendezvous with fleet transports to ferry the army across New York Bay at Sandy Hook.

Washington was determined to attack Clinton while he was in the open and not protected by the Royal Navy and the natural defenses of New York City. Accordingly, he followed Clinton looking for an opening to attack part of the British force. Clinton's large baggage train meant his army was strung out for miles in the New Jersey countryside.

Washington, having decided to mass against the British rear guard under Lieutenant General Charles Cornwallis, divided his army into two wings, the advanced wing, initially under Major-General Marie Joseph Paul Yves Roche Gilbert du Motier, the Marquis de Lafayette, then under Major-General Charles Lee, and the main body under himself. Lee's command, with seven brigades, was ordered to attack the rearguard before they reached the safety of high ground just south of Sandy Hook, less than a day's march away.

Lee, an ex-British officer, shared many of the same low opinions of American fighting qualities that his former peers did despite glaring evidence to the contrary. His belief in the low quality of his troops made him a timid field commander and a poor choice to head up a mission requiring daring and aggressiveness. But, aside from Washington, Lee was the senior officer in the Army and he insisted on the command after Washington had initially given it to the much more optimistic and energetic Lafayette.

When the army got within striking distance of Clinton's rear guard, Washington ordered Lee to attack the next day. Instead of developing a plan for this, Lee told his subordinates to be prepared to receive orders on the battlefield. The next day, 28 June 1778, Lee advanced on Cornwallis' force just north of Monmouth Court House. Despite outnumbering the strung-out British more than two to one, the lack of an overall plan, and Lee's attempts to move units on the cuff resulted in great confusion, piecemeal attacks, and then retreat when the British counterattacked. Washington arrived on the scene and personally rallied Lee's command, organizing them to delay the now reinforced British until the rest of the army could form a defensive line. This worked and the American forces, now on the defensive, beat back the British attack. The American organizational structure's flexibility allowed quick recovery even from poor leadership above the brigade and division level. Lee was subsequently court-martialed and cashiered.

Brigades and Brigadier-Generals

While Washington reserved the right to move regiments around between brigades as he saw fit, he realized it was more practical to stabilize organizations as much as possible.[19] The Army was recruited by state quota, meaning each state was required to recruit a certain number of regiments or smaller units from its population, and, whenever possible, brigades were made up of regiments from the same state. While in reports brigades were usually referred to by their commander's name, later in the war most brigades were designated by state. States with large contingents had several brigades numbered consecutively, for example, the 2d Massachusetts Brigade. Such unique formal brigade designations would not return again to the US Army until World War I.

The number of operational brigades in the Continental Army fluctuated based on the need to counter British activities. Fortunately for Washington, during most of the war the British maintained only one active area of operations at any given time. An exception to this was the summer of 1777, were two major-operations, Howe's advance on Philadelphia and Lieutenant-General John Burgoyne's advance from Canada south along the Hudson Valley. To counter these twin thrusts, the number of active Continental Army brigades was increased to over 22 in the spring of 1777. This number stayed relatively constant, as indicated in Figure 2, until the loss of five entire brigades with the surrender of Charleston, South Carolina, in May 1780. These brigades, consisting of most of the Continental Army contingents from Virginia, the Carolinas, and Georgia, were never replaced.[20] The total number of operational brigades remained between 10 and 15 for the rest of the war. After the victory at Yorktown, in late 1781, the Continental Army was mainly concerned with watching the British garrison in New York. With peace on the horizon, the Army was allowed to shrink as regiments were disbanded and returned home. The number of brigades, accordingly, also shrank throughout 1783 until the British finally evacuated the city, ending the need for the Army. Tied directly to the number of brigades was the number of brigadier-generals. Washington clearly saw this connection and thought it essential that brigade commanders be general officers.[21]

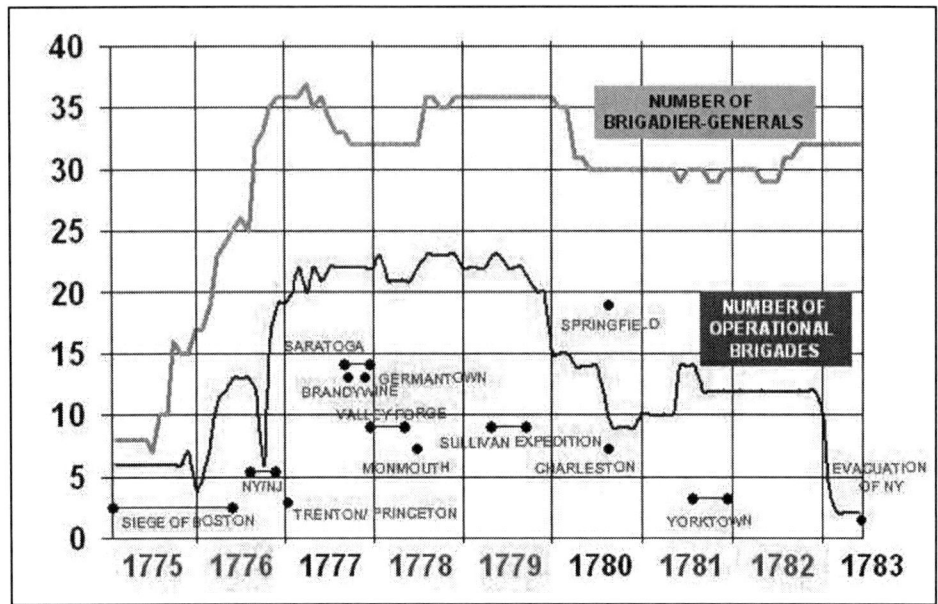

Figure 3. Number of Continental Army Brigades, 1775-1783

The Continental Army adopted the grade of brigadier-general from the British army. But, unlike the American use of the grade as a substantive rank, brigadier-general had developed in the British army as a positional grade much like the grade of commodore in the Royal Navy. In the Royal Navy, for most of its history, the rank of commodore was held by a senior captain who commanded more than just his own ship, in other words, a naval captain acting with the prerogatives of a flag officer, an admiral. The grade came with no additional pay, but the commodore was allowed to fly a flag, euphemistically referred to as a "broad pennant" from his own ship to indicate his position. Similarly, a British brigadier-general was a colonel or, more usually, a lieutenant-colonel, who commanded more than just his own regiment. As with commodore in the Royal Navy, the grade was temporary; only granted to the holder under specific conditions. In the British army, this often meant the grade was only active when the holder was serving in North America. The grade of brigadier-general, also called, almost interchangeably, brigadier, first appeared in the British army during the reign of King James II. A warrant of 1705 placed the grade directly below major-general, but the appointment was always considered temporary and not continuous. The British were ambiguous over whether

8

the holder was considered a general officer or a senior field grade officer. However, when the British adopted shoulder boards with rank insignia in 1880, the brigadier-general insignia included the crossed sword and baton worn by the other general grades. By uniform, in any event, a brigadier-general was considered the lowest grade of general. In 1920, the grade was abolished and two new substantive grades were created, that of colonel-commandant and colonel of the staff. In 1928, these two grades were merged into a new grade, brigadier, which still exists in the British army today. That this current grade of brigadier is considered the senior grade of field grade officer, rather than a general officer, is clearly indicated by its rank insignia, which is similar to a colonel's with an extra pip added.[22]

As with the Army as a whole, brigadier-generals were supposed to be tied to a quota based on the number of troops the respective state supplied. While the total number of brigadier-generals always exceeded the number of brigades by about 10 officers, the number in field command was often less. Some brigadiers were diverted to perform administrative duties. Others, with no retirement system in place, were still on the rolls though unfit for field duty. The number of brigadier-generals reached a high of 35 in 1778, and remained at or near this number for the rest of the war. Later in the war, Congress was stingy on promotion, only appointing new brigadiers to replace losses. As this also applied to major-generals as well, Wayne, promoted to brigadier-general in 1777, remained such for the rest of the war, despite his commanding a division at Brandywine, Germantown, and Monmouth. Because of seniority, Wayne often reverted back to brigade command long after he had shown his prowess at the higher echelon. Statistics for brigadier-generals during the war are as follows:

Table 1. Number of Brigadier-Generals, 1775-1783

Year	Appointed	Promoted	KIA	Other Deaths	Resigned	Total BGs EOY
1775	9	1	0	0	1	7
1776	26	6	0	1	1	25
1777	22	8	4	0	2	33
1778	0	0	0	0	2	31
1779	5	0	0	0	1	35
1780	1	2	0	2	2	30
1781	0	1	0	1	0	28
1782	1	2	0	0	0	27
1783	3	0	0	0	0	30
Total	67	20	4	4	9	

Washington employed brigades much as Napoleon Bonaparte would use the army corps 20 years later to revolutionize European warfare, "capable of independent action, but primarily ... to be an interchangeable part in the big picture."[23] He tried to keep brigades at equal sizes and use them as standardized units commanded by experienced general officers to execute what would otherwise be hopelessly complex battle drills. "In short, each brigade should be an epitome of the great whole, and move by similar springs, upon a smaller scale."[24] The US Army would not again see the brigade play such a prominent role in its operational doctrine for almost 200 years.

NOTES

1. J.A. Simpson and E.S.C. Weiner, *The Oxford English Dictionary*, 2d ed. (Oxford: Clarendon Press, 1989) Vol. I, 148 and Vol. II, 548.

2. Jack S. Radabaugh, "The Militia of Colonial Massachusetts," *Military Affairs* 18 (Spring 1954), 2-5.

3. Frederick S. Aldridge, *Organization and Administration of the Militia System of Colonial Virginia*, Ph.D. diss. American University 1964, 25, 62, 64.

4. George M. Bodge, *Brief History of King Philip's War* (Boston: Printed Privately, 1891), 182-83.

5. The 4,000-man force raised by Massachusetts Bay Governor William Shirley included eight regiments from Massachusetts, including the district of Maine, one each from Connecticut and New Hampshire, and three companies from Rhode Island. William Pepperrell, as a colonel, had been the militia commander for the portion of the Massachusetts militia from Maine. See the Canadian Parks Service Louisbourg website: <http://www.louisbourg.ca/fort/siege1745.htm>, accessed 1 May 2003.

6. Douglas E. Leach, *Arms for Empire: A Military History of the British Colonies in North America, 1607-1763* (New York: Macmillan, 1973), 236-41.

7. A more detailed discussion of the rank of brigadier-general, and the later rank of brigadier, can be found on pages 7 through 9. The grade in the British service was not substantive, being given to lieutenant-colonels and colonels only while they were in brigade command. (Ranks were hyphenated until after the Civil War.)

8. The officers were Lieutenant-Colonel James Wolfe, 20th Regiment of Foot; Lieutenant-Colonel Charles Lawrence, 40th Regiment of Foot and governor of Nova Scotia; and Colonel Edward Whitmore, 22d Regiment of Foot. <http://www.militaryheritage.com/40th.htm>, accessed 1 May 2003; J.W. Fortesque, *A History of the British Army*, Vol. II (London: MacMillan, 1910), 322. In the British service, the regiment was the administrative unit, the battalion the tactical unit. Some regiments had more than one battalion but they always fought separately, even when part of the same army. With a few unique exceptions, the US Army would also retain single battalion regiments until the 1890s.

9. Walter O'Meara, *Guns at the Forks* (Englewood Cliffs, NJ: Prentice-Hall, 1965), 208; Douglas Leach, *Arms for Empire*, 443; James P. Myers, Jr., "General Forbes Roads to War," *Military History* 18:5 (December 2001), 30-36. Forbes' substantive rank was colonel, 17th Regiment of Foot. The other two brigades were commanded by Lieutenant-Colonel Henry Bouquet, 1st Battalion, 60th Regiment of Foot, and Lieutenant Colonel Archibald Montgomery, 77th Highland Regiment of Foot.

10. Robert Wright, *The Continental Army*, 26, 29; *Journals of the Continental Congress, 1774-1789*, 34 Vols., Worthington C. Ford, ed. (Washington, DC: Government Printing Office (GPO), 1904-1937), Vol. 2, 93-94 (hereafter cited as *JCC*).

11. Brendan Morrissey, *Boston 1775: The Shot Heard Around the World*. Osprey Campaign Series Number 37. (Osprey: London, 1993), 75-76; John B. Wilson, *Maneuver and Firepower: The Evolution of Divisions and Separate Brigades*. Army Lineage Series (Washington, DC: GPO, 1998), 3.

12. Wright, 25; Wilson, 3.

13. Wilson, 4-5.

14. Wright, 98, 152; E-mail from Dr. Robert Wright to author, 14 January 2003; Wilson, 5-6.

15. Craig L. Symonds. *A Battlefield Atlas of the American Revolution* (Baltimore, MD: Nautical and Aviation Publishing, 1986), 30-33.

16. Wright, 97-98.

17. Wright e-mail, 14 January 2003; Wright, 152.

18. Ibid. Clinton's comments can be found in his *Headquarters Intelligence Books*, archived at the New York Public Library.

19. *The Writings of George Washington*, Vol. VII 1778-1779, Worthington C. Ford, ed. (New York: Putnam's Sons, 1890), 60-61.

20. Brigades, which surrendered on 12 May 1780 at Charleston, included the 1st Virginia Brigade; the North Carolina Brigade; Armstrong's Brigade, of North Carolina troops; the South Carolina Brigade; and the Georgia Brigade.

21. *JCC*, 102, 315.

22. Wright, 26; *The Writings of George Washington*, Vol. 2, 93-94, 97; Commander (RN) W.E. May, W.Y. Carman and John Tanner, *Badges and Insignia of the British Armed Service* (New York: St. Martin's Press, 1974), 141.

23. Wright e-mail, 14 January 2003; Wright, 152.

24. *The Writings of Washington*, 315.

Chapter 2

THE BRIGADE FROM 1783 TO 1861

From 1783 to the War of 1812

Throughout the 19th century, the largest permanent organization in the regular Army was the regiment, usually consisting of 10 subordinate companies. The brigade was a temporary organization only established to control forces of multiple regiments, usually more than three. Only during the War of 1812, the War with Mexico, the Civil War, and the War with Spain were brigades formally established. In all cases they were disestablished almost immediately upon the cessation of hostilities. Occasionally in the course of the Indian Wars or domestic operations, such as the Mormon Expedition, short-term brigades were sometimes formed in the field.

After the successful conclusion of the War for Independence, the United States' standing Army was allowed to shrink to microscopic proportions. The experience with the self-contained combined arms brigade was mostly forgotten except for a brief experiment on a larger scale, with the US Legion from 1792 to 1796. The Legion, which was the standing Army as a whole, was divided into four sub-Legions, each commanded by a brigadier-general and authorized 1,280 men. Subordinate organizations included two battalions of infantry, one battalion of riflemen, a company of artillery, and a troop of dragoons.[1] After 1796, the Army reverted back to a more conventional single branch regimental organization, with no established permanent units above the regiment.

In 1792, with a small standing Army and a militia tradition, Congress established a structure for larger units of the militia, for possible use in time of emergency, providing for, at least on paper, brigades and divisions. A militia infantry brigade's strength would be roughly 2,500 men, with four subordinate regiments, each divided into two battalions of four companies. The latter was a departure from Continental Army regiments, which generally had its eight companies organized as a single battalion. The brigade staff, unlike in the later stages of the Revolutionary War, was small, being limited to the brigade commander and his primary assistant, called either the brigade major or brigade inspector. This system was, however, not implemented in practice. No state raised any unit larger than a battalion for Federal service. Congress additionally added a third component of the Army, to go along with the Regular Army and the militia, with the calling up of volunteers. The volunteers, until requested, would not be part of any standing, organized force. With the extensive legal restrictions on the use of the militia, the use of volunteers would be the primary method by which the United States mobilized large forces for use in wartime in the 19th century.[2] An exception to this was that the War of 1812, fought in or near many of the largest states, saw the extensive use of militia.

The War of 1812

When the new war with Britain began in 1812, Congress immediately raised forces by expanding the size of the Regular Army, while calling for volunteers and mobilizing the militia. The largest new units raised were regiments. The use of higher units—brigades and divisions—was a lot more of an ad hoc nature than it had been in the Revolutionary War.

Usually a field commander would organize his army into brigades at the start of a campaign or whenever reorganization was necessary. Most army commanders controlled brigades directly, forces usually being somewhat smaller than during the Revolutionary War. Typically regiments would be assigned to brigades based on seniority, with brigades numbered according to the seniority of their commanders. Given the ad hoc nature of this organizational structure, brigades could vary in strength from 400 to 2,000 soldiers. As a general rule, regular regiments, militia regiments, and volunteer regiments were brigaded separately under commanders from their own components. While Army documents of the era stated that a brigade staff would only consist of the brigade major, public law provided for a staff similar to that employed in the later years of the Revolutionary War: five officers on the brigade staff (brigade inspector, brigade subinspector, brigade quartermaster, wagon master, chaplain) and, on the brigade commander's personal staff, the brigade major and several aides de camp.[3]

The rank of brigadier-general was, again, tied directly to the brigade. The peacetime Army of 1812 had three generals: one major-general, and two brigadier-generals. During the war, a total of 25 additional officers were appointed to the rank in the Regular Army. Several more served temporarily in the militia and volunteers. Given promotions, battlefield losses, and resignations, Congressional oversight kept the number of brigadiers at 12 for most of the war:

Table 2. Brigadier-Generals, War of 1812

Year	Appointed	Promoted	KIA	POW	Off Rolls	Total BGs EOY
1812	12	0	0	0	0	12
1813	9	4	1	3	0	13
1814	6	2	0	0	5	12
1815	0	0	0	0	0	12
Total	27	6	1	3	5	

In Congressional hearings on the number of generals to be appointed, the War Department formally gave its opinion that a brigade consisting of 2,000 men organized in two regiments was the appropriate command for a brigadier-general. With the Regular Army expanded to 37 infantry regiments for the war, seven prewar, 10 more in 1812, and 20 more in 1813, the number of brigadier-generals actually averaged about one for every three regiments, though several, instead of commanding brigades, commanded one of the nine geographic military districts.[4]

After the War of 1812, the Army was reduced to seven infantry regiments and three brigadier-generals. Despite the small size of the force, the Army Regulations of 1821, drawn up by Brigadier-General Winfield Scott, one of the most successful brigade commanders of the war, envisioned much larger organizations, including the army corps, to consist of two or more divisions. The brigade was to consist of two regiments and only the brigade major remained on the staff. Brigades would be numbered according to the seniority of their commanders, but, in official reports, they would be referred to by their commander's name. A further revision to the regulation in 1841 allowed for a bigger brigade staff, but stated that its size and composition would be based on the specific mission of the unit. All this organizational thought was purely notional as the Army did not operationally field units larger than a regiment.[5]

The Mexican War

At the start of the Mexican War in 1845, the Army had eight infantry regiments, two dragoon (mounted infantry) regiments, and four artillery regiments. In early 1846, a third mounted regiment, the US Mounted Rifles, was added. In 1847, eight additional infantry regiments, a rifle regiment, and a third dragoon regiment were added to the regular Army for the duration of the war. As the war was to be fought mostly on foreign soil, the militia was not called out. Instead, Congress authorized 50,000 volunteers in May 1846, of which 18,210 were mustered into Federal service, the small number based on belief in a short war. When the war continued into fall and winter of 1846, many of the volunteer units were due to be mustered out, as their terms of service were for only 12 months. Accordingly there was a second call for volunteers that enlisted 33,596 men whose term of service was for the duration of the war.[6]

Both regular and volunteer units were organized permanently at no higher than regimental level. Volunteer regiments and smaller units were recruited and organized on a state basis. Field commanders then organized brigades and divisions in the field. For example, in early 1846 Zachary Taylor organized his force, which advanced from Texas into Mexico with 3,500 men in five regular Army infantry regiments, one dragoon regiment, and several batteries of artillery and parts of four artillery regiments fighting as infantry, into three brigades.[7]

The grade of brigadier-general remained tied to the number of brigades or brigade equivalents fielded by the Army. In 1845, there were one major-general and three brigadier-generals in the peacetime Army, one of the brigadiers serving in the staff position of quartermaster general. An additional two officers held the rank of brigadier-general by brevet only.[8] A brevet rank was an honorary one. In the days before medals, a brevet promotion was one of the few ways an officer could be recognized. In the Mexican War, brevet rank was used whenever the command consisted of soldiers from more than one Army component. Since all the forces used in the war consisted of a mix of regulars and volunteers, brevet rank was to be significant.

Including the two brevet appointments and ignoring the staff brigadier-general, the quartermaster general, there were four brigadier-general equivalents in an Army with only eight infantry regiments and two cavalry regiments, giving a ratio of one brigadier-general for roughly every two and a half regiments, not far removed from the two regiment brigade structure officially envisioned by Army regulations. At the height of the war, when the Regular Army had been expanded to 18 regiments of infantry and cavalry, there were three line brigadier-generals and three by brevet only. The ratio of brigadiers to regiments rose slightly to three to

Table 3. Brigadier-Generals, Mexican War

Year	Brevet Brigadier-Generals Regular Army	Brigadier-Generals Regular Army	Volunteers
1845	2	3	-
1846	1	4	7
1847	3	4	12
1848	3	4	10
1849	3	4	-

In addition, nine regular officers served as acting brigade commanders; one major, five lieutenant colonels, one Marine lieutenant colonel, and two colonels one. In the volunteer service, where 42 regiments were raised for 12 months service in 1846 and 1847, 12 brigadier-generals were appointed, giving a slightly higher ratio of 3.5 regiments per general for the volunteer service. A breakdown of appointments is shown in Table 3.

As in the War of 1812, brigades were generally organized and used in the Mexican War as temporary expedients or as part of a larger unit, usually a division. For the first time, large volunteer forces were raised. These were also formed into brigades and, in some cases, into divisions. Regular and volunteer regiments were usually not brigaded together. Unlike in the later Civil War, most of the senior officers commanding volunteer brigades and divisions were themselves holders of exclusively volunteer commissions. Since the Regular Army was in the field, its officers were needed to command their own units. A typical brigade consisted of two 500-man regiments. In the volunteer force, regiments from the same state were generally brigaded together. Sometimes the senior volunteer officer from the state was made brigadier-general of volunteers to command such a brigade. For example, Colonel Gideon J. Pillow, 1st Tennessee Volunteers, was commissioned as brigadier-general of volunteers and made commander of the Tennessee Brigade, consisting of the 1st and 2d Tennessee Volunteer Regiments. But even such arrangements could prove to be transitory—in the case of the Tennessee brigade, Taylor reassigned its units as he saw fit almost immediately after the brigade came under his command.[9]

While usually part of a larger organization, most brigades were supported directly by one or more companies of artillery and some also by mounted infantry or dragoons. Although the current version of the Army regulations maintained that brigade staffs would not be fixed and would be based on the specific mission of the brigade, President James Polk and Congress did authorize a staff consisting a quartermaster and assistant, a commissary officer and assistant, a surgeon and his assistant, and a chaplain.[10]

The Utah Expedition

After the end of the Mexican War, the volunteers were mustered out and the Regular Army was reduced back to its small permanent size of eight infantry regiments, one mounted rifle, two dragoon regiments, and four artillery regiments, as well as four brigadier-generals, counting the quartermaster general. The Army settled down to frontier security, constabulary, and coast defense duties.

In 1857, however, Mormon defiance of Federal authority in the Utah territory compelled President James Buchanan to order the Army to assemble the largest peacetime force of the era to occupy Utah and enforce Federal governmental authority. Accordingly, a detachment of 5,606 soldiers was ultimately assembled, including four regiments of infantry, one regiment each of dragoons and cavalry, and three companies of artillery. Brigadier-General Persifer F. Smith was assigned to command the force, serving in his brevet rank of major-general. Upon assembly, Smith was directed to form his command into two brigades headed by his two senior officers, Colonels Albert S. Johnston and William S. Harney. Both Harney and Johnston would be serving in their brevet rank of brigadier-general. However, Smith died before he could arrive and assume command. The Mormon crisis was settled through diplomacy and there was no longer a need for such a large force. Johnston, now in command, moved into Utah with a reduced force, and the brigades were never actually formed.[11]

Within three years of the Utah Expedition, much larger forces would be assembled to fight the insurrection the southern states started in reaction to the election of Republican Abraham Lincoln as Buchanan's successor.

NOTES

1. James Sawicki, *Cavalry Regiments of the US Army* (Dumfries, VA: Wyvern Publication, 1985), 15-16.

2. John B. Wilson, *Maneuver and Firepower: The Evolution of Divisions and Separate Brigades.* Army Lineage Series (Washington, DC: Government Printing Office, 1998), 6-7.

3. Ibid., 8-9.

4. James Sawicki, *Infantry Regiments of the US Army* (Dumfries, VA: Wyvern, 1981), 2.

5. Wilson, 9.

6. *The United States and Mexico at War: Nineteenth-Century Expansionism and Conflict*, Donald S. Frazier, ed. (New York: Simon & Schuster Macmillan, 1998), 24-27, 464-65.

7. Ibid., 27, 308.

8. The brigadier-generals were Edmund Gaines, John E. Wool and the Quartermaster General Thomas S. Jesup. The brevet brigadier-generals were Zachary Taylor, colonel, 6th Infantry, and William J. Worth, colonel, 8th Infantry.

9. Frazier, 321. Pillow was later made a major-general in the Regular Army, an appointment he resigned at the end of the war.

10. Wilson, 10.

11. Headquarters of the Army Circular, dated 11 January 1858; General Orders Number 7, Headquarters of the Army, dated 15 April 1858; General Orders Number 14, Headquarters of the Army, 21 May 1858; General Orders Number 17, Headquarters of the Army, dated 29 June 1858; Robert W. Coakley, *The Role of Federal Military Forces in Domestic Disorders 1789-1878* (Washington, DC; US Army, 1988), 196-200; 210-15.

Chapter 3

BRIGADES IN THE CIVIL WAR

Organization

In sheer numerical size, the United States raised its largest force of brigades ever in the American Civil War. Between 1861 and 1865 the United States, or Union, forces established over 200 brigades to fight the war. These brigades were almost always part of a higher command, division and army corps, as the division was then considered the Army's basic administrative and organizational unit. The army corps, as a headquarters controlling two or more divisions, made its first appearance in the US Army organizational history. While unit designations evolved during the course of the war, the army corps became the uniquely designated command, retaining its numerical designation even when it was shifted to a different command. Divisions and brigades, on the other hand, were numbered sequentially within their respective higher command and called in official reports by their current commander's name. As an exception to this, before 1863 in the portion of the Army fighting in the Western theater, brigades were numbered sequentially within their respective army.[1]

Similar to events in the Mexican War, the US government called up a large number of volunteers to fight the war. Unlike the Mexican War, the pure numbers of the volunteers dwarfed the small Regular Army. Additionally, regular officers were allowed to accept higher commissions in the volunteer service, thus fairly wrecking the chain of command of the regular units. With recruiting difficulties, the Regular Army, despite being expanded at the beginning of the war, basically withered away during the conflict. The war was fought primarily by the volunteers.

Similarly to the Revolutionary and Mexican Wars, brigades often started with regiments all from the same state, or composed exclusively of regular regiments. Attrition and a virtually nonexistent replacement system broke this down rather quickly. As in the Revolutionary War, commanders sought to keep brigades up to a strength of at least 2,000 men by adding additional regiments, even as the more veteran regiments grew smaller and smaller. Initially the minimum number of regiments in a brigade was two, but this was soon changed to four. At Chancellorsville, Virginia, in 1863, Union brigades averaged 4.7 regiments with a strength of 2,000. At Cold Harbor, Virginia, a year later, they averaged 5.5 regiments with the same strength. In the later stages of the war, whole brigades were amalgamated, as were several whole corps, to retain commands of adequate strength.

Only one brigade retained its organization throughout the entire war, the Vermont Brigade, formally the 2d Brigade, 2d Division, Sixth Corps. This brigade, raised in early 1862, retained the 2d, 3d, 4th, 5th, and 6th Vermont Volunteer Infantry Regiments throughout the war and added the 11th Vermont, formerly the 1st Vermont Heavy Artillery Regiment, in 1864. The brigade was able to stay together because all its regiments reenlisted when their enlistments ran out in 1864. The brigade also, naturally because of its long, continuous service, suffered the most fatal combat casualties of any brigade in the war, with 1,172 men killed or dying of wounds while serving in its ranks. These losses were distributed almost evenly throughout the brigade:

Table 4. Vermont Brigade Losses, 1862-1865

Brigade	Killed/ Died of Wounds
2d Vermont (1862-1865)	224
3d Vermont (1862-1865)	206
4th Vermont (1862-1865)	162
5th Vermont (1862-1865)	213
6th Vermont (1862-1865)	203
11th Vermont (1864-1865)	164
Total	1,172

As with many units in the east, the Vermont Brigade's toughest week was when it participated in the Battles of the Wilderness and Spotsylvania. During that week the brigade suffered 266 killed, 1,299 wounded, and 80 missing, a total of 1,645 casualties out of a command that started with 2,800, giving a loss rate of 58 percent. The hardest single 24-hour period was 5-6 May 1864, in the Battle of the Wilderness when the brigade lost 195 killed, 1,017 wounded, and 57 missing, a total of 1,269 men.

Despite the relative stability of the brigade, the Vermont Brigade had two permanent commanders and four temporary commanders during the war. The original commander, Brigadier General William T.H. Brooks, a Regular Army infantry major, was promoted to division command late in 1862. He resigned in 1864 because of ill health, after failing to be promoted to major general of volunteers because of his part in his superior's, Major-General William Franklin's, attempt to discredit Army of the Potomac commander, Major-General Ambrose Burnside. Then Colonel Lewis A. Grant, commander, 5th Vermont, a former schoolteacher and lawyer, replaced Brooks and remained the permanent commander of the brigade until the end of the war. He later received the Medal of Honor for his actions at Salem Church during the Battle of Chancellorsville, and was promoted to brigadier general of volunteers in 1864. After the war he returned to his law practice.[2]

Four hundred and fifty men were commissioned as brigadier-generals in either the Regular Army or the volunteer service during the Civil War. Theoretically, all brigades were supposed to be commanded by brigadier-generals. However, the creation of the army corps as a level of command and the extensive use of field armies made up of several army corps created two new levels of command. Unfortunately, at the same time, Congress, except for appointing Ulysses S. Grant as the sole lieutenant-general in 1864, did not promote officers past the grade of major-general, the standard grade for a division commander. Accordingly, major-generals commanded armies and corps, as well as divisions. Brigadier-generals frequently commanded divisions, as well as brigades, often by using brevet promotions to major-general. Brigades, therefore, were often commanded by the senior regimental colonel rather than a general officer, most of whom were also brevet brigadier-generals. Authorizing officers to serve in their brevet grade had previously been a right reserved for the president, but in February 1865, this authority was delegated directly to the Army's commanding general, Lieutenant-General Ulysses Grant. For the first time in US military history, the grade of brigadier-general was no longer tied to the number of brigades the Army could assemble. From this time forward, it was simply the lowest grade of general officer.[3]

Although most brigades served just as a component of a corps, some retained distinctive nicknames even when their official designation changed. A good example of this is the famous Iron Brigade, which earned its nickname at Second Bull Run while officially designated 4th Brigade, 1st Division, Third Corps, Army of Virginia. Later at Gettysburg, Pennsylvania, it re-affirmed its nickname while designated officially as the 1st Brigade, 1st Division, First Corps. Another famous brigade was the Irish Brigade—2d Brigade, 1st Division, Second Corps—originally composed of regiments recruited from the Irish immigrant population of New York City. Both brigades were eventually broken up when combat losses were not replaced.

While being almost purely a tactical unit consisting of only either infantry or cavalry regiments, the Civil War brigade did acquire a small staff as the war progressed: two aides de camp; a captain assistant adjutant general, who wrote out orders for the command; a surgeon; an assistant quartermaster; and a commissary officer. The brigade headquarters was also authorized three wagons to carry supplies. Each subordinate regiment was authorized an additional six wagons.[4]

For the first time, brigades had distinctive identifying flags for use on the battlefield. After abandoning an elaborate, but generic, flag system used early in the war, a new triangular flag was adopted for brigades. The flag would have the symbol used by parent corps on it and was color coded to indicate brigade and division number within the corps.

Infantry brigades in the Civil War consisted almost exclusively of infantrymen. Early war experiments placing supporting units of artillery and cavalry in the brigade were abandoned. Since brigades seldom fought separated from their parent corps, artillery eventually came to be consolidated at the corps level in a command, an artillery brigade. Despite the name, a typical corps artillery brigade consisted of between four and six artillery companies and was commanded by an artillery officer, usually a colonel, but sometimes a more junior officer.

Cavalry was rarely organized into units larger than the regiment before the Civil War. The branch had previously been divided into three components, dragoons, or mounted infantrymen, who were supposed to fight dismounted; mounted riflemen, who were dragoons equipped with rifled firearms; and cavalry, which was a lightly armed force designed to fight mounted. On the eve of the war, all three elements were consolidated into one branch, called, simply, cavalry. Unlike infantry regiments, cavalry regiments were usually divided into subordinate units, squadrons, and fought that way on the battlefield. After experiments in attaching cavalry directly to lower units, most army commanders organized their cavalry as a separate unit reporting directly to them. Depending on the amount of cavalry available, this unit would be a corps or division, each with subordinate pure cavalry brigades and one or two small brigades of horse artillery.

In the Civil War, the maneuver brigade was a purely tactical organization, almost always consisting of regiments belonging to one arm of the service, either infantry or cavalry. Additionally, brigades were almost always parts of larger organizations, divisions, which were, except for early in the war, themselves components of corps. The use of brigades in the Civil War was a continuation of their usage in the War of 1812 and the Mexican War, but on a larger scale. The poor regimental replacement system, which often left veteran regiments at skeletal strength, while raising new unblooded regiments, left the brigade as the basic fighting unit of consistent size. Since brigades were supposed to be commanded by general officers, their size remained constant at about 2,000 soldiers, the difference being made up for by adding additional small regiments to the command. Consequently, in the war of attrition that the Civil War became, the brigade remained a unit of constant size that commanders could maneuver.

Little Round Top: A Civil War Brigade Action

Brigades were essential to the smooth execution of both offensive and defensive operations in the Civil War. While most brigades fought as part of a larger unit, an example of an action where two brigades were detached from their parent units to defend a key piece of terrain at Gettysburg will be used to illustrate how a brigade was fought during the war.

On 2 July 1863, the second day of the three-day Battle of Gettysburg, a corps-sized Confederate force under Lieutenant-General James Longstreet was ordered to attack the opposing Union army's left flank, which was anchored on a small ridge line, Cemetery Ridge, south of Gettysburg. Longstreet chose to attack in echelon from his right to left, with each of his divisions attacking in turn. His leftmost division, commanded by Major General John Hood, would begin the advance against the Union's left flank near a rocky outcrop, later called Devils Den, and a small rocky hill, locally called Little Round Top. Little Round Top's forward slope, facing the Confederates, had been cleared of vegetation by a farmer before the battle increasing its military importance. Its occupation by the Confederates threatened the whole

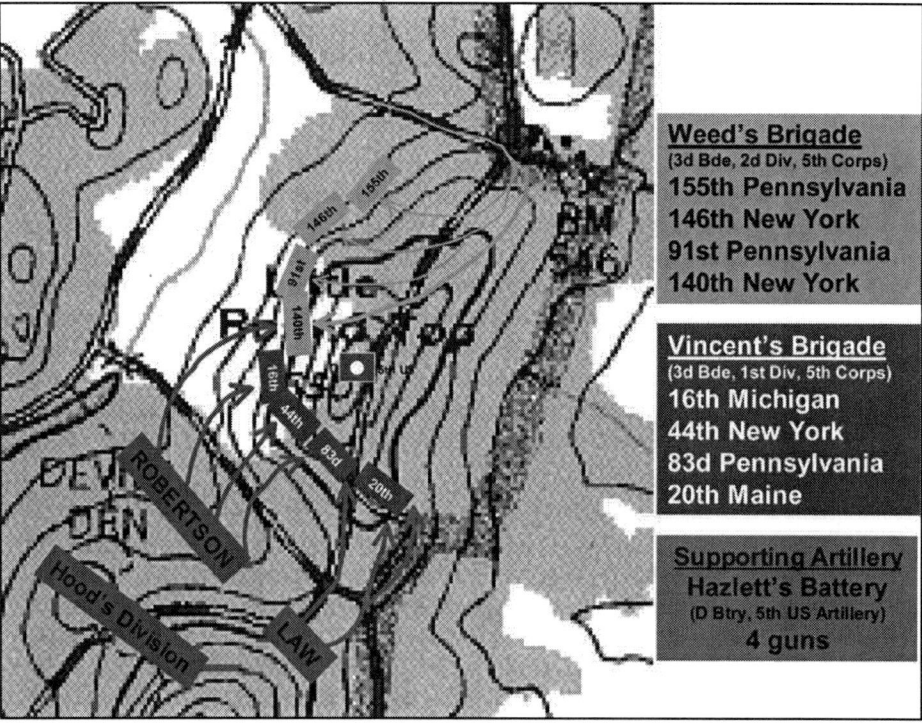

Figure 4. Action at Little Round Top, 2 July 1863

Union position. Its occupation by the Federal forces threatened any Confederate attack on the Union's left flank.[5]

However, the Union's left flank was in an uproar as Longstreet began his late afternoon attack. Major General Daniel Sickles had unilaterally moved his command, the Third Corps, forward of its assigned position. This move not only made him vulnerable to Longstreet's attack, but it also uncovered the Union's left flank near Little Round Top, exactly where Hood's leftmost brigades were poised to strike. Fortunately for the Union forces, Brigadier General Gouverneur K. Warren, the chief engineer officer, discovered the mistake and sent his aides out to find troops to defend Little Round Top.

The 3d Brigade, 1st Division, Fifth Corps, was commanded by Colonel Strong Vincent, 83d Pennsylvania. Aside from his own regiment, the brigade consisted of the 16th Michigan, 44th New York, and the 20th Maine. Vincent had assumed command in May when the previous brigade commander, Colonel Thomas Stockton, 16th Michigan, suddenly resigned. The brigade was greatly reduced in strength, with about 1,000 men bearing arms; the 20th Maine being the largest regiment at about 350 men, the 16th Michigan the smallest at about 200.[6] In the late afternoon of 2 July, the Fifth Corps was under orders to reinforce the Third Corps on the Union's left flank. But when Warren's aide, Captain Ranald Mackenzie, rode up to Major General George Sykes, commander, Fifth Corps, and asked for a brigade to hold Little Round Top, Sykes promptly ordered his First Division commander, Brigadier General James Barnes, to dispatch a brigade. Barnes chose Vincent's, as it was on a nearby road lined up in column.

There was a sense of urgency in this deployment, as Confederate troops were expected to advance on Little Round Top from the southwest momentarily. Vincent, therefore, set his brigade in motion toward Little Round Top to the south. As the brigade column stretched out for about a quarter mile, Vincent rode ahead to examine the ground he was to defend and select positions for the brigade on the south side of the hill in the direction the Confederates were expected to come. Vincent's energetic execution of his new mission and ability to place his troops in the best possible location to execute that mission would prove to be critical.

As each regiment arrived, Vincent brought the regimental commander up and showed him the regiment's position. The 20th Maine, under Colonel Joshua Chamberlain, was first and was posted on the extreme left. Vincent had to caution Chamberlain that, while his right would be tied into the next regiment, his left would be tied into nothing, becoming the left flank of the entire army. The main Union wagon train was also parked not far to the rear of Chamberlain's right flank, making this flank doubly important. Posted to the right of the 20th Maine was the 83d Pennsylvania. The small 16th Michigan was next, but Colonel James Rice, 44th New York, asked that his regiment be placed next to the 83d, as they had always fought side by side. Vincent agreed and the 16th Michigan was placed on the brigade's left flank, in the open area of Little Round Top facing Devil's Den. The 16th's left tied into the 44th New York, but its right was in the air. This was less crucial than the 20th Maine's left flank, though, as the Third Corps' 4th Maine Regiment was posted on the valley floor north of Devil's Den, as the left flank of a Third Corps brigade. There was, however, a sizeable gap between these two units.[7]

The regiments formed up in two lines across their assigned fronts. Soldiers stood shoulder to shoulder where possible. While later in the war the troops would have immediately dug entrenchments or thrown up vegetation as natural breastworks, at this stage of the war they just used trees and boulders for cover where available. Each line in the regiment would fight by firing massed volleys at the attackers. As a standard measure, the regiments posted a company of troops in front of it to act as skirmishers. The skirmishers were designed to provide early warning of the enemy's approach. They fought in small groups and fired individually, using all available cover to break up the enemy attack before it reached the main line. The skirmishers would then fall back into their regiments. Chamberlain placed his Company B to cover the regiment's front and the brigade's left. The 16th Michigan dispatched two companies, including one of attached sharpshooters, to protect the brigade right flank.[8]

Vincent's troops were in position at approximately 1600. The Confederate advance reached Little Round Top within the next 15 minutes. Almost as soon as Vincent's skirmishers were posted, they encountered the main enemy line advancing. The right two brigades of Hood's division, Brigadier-General Jerome Robertson's composed of Texas and Arkansas regiments and Brigadier-General Evander Law's of Alabama troops, were to advance on Little Round Top roughly side by side from the southwest to flank the positions of the Federal Third Corps, which the left portion of Hood's division was about to assault. The skirmishers immediately withdrew. The 20th Maine's skirmishers, however, had been passed by the advancing Confederates and remained on the brigade flank waiting for an opportunity to rejoin the regiment.

The Confederate assault was somewhat uncoordinated. Advancing from covered terrain and on a front wider than that Vincent's men were defending, Robertson and Law had an excellent chance of overwhelming or outflanking the Federal brigade, which had both of its flanks in the air. After a pause to redress their lines, the rebel brigades advanced up the wooded, southern face of the hill. The attack developed first against the center regiments, 44th New York and 83d Pennsylvania, and then spread to the right to the 16th Michigan, and then on to the 20th Maine on the left. Robertson's brigade, the 4th and 5th Texas, made several abortive assaults against Vincent's center, having to break formation to pass between the large boulders that littered that part of the slope of Little Round Top.

To Robertson's left, Law's 4th Alabama also attacked the center of Vincent's position. This attack was not coordinated with the Texans or with Law's two other regiments on the right. These two regiments, the 15th and 47th Alabama, had fallen behind because of the exertion of scaling the heights of Round Top, the large, wooded hill south of Little Round Top. Colonel William Oates, 15th Alabama, was in command of both regiments with orders to seize Little Round Top, and, as the extreme right of the Confederate Army, to turn the Union flank. After a short rest on Round Top, Oates dispatched a company to capture the Union wagon train, and then set out to seize Little Round Top. Skirmishers kept the wagons safe. Oates' delay allowed the 20th Maine to volley fire into the 4th Alabama advancing to the right against the 83d Pennsylvania. Soon, however, Oates was giving the Maine men the fight of their lives.

Vincent directed his brigade's defense of Little Round Top from a position located behind the center of the unit. The battle soon developed into waves of attacks, the first two being disjointed regimental attacks, the third an all out attack in the pending twilight by the six regiments of the two Confederate brigades. As the battle raged over the course of an hour and a half, Vincent dispatched aides to both flanks to keep him informed and other runners to bring back additional ammunition and find reinforcements.

Figure 5. Vincent Directs His Brigade's Defense of Little Round Top
"Don't Give Up an Inch" by Don Troiani

Both sides were fatigued and the Union brigade had suffered heavy losses and was low on ammunition when the two rebel brigades advanced for the third time. While Vincent's center was firm, naturally entrenched behind boulders, Oates was trying to maneuver the 15th Alabama around the 20th Maine's left to turn the Union brigade's entire left flank. On the other flank, the 16th Michigan began to give away when an officer ordered a poorly timed short withdrawal. In the confusion, a third of the regiment, 45 men, were separated from the main line and out of the battle. After ordering the 44th New York to fire into the flank of the Confederates attacking the 16th, Vincent rushed to rally the Michiganers and was fatally wounded. He would be promoted to brigadier general of volunteers before he died, five days later. Rice, 44th New York, immediately assumed command of the brigade.[10]

Vincent was not alone in his quest for reinforcements. Warren had remained atop the northwest face of Little Round Top while Vincent deployed. Vincent's march passed out of Warren's view on the east side of the summit, so he was still in search of units to garrison the hill. Barnes, one of the Fifth Corps division commanders, had dispatched First Lieutenant Charles Hazlett's four-gun battery, D Battery, 5th Artillery, to Little Round Top to support his division's advance forward of the hill. Hazlett met Warren at the summit and, despite the rugged terrain, the guns were manhandled to the top and soon were firing at the Confederates attacking Vincent's left and beyond near Devil's Den.

Warren needed infantry and, with his aides already out, he went looking for some himself. North of Little Round Top the bulk of the Fifth Corps was now marching to support the Third Corps, which was being attacked by the bulk of Longstreet's force. Warren came upon elements of the 3d Brigade, 2d Division, Fifth Corps, waiting to move up. In an ironic twist, this was his old command. The previous September he had commanded this brigade when it had unsuccessfully tried to hold the Union's left flank against Hood's Texans at the Battle of Second Bull Run. Now Warren found the commander of the lead regiment, Colonel Patrick O'Rorke, 140th New York, with his regiment just north of Little Round Top. On his own authority, he gave O'Rorke, who knew him well, orders to move to Little Round Top. The regiment, 526 men strong, was formed on the road to the Wheatfield, the main east-west road running north of Little Round Top, in a column of fours. O'Rorke, not hesitating, turned the head of his column to the left and advanced at a slow run in a column of fours to the top of the hill. Sykes had intended to send the brigade O'Rorke's regiment was in, commanded by Brigadier General Stephen Weed, to Little Round Top even before Warren snatched up the regiment. However, the order got muddled in the sending and Sykes had to reiterate it to Weed, who was not with his brigade when the 140th moved. Weed acted promptly upon returning to his command, leading the rest of his brigade to Little Round Top behind O'Rorke's troops.[11]

The 140th New York, with O'Rorke in the lead, reached the forward slope of Little Round Top just as the 16th Michigan was about to give way. The 140th, still in a column of fours advanced forward, halted, and fired into the Confederate attackers. The timely arrival of these reinforcements quickly secured the flank and blunted the impetus of the Confederate attack. However, O'Rorke, like Vincent minutes before, was mortally wounded by a minié ball and died before he hit the ground. The rest of Weed's brigade, the 91st Pennsylvania, 146th New York, and 155th Pennsylvania, formed up on the 140th's right, securing that side of Little Round Top.

There were no reinforcements coming to secure the critical left flank where the 20th Maine, low on ammunition and reduced in strength, was attempting to prevent being outflanked by one Alabama regiment while being attacked frontally by another. Both attacker and defender had almost reached the breaking point on this flank. Chamberlain, in order to defend against both threats, had thinned his line out and swung his left back to form an inverted V. Still the Confederates came on. In desperation born of a lack of ammunition resupply, Chamberlain ordered a bayonet charge with his regiment swinging from left to right across the regimental front. The shock effect of this unexpected maneuver, along with the opportune reappearance of the 20th Maine's company of skirmishers, along with some US sharpshooters, routed the Alabamans. The 20th Maine quickly took over 450 prisoners, including some troops from the two Texas regiments.

Vincent's brigade, reinforced by the 140th New York, had conducted, perhaps, the most important brigade defensive action of the war. While the main attacks were over, balls were still flying and both Weed and Hazlett were mortally wounded. The day's action had cost the Union forces two brigade commanders, a regimental commander, and an artillery commander. Total losses for the brigade in the battle were 88 killed, 253 wounded, and 11 missing or captured, roughly 35-percent losses. A year and 10 months later at Appomattox, the brigade was part of the honor guard specially selected to accept the Confederate surrender. The remnants of all the

Gettysburg regiments, except the 44th New York, were still part of the brigade, along with six other regiments, including the 91st and 155th Pennsylvania, which had been in Weed's brigade on Little Round Top.[12]

Brigades in the War With Spain

After the Civil War, the Army again was reduced in size and no permanent units above regimental level were retained. It was not until the 1890s that the Army made any significant organizational changes, the most important being the reorganization of the regiment with three subordinate battalions. When an army was raised in 1898 to fight Spain, many of the precedents established in the Civil War were followed. Volunteers were called out and eight corps were raised. At full strength, each corps had three divisions with three brigades each. When a corps' strength was less than a full division of three brigades, the extra brigade or two were considered "separate" and fell directly under the corps headquarters. An act of Congress in 1898 had established the brigade as consisting of three or more regiments, though in practice some would only have two. Brigade designations followed the pattern established in the Civil War, with brigades numbered sequentially by division and corps, with no unique designations.

Unlike the previous war, the Regular Army was kept mostly intact during the short war with Spain. Most brigades were either all regular troops or all volunteer. The regiments of the regular force were mostly consolidated into the brigades of the Fifth Corps, with some in the Fourth Corps. Most volunteers raised did not see action. The Fifth Corps provided the attack force for the expedition to Cuba. The Fourth Corps served in an occupation role in Cuba and Puerto Rico. The Eighth Corps served as the Philippine Expedition and was active in those islands long after the other corps had been disbanded.

While almost every state and several territories contributed at least one regiment of infantry or cavalry volunteers, no brigades were formed with regiments all from the same state. A special category of volunteers, recruited from the nation at large, rather than from particular states, was used extensively during the war itself in 1898 and in operations in the Philippines in 1899-1901.[13]

The Philippine Expedition, which formally lasted from 1898 to 1901, saw the Eighth Corps, the command headquarters in the islands, organized into as many as seven brigades at its largest size in January 1900. The organization in the Philippines was a lot more flexible than elsewhere. Artillery batteries were often attached directly to brigades and infantry and cavalry regiments were sometimes brigaded together.

As in previous wars, the authorized grade of a brigade commander was brigadier general. However, with the paucity of general grades, like in the Civil War, regimental colonels and lieutenant colonels often commanded brigades for extended periods of time, the most famous being Lieutenant Colonel Theodore Roosevelt, 1st US Volunteer Cavalry, who commanded the 2nd Brigade, Cavalry Division, Fifth Corps, in July 1898, after the Battle of San Juan Hill.[55] The war itself had two phases, a short campaign against Spain in April-July 1898, and a longer war from 1898 to 1901 in the Philippines against Filipino insurgents. This duality saw the unusual situation of some general officers holding two volunteer commissions, one for the 1898 campaign and a subsequent one, sometimes at a lesser grade, in the Philippines. While most volunteer appointments went to senior Regular Army field grade officers, several were given to former Union and Confederate Civil War general officers directly from civilian life.

At the end of the century, the maneuver brigade remained a temporary organization consisting of little or no headquarters staff and troops from a single branch, infantry, or cavalry. The brigade structure had changed little from the establishment of the first brigades in the War of 1812. The main reason for this static organizational development was, that, despite technological advances in weaponry, infantry and cavalry tactics were generally unchanged. And a brigadier general could still control on the battlefield a force of 2,000 men divided into several large regiments or several more smaller regiments. However military and technological advances would see changes in the next century.

NOTES

1. Mark M. Boatner III, *The Civil War Dictionary* (New York: Vintage Books, 1991), 611.

2. Ezra Warner, *Generals in Blue: Lives of the Union Commanders* (Baton Rouge: Louisiana State University Press, 1984), 47, 182-44. The Franklin affair was an incident where several generals, Brooks included, complained directly to President Abraham Lincoln concerning their army commander, Major General Ambrose Burnside, after the Battle of Fredericksburg in December 1862.

3. To further confuse things, brevets that had formerly been exclusively granted solely in the regular service, were also granted in the volunteer service after 3 March 1863. The first brevet brigadier-general of volunteers was appointed in June 1864. A Regular Army officer could, therefore, hold four grades in the Civil War—his substantive regular grade, a brevet regular grade, a substantive volunteer grade, and a brevet volunteer grade. At Appomattox, for example, the famous George Custer was a regular army captain, 5th Cavalry, a brevet major-general in the regular army, a brigadier-general of volunteers, and a brevet major general of volunteers. Two weeks later, he was promoted to the substantive rank of major-general of volunteers. In 1866 when the volunteer force went away, he was a captain in the Regular Army again. See Roger D. Hunt and Jack R. Brown, *Brevet Brigadier Generals in Blue* (Old Soldier Books, 1998), vi-vii.

4. John B. Wilson, *Maneuver and Firepower: The Evolution of Divisions and Separate Brigades.* Army Lineage Series (Washington, DC: Government Printing Office (GPO), 1998), 14.

5. Best source for the background of the Little Round Top battle is Henry Pfanz, *Gettysburg—The Second Day* (Chapel Hill, NC: University of North Carolina Press, 1987), 113-15, 149-67.

6. *The War of the Rebellion: A Compilation of the Official Records of the Union and Confederate Armies.* Series 1, 53 Vols. (Washington, DC: GPO, 1881-1898) (hereafter *OR*), Series I, Volume XXVII, Art 1, Book 43, 616-20.

7. Pfanz, 211-14.

8. Ibid., 214.

9. Pfanz, 220-23.

10. Pfanz, 225-27.

11. *OR*, Series I, Volume XXVII, art 1, Book 43, 771; The 44th New York was mustered out in October 1864 when its three year enlistment ran out.

12. John McGrath, *Organization of the Army During the Spanish-American War*, unpublished monograph, US Army Center of Military History, 2002. As US volunteers, three regiments of infantry, three of cavalry, and three of engineers were raised in 1898 for service in the Philippines, 24 regiments of infantry and one regiment of cavalry were raised in 1899, serving until 1901. The latter regiments were numbered above the highest numbered regiments in the regular service; 10th in the cavalry and 25th in the infantry.

13. Ibid. Roosevelt commanded in the absence of Brigadier General Samuel B. M. Young. The brigade consisted of Roosevelt's regiment and the regular 1st and 10th US Cavalry. Though designated cavalry, the regiments fought on foot during the war as infantry.

Chapter 4

THE BRIGADE IN THE EARLY 20TH CENTURY, 1902-1919

Organizational Reforms

After almost a century of unchanging organizational structure at the brigade level, technological and organizational advances would transform both warfare and the brigade in the early 20th century, resulting in the eventual adoption of a permanent brigade organization with organic supporting arms. Participation in a European war would directly spur most aspects of these changes. But as the century started, these dynamic events were still in the future.

With the volunteers in the Philippines mustered out in 1901, the regiment returned to its status as the largest permanent unit in the Regular Army. However, the period before the US entry in the World War I was one of great reforms in the US Army, some in reflection of the experience of the war with Spain, others from observing the large conscript armies maintained by most of the European powers. As a first response to this, Secretary of War Elihu Root established an Army general staff in 1903. Army planners in this new agency soon turned their attention to units larger than regiments.

Before World War I, the basic unit in European armies was the army corps, usually consisting of two infantry divisions, each with two brigades of two regiments. The European corps also contained cavalry, engineers, and field artillery. The US Army, too, had used the corps as its basic unit in both the Civil and Spanish-American Wars. But in the new 1905 version of the Army's regulations, the division became the US Army's basic unit. While the regulation did not organize permanent larger units, it directed commanders to form provisional brigades and divisions during maneuvers. A division of either infantry or cavalry was to consist of three brigades, each with two or more regiments.[1]

The Dick Act of 1903 reformed the role of the militia, now universally referred to as the National Guard. Where formerly the militia had been restricted in its use, necessitating the employment of the volunteer component, under the new law, National Guard units could be called upon by the Federal government for unrestricted service in times of national emergency. The Guard was also tasked to maintain units with the same organizational structure and standard as the Regular Army. Pennsylvania had maintained a nonstandard division since 1879, and New York organized a division in 1908. These were the first peacetime permanently organized brigades and divisions in the Army's force structure. The Dick Act led to annual joint maneuvers and plans to organize the part-time and full-time forces together into permanent larger units. In 1909, the War Department divided the country into eight districts. The theory was to organize brigades and divisions from the Regular Army and National Guard units stationed in each district. The scheme was voluntary for the National Guard, and by 1910 most states in the northeast had agreed to participate, though no brigades were actually formed.[2]

Between 1910 and 1914, various notional organizations were proposed and authorized. The division was now to be uniquely numbered in order of creation, while brigades remained being numbered consecutively within the division. Only in 1911 was theory put into practice. That year, disorders in Mexico led to the assembly of part of the Regular Army on the border in Texas and California. The portion in Texas was organized into a division at San Antonio,

Texas, the Maneuver Division, consisting of three infantry brigades and a separate cavalry brigade, the Independent Cavalry Brigade. At Galveston, Texas, 36 companies of coast artillery were reorganized into three infantry regiments, forming a provisional brigade guarding the coast. In San Diego, California, another brigade was formed from two infantry regiments and small detachments of medical, signal, and cavalry. This concentration lasted five months, the brigades being discontinued in June and July 1911. In 1913, the Secretary of War, Henry Stimson, as part of a general review of Army organization, accepted a proposal to organize the Army permanently into divisions and brigades. The Regular Army was to organize one cavalry and three infantry divisions and the National Guard an additional 12 infantry and three cavalry divisions. For the first time the Army produced formal tables of organization. A division had three brigades and each brigade three regiments. Cavalry brigades were, however, reduced to two regiments, primarily to save road space, not out of any belief in the organizational soundness of a two-regiment brigade. Brigades in the divisions were numbered consecutively within the Army, the 1st Division containing the 1st, 2d, and 3d Brigades; the 2d Division containing the 4th, 5th, 6th Brigades; and so forth. Where several brigades were not filled (3d and 9th Brigades), the numbers were retained for future use. Cavalry brigades were numbered separately.[3]

Unlike previous plans, the Stimson Plan was implemented in fact in 1913-1914. The Army organization is illustrated in Figure 6. Aside from a commander and very small staff, division and brigade headquarters staffs were not organized as such. Personnel for these would be taken out of hide from the administrative departments or from subordinate regiments, a long standing Army practice. The division was to be a self-contained, combined arms organization, while the brigade remained purely branch specific. The divisions and some of the brigades were

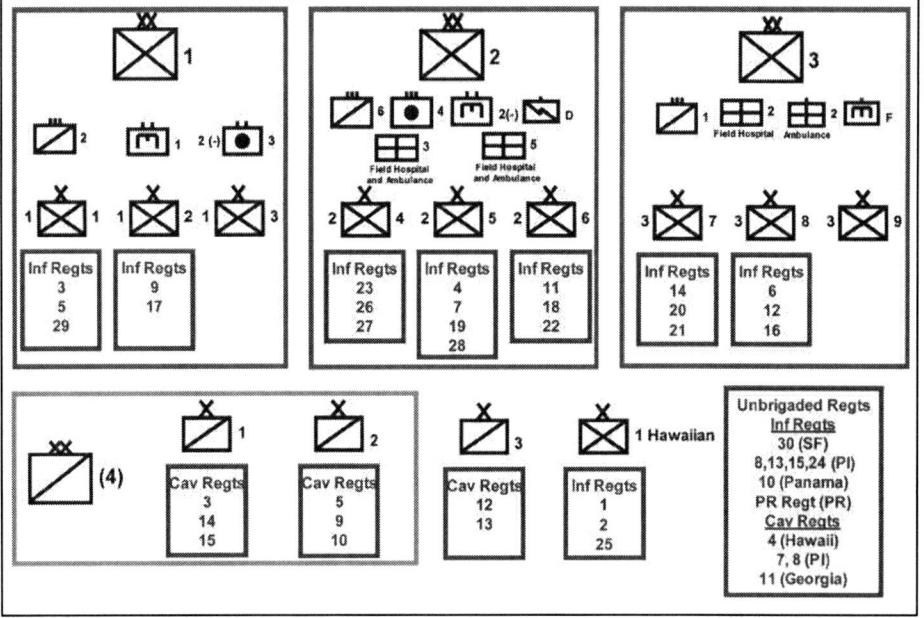

Figure 6. First Peacetime Brigades, 1914

30

scattered at various posts and would not be considered operational until they were mobilized. The organization would soon be tested again on the Mexican border.

Mexican Expeditions

In February 1913, when the Mexican disorders climaxed in a coup d'etat, President William Taft ordered a show of force on the Texas border. The new 2d Division, the only division with three full brigades, moved to locations on the Texan Gulf coast. In April 1914, the new president, Woodrow Wilson, ordered naval action against the port in Vera Cruz, Mexico, to protect American citizens and interests. The 5th Brigade, 2d Division, augmented with cavalry, field artillery, signal, aviation, engineers, and quartermasters, landed at the port to relieve the Navy personnel, in effect becoming the first brigade combat team in Army history. The brigade, under Brigadier General Frederick Funston's command, stayed until November 1914. In Texas, the 2d and 8th Brigades from the other two divisions moved to the border to replace the 2d Division elements. In December 1914, the 6th Brigade of the 2d Division deployed to the Arizona border. The 2d Division remained on station until October 1915, when it was demobilized after a hurricane in Galveston killed a number of soldiers and made the public question the necessity for the continuation of the deployment.[4]

The situation reversed itself again in March 1916 when Mexican bandits raided Columbus, New Mexico. The commander of the Southern Department, now Major General Funston,

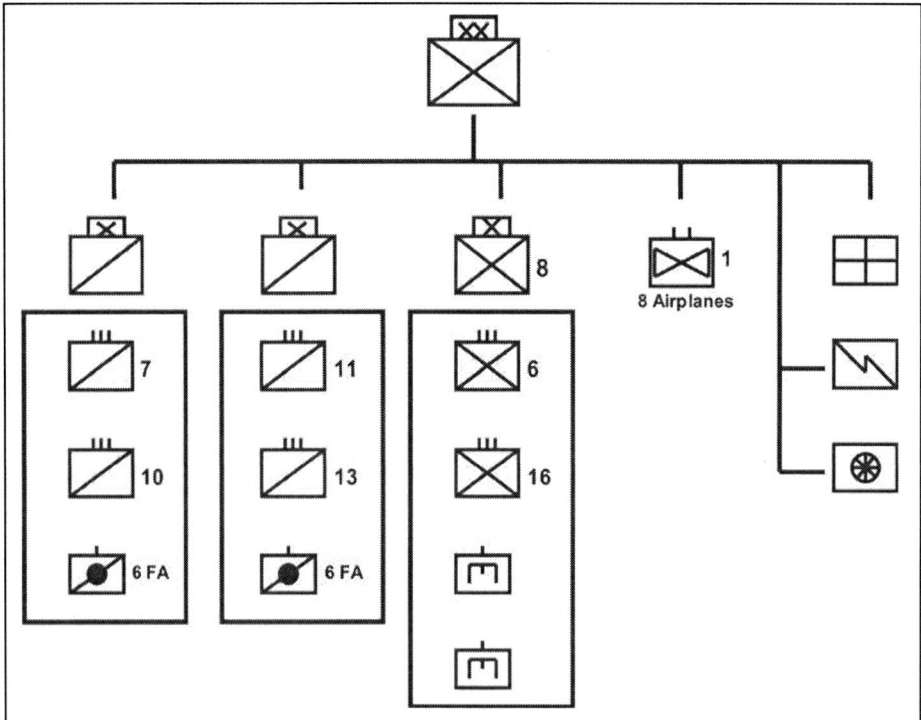

Figure 7. Pershing's Provisional Division, 1916

ordered Brigadier General John J. Pershing, commander, 8th Brigade, to chase down the attackers. Pershing organized a provisional division, the Punitive Expedition, US Army, out of his own brigade and additional troops given him. The divisional organization was of Pershing's own devising, and consisted of three combined arms brigades: two cavalry brigades, each with two cavalry regiments and a field artillery battery, and an infantry brigade with two infantry regiments and two engineer companies (see Figure 7). Pershing planned to pursue the Mexicans with the cavalry and use the infantry for security.[5]

In June 1916, as Pershing was preparing his expedition, violence on the border increased to the point that President Wilson federalized all the National Guard units assigned to divisions and brigades under the Stimson Plan. Except for the New York and Pennsylvania divisions, the planned mobilization of brigades and divisions worked poorly. In August, the War Department directed Funston to form the Guard units into 10 provisional divisions and six separate brigades. The border calmed down over time. The first Guardsmen were demobilized in the fall, with most released from Federal control by March 1917. Pershing's expedition remained south of the border until February 1917. Pershing then replaced Funston, who had died suddenly, as Southern Department commander. As such, he organized the Regular Army units in the department into three provisional infantry divisions and a cavalry brigade. In April, the United States entered World War I and Pershing disbanded his divisions and brigades as the Army again reorganized, this time to send an expeditionary force to Europe.[6]

The Brigade and World War I: The Square Division

The major European powers had been at war since August 1914 when the United States entered the conflict in April 1917. The continental European armies began World War I with large conscript armies organized rigidly into corps of two divisions, each with two infantry brigades. Each brigade consisted of two infantry regiments. The powers deployed machine guns differently. In the German army, a separate machine gun company was found at the regimental level. The French had only a platoon at the regiment. The reality of fighting entrenched infantry equipped with machine guns and supported by massed, quick-firing field artillery, made the French and Germans change the structure of their divisions during the course of the war. With attrition and the accompanying agony of trench warfare, the French and Germans had, by 1916, reduced their divisions from four infantry regiments to three. Operationally, the regiments reported directly to the division commander, though the Germans retained a brigade headquarters to control the three regiments administratively. At the same time, machine guns were increased. Both placed a machine gun company in each infantry battalion (there being three per regiment) by 1918. Smaller divisions allowed divisions worn out by trench warfare to be replaced in the line by a similar unit.[7]

American planners looked at the French and British experience. Ironically, however, a study completed in May 1917 by the War Department's War College Division, recommended an organization structurally similar to the French and German 1914 divisions. This was the square division, organized with two infantry brigades, instead of the traditional three, each with two subordinate infantry regiments. Though machine gun units were organized at three echelons, regiment, brigade, and division, the structure also provided, once organized for combat, for one machine gun company to support each infantry battalion. The design was approved, though it was tweaked and changed numerous times in 1917-1918. The theory behind the organization

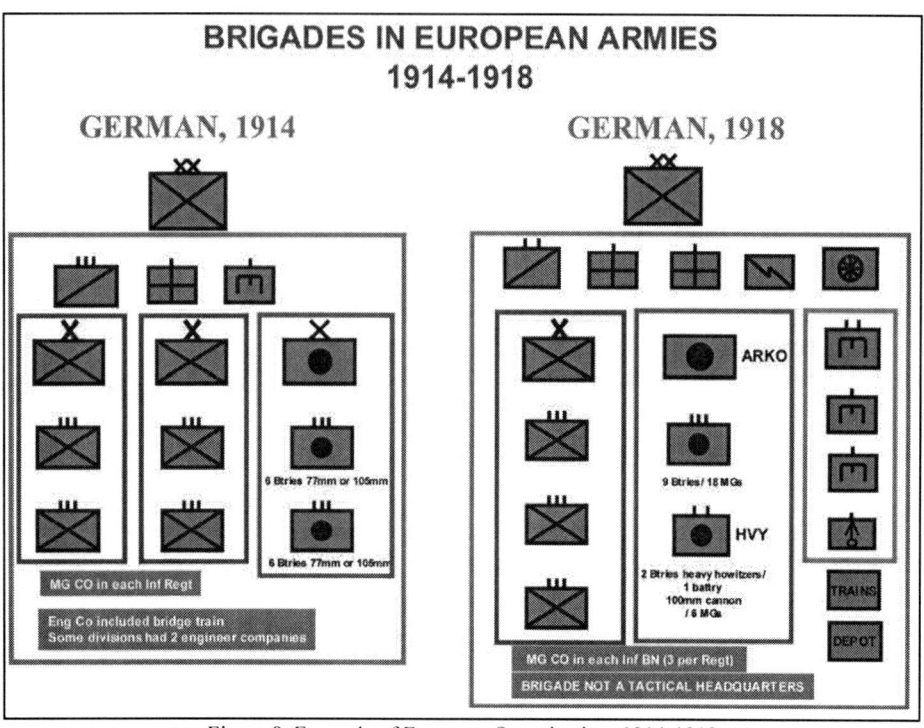

Figure 8. Example of European Organization, 1914-1918

was that the division would normally defend or attack with its two brigades side by side, but with each brigade having one regiment forward and the second regiment in reserve directly behind it. The regiments would typically deploy its battalions in a column for either an in-depth defense or to allow the rotation of fresh battalions in the offensive, with the reserve regiment either then taking over to continue the attack or to consolidate the position gained.[8] Therefore the brigade was to be the basic US Army tactical unit for trench warfare. This was different from the French, British, and Germans who used the division in this role. The brigade commander, leading a purely tactical unit, would be able to remain forward and leapfrog regiments as necessary, given his ability to respond to the battlefield situation quickly.[9]

The square divisional brigade was almost purely a tactical unit, with no logistical or administrative functions. While commanded by a brigadier general, its staff was small, consisting of three aides, a brigade adjutant, and 18 enlisted men who provided mess, communications, and transportation support. Assigned directly to the brigade were two infantry regiments, a small ordnance detachment, and a machine gun battalion. Each infantry regiment consisted of a headquarters company, a machine gun company, medical section, and three infantry battalions, each consisting of four rifle companies.

Public law complicated the concept of employment of machine guns. The National Defense Act of 1916 restricted the size of the infantry regiment. While the Army wanted one machine gun company for each rifle battalion, to place the three required companies under the regiment

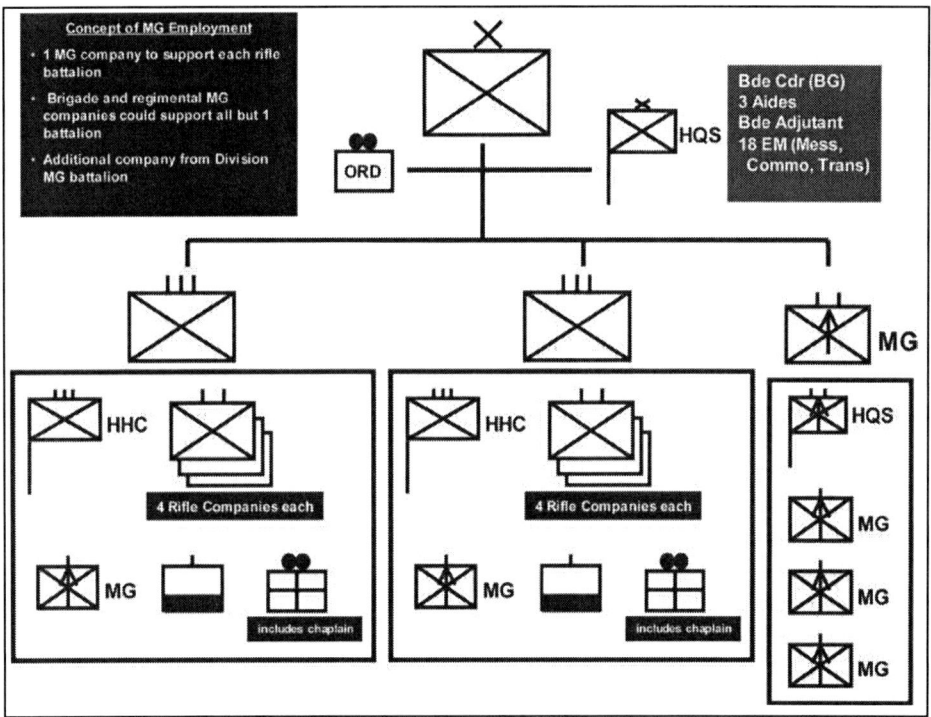

Figure 9. The Square Divisional Brigade, 1917

would mean a loss of two rifle companies. To get around this restriction, each brigade had a three-company machine gun battalion. When reorganizing for combat, the brigade could provide a supporting machine gun company to each battalion except one. To make up for this, the division also had a machine gun battalion of three companies, which habitually provided the extra company. In 1918, the organization was tweaked to give the brigade the additional company directly.[10]

For service in World War I, the Army raised 112 infantry brigades, all assigned or projected to be assigned to divisions. The mobilization of 1917-1918 saw the Army divided into three components: the Regular Army, the mobilized National Guard, and the National Army. The National Army, filled with draftees, replaced the former Volunteer Army used in the Civil and Spanish-American Wars. While the new unit designation scheme adopted by the Army in 1917 reflected the three-component distinction, it was later blurred. Divisions were numbered consecutively by component, with numbers 1-25 reserved for the Regular Army, numbers 26-42 reserved for the National Guard, and numbers 76 and higher reserved for the National Army. Brigades were numbered consecutively, but their numbers reflected their component. For example, the 1st Division had the 1st and 2d Brigades, the 2d Division the 3d and 4th, and the first National Guard division, the 26th, had the 51st and 52d Brigades. Regular Army brigades included the 1st through 40th; brigades above the number 40 were never organized. National Guard brigades included the 51st through 84th and the 185th. The National Army brigades were the 151st through 184th, 186th, 192d, and 194th.[11] Machine gun battalions were numbered sequentially within each component using the numbering system used by regiments: the Regular Army had numbers 1 to 100, the National Guard 101 to 300, and the National Army 301 and higher. For example, the 26th Division's divisional machine gun battalion was numbered 101st, the 51st Brigade's 102d, and 52d Brigade's 103d.

Of the 112 infantry brigades raised for the war, 88 deployed to Europe: 58 brigades saw combat, 14 were converted to depot units in France, four were skeletonized, 10 were stripped of personnel to provide replacements and two arrived after the fighting ended. The wartime buildup lasted 18 months and was immediately halted upon the signing of the armistice on 11 November 1918.[12] A listing of the wartime, and postwar, brigades can be found in Appendix 3.

With the large number of draftees coming into the Army in 1917, a specialized brigade was established, the depot brigade. These brigades, organized for each National Guard and National Army division, processed new draftees and provided basic training. Each depot brigade had from two to seven training battalions, though some were organized with one or two training regiments as well. These units were eventually removed from divisions and placed directly under cantonment commanders.[13]

The brigade of the square division, with its 8,000 assigned personnel, was the largest brigade ever fielded by the US Army and, in 1918, was as large as the average French or British division. Accordingly, whenever US forces were placed under Allied command, it was common for the French or British commander to ignore US doctrine and place the division in a corps sector by itself and deploy the four regiments with three in the trenches and one in reserve or with both brigades abreast.[14]

Tank Brigades

Technical innovations created a whole new maneuver arm during World War I: the Tank Corps.[15] Tanks, though thought of at the time as primarily infantry support weapons, were organized into their own battalions and brigades as a separate branch of the Army. Tanks were considered an army or corps asset. The Tank Corps developed in two separate branches, the Tank Corps, American Expeditionary Force (AEF), in France, and the Tank Corps, National Army, in the United States. The AEF formed four tank brigades, initially called the 1st through 4th Provisional Tank Brigades, in August and October 1918. In November these brigades were redesignated as the 304th through 307th Tank Brigades. A shortage of tanks severely restricted their employment in 1918. The 2d and 4th Brigades were still forming when the war ended.[16]

Initially, tank support was conducted only at the battalion or lower level. Separate tank battalions supported one or two divisions. Each battalion was a self-contained unit designed to support a division or brigade in an assault. But later two tank brigades did see combat, the 1st/304th and the 3d/306th, commanded respectively by Lieutenant Colonel George S. Patton, Jr., and Lieutenant Colonel Daniel D. Pullen. While the AEF had formed five heavy and 10 light tank battalions, most of these were used as army- or corps-level assets. Patton's brigade consisted only of two light tank battalions, two repair and salvage companies, and a motor maintenance detachment (see Figure 10). Pullen's command served primarily as a liaison detachment with supporting French tanks and also as a command headquarters for some French tank units supporting the Americans.[17]

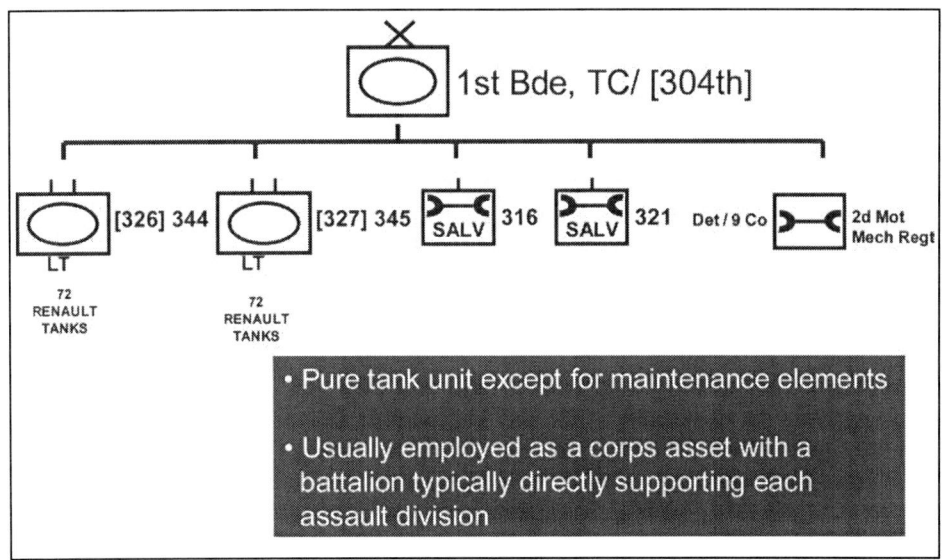

Figure 10. World War I Tank Brigade

Patton's brigade, with an attached group—roughly equivalent in size to an American battalion—of French tanks, participated in the Saint Mihiel offensive in September 1918. The brigade supported the 1st and 42d Divisions, with a battalion supporting each division.

Both brigades participated in the subsequent Meuse-Argonne offensive that started in late September 1918 and continued right up to the 11 November armistice. For this operation, Patton's brigade was assigned to support the 35th Division, I Corps. Because of terrain and maintenance considerations, Patton deployed the brigade differently than at Saint Mihiel, leading with one battalion supporting the infantry and his second battalion following a mile to the rear. The brigade initially supported the 35th Division from 26 to 30 September 1918, before being withdrawn for refitting. Two days later, the 35th was withdrawn after suffering almost 8,000 casualties in the four-mile advance that opened the offensive. Patton was wounded early on the first day of the offensive, but the brigade he had trained fought well under his replacement, Major Sereno Brett. The brigade returned to the line for short periods throughout the rest of offensive, supporting the I and V Corps. Pullen's brigade, after initially serving as a liaison headquarters for the French tanks supporting the II and V Corps between 26 September and 10 October, was reorganized with two light tank battalions. It replaced Brett's brigade in early November, but did not participate in any action before the war ended. The tank brigades, though sometimes employed as complete brigades, were pure tank formations in World War I whose focus was on supporting the maneuver of the infantry, rather than maneuvering on their own.[18] After the war, the Tank Corps was disbanded and tanks became a purely infantry support weapon, without an independent role.

The 154th Infantry Brigade in the Argonne

The 77th Division, consisting of the 153d and 154th Infantry Brigades, served as the left flank division of the I Corps, part of the American First Army, at the start of the Meuse-Argonne

36

offensive. By Wednesday, 2 October 1918, the division had been attacking for seven days in sector as part of the I Corps. Fighting in the Argonne Forest's rugged terrain, the division had initially, through tactical surprise, pushed the Germans back almost 4 miles, ejecting them from their first defensive line. The Germans were now in their second defensive line.

On 2 October 1918, the 77th was ordered to conduct a general assault and take the second German defensive line in a sector facing north, which had the 28th Division on the right and the French Fourth Army on the left. The day's objective, an advance of roughly 2,000 meters, was to high ground on which was the line of an east-west road and a railroad that paralleled it to the north. This was to be a repeat of an unsuccessful attack executed the previous day.

The 154th Infantry Brigade, the subject of this case study, was composed of the 307th and 308th Infantry Regiments and the 306th Machine Gun Battalion. While the division had been recruited as a National Army unit from the New York City area, attrition and replacements had complicated the complexion of the unit. For example, Company K, 307th Infantry, had been redesignated from the former Company L, 160th Infantry, California National Guard. The company had belonged to the 40th Division, which had been converted into a depot division in August 1918. The brigade had been in the line with only a few breaks since August, participating in the Oisne-Aisne operation where it was on the right flank during the German retreat to the Aisne, suffering heavy casualties. The unit was trucked from the Aisne front directly to the Argonne and attacked almost immediately. Due to attrition from these previous battles, some battalions were commanded by captains and one regiment, the 307th, was commanded by a lieutenant colonel. On the eve of the attack, the brigade received about 1,500 replacements from the 41st Division, which had been converted into the depot division for the I Corps. The replacements had been rushed to join the unit before their training was complete.[19]

The division commander, Major General Robert Alexander, directed the 154th Infantry Brigade's commander, Brigadier General Evan M. Johnson, to continue attacking in sector on 2 October northward against the entrenched Germans. Alexander directed Johnson to advance vigorously in disregard of the units on his flanks. The Germans were felt to be withdrawing and the units on the flanks, elements of the French Fourth Army's XXXVIII Corps, and the 28th Division, were expected to also be advancing vigorously.[20]

The terrain was the harsh easternmost portion of the Argonne Forest. The first German defensive line had been taken in the previous days. Despite that, the defense was still solid. The Germans had held positions in the Argonne since 1914 and part of the Battle of Verdun had been fought in the forest's eastern side in 1916. The German defenders in the western half of the brigade sector were seasoned veterans of the I Reserve Corps, Third Army. The 254th Reserve Infantry Regiment, 76th Reserve Division, held the line itself. The boundary between the I Reserve Corps and the easterly 2d *Württemberger Landwehr* Division ran along a ravine in the left portion of the 154th Brigade's sector. This boundary was not just between two divisions; it was also the boundary between the German Third and Fifth Armies. The 122d Infantry Regiment, 2d *Landwehr* Division, considered the weakest category of German unit by US intelligence, held the line in the west half of the brigade sector.[21]

The terrain in the brigade sector was thickly forested with high ground to the north cut by the lower reaches of the Charlevaux stream. The thickness of the foliage made the maneuver of units difficult and hindered the adjusting of supporting artillery fire.

In the left portion of the brigade sector, the prominent feature was the ravine, the German army boundary. This ravine, an outshoot from the stream, ran roughly southwest to northeast from the brigade front line to the German rear area near the high ground that was the day's American objective. Though the German first defensive line had been taken in earlier attacks, the German defense was an in-depth defense, with their second line now reached, consisting of well-placed trench lines and machine gun positions, but the ravine was a natural weak point in the defensive position. While it was covered by fire and trenches at its southern end, the extensive barbed wire obstacles, usually found in front of the German trenches, were lacking here. This oversight was a consequence of the ravine being the boundary between two large units, where coordination between the forces on each side was harder than normal. A determined unit could surprise the defenders on each side in the first line. Once past that line, the ravine provided a covered, natural corridor into the rear of the German position.

The 154th Infantry Brigade led the assault with two regiments attacking side by side in sectors roughly 2,000 meters wide, the 308th on the left (west), 307th on the right (east). Each regiment led with one battalion, followed closely by a second battalion in support. The third battalion of each regiment was in reserve, the 3d Battalion, 308th (3/308), serving as the brigade reserve and the 1st Battalion, 307th (1/307), serving as the division reserve. Each regimental machine gun company was parceled out to the assault and support battalions by platoons. Additionally, each assault and support battalion had machine gun platoons from the 306th Machine Gun Battalion attached to them.

The 2 October morning attack failed. Johnson called the division commander and received firm instructions to try again. Johnson now clearly felt his job was on the line and directed his subordinate regimental commanders to attack after noon without worrying about what the units to the left and right were doing.

The assault battalion of the 308th, 1/308th, commanded by Major Charles Whittlesley attacked with three of its companies on line. The fourth company was covering the battalion's left flank where the French were supposed to be advancing. The support battalion, the 2d, under Captain George McMurtry, followed closely behind with three companies, one company also covering the left flank. Whittlesley was a determined commander and the two battalions found the gap in the German wire at the ravine and capitalized on it, quickly advancing almost 1,000 meters to the high ground just south of the day's objective. In the advance, the Americans captured two German officers, 28 enlisted men, and three machine guns, while receiving about 90 casualties from machine gun fire. Whittlesley set up a perimeter defense for the night and maintained contact along the ravine with the rear area by setting up a series of runner posts. The brigade reserve battalion had the responsibility to bring forward supplies along the line of these posts.[22]

Unfortunately for Whittlesley, the units on both of his flanks were stopped cold by the combination of German machine guns, mortars, and wire obstacles. The 307th Infantry, on the right, was stopped in front of the German defensive line, except for a little progress on the right, which was negated by the lack of progress of the 153d Brigade to the east. On the left, the French forces were retreating slightly rather than advancing.

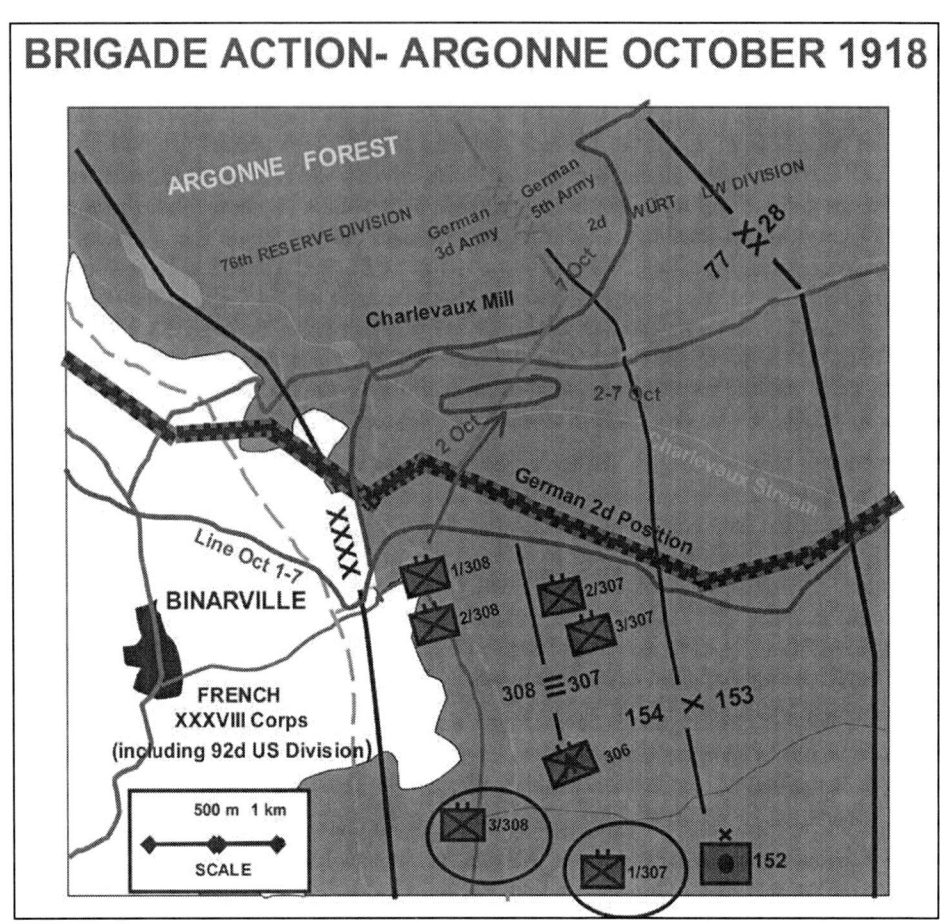

Figure 11. Operations of the 154th Infantry Brigade, 2-7 October 1918

Johnson relocated his command post to the rear of his two regiments and used runners to communicate with his subordinate regimental commanders. Near the end of the afternoon after receiving news of the 308th's success from Colonel Cromwell Stacey, commander, 308th Infantry, Johnson, realizing both the precarious position of the units with Whittlesley and the opportunity the gap in the German lines gave him, directed Lieutenant Colonel Eugene Houghton, commander, 307th Infantry, to send a battalion from his regiment to hold open the gap. Houghton immediately set his 3d Battalion in motion to comply with the orders. In the darkness the lead company, Company K, led by Captain Nelson Holderman, managed to get through, but follow-on units were stopped cold by the now alerted Germans.

The Germans responded to the apparent breakthrough swiftly. The breakthrough in the sector of the 254th Regiment, 76th Reserve Division, cut communications with the units of the German Fifth Army on the other side of it and threatened the whole German defensive position.

The 76th's front extended across the French sector, with only its left (eastern) flank opposite the US 154th Brigade's sector. The Ia, or the 76th's Operations Officer, Captain von Sybel, directed that the divisional engineer battalion, the 376th, several detached engineer companies, and the 76th and 77th, be sent to restore the main defensive line even though it was after dark. Major Hünicken, commander, 254th Reserve Regiment, would oversee this operation. Coordination at the corps level assured that elements on the other side of the army boundary would support the counterattack. During the night, the Germans moved in along the ravine between the American forward position and their own main line. In the process, they knocked out the string of runner posts Whittlesley had established and prevented all but K Company, 3d Battalion, 307th US Infantry from getting through the gap.

Before dawn, patrols from the German 254th Reserve Infantry Regiment infiltrated and cut the line of runner posts, killing two runners, capturing another, and driving the rest off. As dawn came, a solid German defense formed both on the main line and around the now isolated elements of the 308th Infantry. In some cases, the Germans posted alternate machine gun nests facing north and south.[23] Contact was restored between the 254th Reserve Infantry Regiment and the 122d *Landwehr* Regiment, providing a continuous defensive line once more. Though they would not know it until daylight, a force of seven companies was surrounded about 1,000 meters behind the German main defensive line. This detachment became known popularly as the "Lost Battalion," even though its location was always evident, to both Americans and Germans alike, and it was almost the size of two battalions.[24]

Despite the successful isolation of the American detachment, the Germans quickly discovered how large the American force was and how weak were their own forces in the area. The Allied offensive had stretched them thin in the western Argonne and reduced most units to a third of their authorized strength. Through a reshuffling of units, the 254th Reserve Regiment was given responsibility solely for the front facing the US 154th Brigade and around the Lost Battalion and the German 76th Division dispatched its reserve, a battalion of the 254th Regiment, to take care of the pocket.[25]

"Lost Battalion"

1st Battalion, 308th Infantry
  Companies A, B, C
  Platoon, Company C, 306th MG Battalion
2d Battalion, 308th Infantry
  Companies E, G, H
  Platoon, Company D, 306th MG Battalion
Company K, 307th Infantry

Figure 12. Units Isolated as the "Lost Battalion," 2-7 October 1918

Notwithstanding personnel shortages, the advantages of the thickly wooded terrain, and a prepared defensive line fortified the defense. Between 3 and 7 October, the Germans would successfully drive off seven attacks designed to free the Lost Battalion and advance the 77th Division's line forward.

Whittesley made the first of these attacks himself. Upon discovering his isolation in the morning, Whittesley dispatched Holderman and his company to reestablish contact with the rest of the brigade. The same German security patrols that had picked off the runner posts discovered Holderman's advance and promptly set up an ambush, which forced Holderman back into the perimeter. Soon the Germans had strung wire and posted machine guns and snipers solidly around Whittesley's perimeter.[264]

Between 3 and 7 October 1918, the 154th Infantry Brigade made the remaining six unsuccessful attempts to relieve Whittlesley and advance the line to the objectives of 2 October. These attempts were all beaten back by the Germans. The brigade reserve, 3/308th, a battalion weakened in previous days of battle, was committed to cover the brigade's left flank along with elements of the brigade machine gun battalion, while Stacey, 308th, led the first three attacks on the 3d and 4th. In the afternoon of the 4th, the 308th commander attacked for the last time with three companies of his own regiment and the division reserve battalion, 1/307th. This attempt to outflank the German positions on the right was defeated by thick underbrush and well-prepared defenders. The brigade and division commanders saw something lacking in Stacey, who lost his command that night on directive from Alexander, after he requested relief based on exhaustion and frayed nerves.[27]

The brigade commander, Johnson, personally led the attack on the afternoon of the 5th. The 307th Infantry had spent the previous few days trying to crack the nut that was the German defensive positions in front of their line. Despite their reputed poor quality, the 2d *Landwehr* Division's soldiers held off every 307th effort to push them back. For his attack, Johnson used the division reserve battalion, now down to 250 men, and the 2/307th, commanded by First Lieutenant Weston Jenkins, an attacking force of four companies. Three companies held the brigade's line. Each company was about 55 men strong, but many of Jenkins' men were raw replacements. Johnson's effort failed too, despite his vigorous leadership. The attacks failed through a combination of rugged terrain, a lack of artillery support due to inability to adjust fires, and the close proximity of the enemy lines to the American line.[28]

Throughout all these efforts, Whittlesley resolutely held on in his pocket, sending messages back by carrier pigeon. Attempts to resupply him by air failed when the drops fell into German lines and the plane was shot down. The men had started out with two days rations, which were stretched to five days. The Germans vigorously shelled the pocket and attacked the perimeter with grenades, finally demanding Whittesley's surrender on the afternoon of 7 October, a demand he refused.[29]

And rightfully so as the German demand was mostly a bluff: the Lost Battalion's ordeal was almost over, though the Germans tried one last, vigorous grenade attack before withdrawing themselves. Earlier in the day at the main line, a crack had appeared in the German defenses on the 154th Brigade's right flank, where the wire obstacles had not been maintained. Both the 154th and the adjacent 153d Brigade advanced into the opening and took up positions where their fire outflanked the German main line. The Germans began withdrawing. The Lost Battalion was relieved by dusk. The original force of 554 was reduced to 194 soldiers capable of walking unaided off the hill they had defended against all comers.[30]

Part of the reason for the German withdrawal was the advance of another American brigade to the east. To ease the pressure on the Lost Battalion, US forces were shuffled to provide fresh troops to attack and outflank the Germans defending in the western Argonne. One of these units, the 164th Infantry Brigade, consisting of the 82d Division's 327th and 328th Infantry and 321st Machine Gun Battalion attacked to the northwest commencing on 6 October 1918. The early success of this attack into the flank of the 2d *Landwehr* and 45th Divisions resulted in a German withdrawal.

As part of this attack, Corporal Alvin York, Company G, 328th Infantry, executed one of the most famous acts of individual heroism in US military history when he single-handedly captured almost an entire battalion of Germans on 8 October, earning the Medal of Honor.[31]

For their part, members of the Lost Battalion also received several Medals of Honor: Whittesley, commander, 1/308; McMurtry, commander, 2/308; and Holderman, commander, K/307th. Additionally, the second highest Army award, the Distinguished Service Cross (DSC) was awarded to 28 members of the Battalion. In the direct attempts to relieve the battalion, three additional Medals of Honor and five DSCs were awarded.[32]

As for the 154th Infantry Brigade, it continued with the offensive and ended the war on 11 November 1918 far beyond the Argonne on the heights overlooking the Meuse River south of Sedan, France. Johnson commanded the brigade until 30 October 1918, when his health failed, necessitating an operation. He had been the brigade's original commander and died shortly after the war.[33]

As can be seen from this case study, the brigade in World War I was a fairly inflexible fixed organization designed to provide continuous combat power to the front in the form of ample reserves ready to continue forward momentum after casualties or terrain had slowed up the initial attackers. A brigade with six infantry battalions would often advance with only two forward battalions, the rest in reserve to either continue the advance or be shifted to a discovered weakness in the enemy defenses. Though the Army maintained a continuous front as in previous wars, in this new war, a brigade did not necessarily attack with soldiers shoulder to shoulder. Consequently, for the first time, a brigade commander had to rely on various command and control means rather than personal contact to control subordinate units. No longer was a whole brigade visible to its commander. Unfortunately, means of communication had not kept up with tactical innovation. The inadequacy of the use of couriers, carrier pigeons, and landline telephones on the tactical battlefield resulted in the uncoordination of brigade offensive operations and the subsequent surrounding of a major portion of the command. Such coordination problems were apparent in earlier wars at higher levels, but now also appeared at the brigade level.

NOTES

1. John B. Wilson, *Maneuver and Firepower: The Evolution of Divisions and Separate Brigades.* Army Lineage Series (Washington, DC: Government Printing Office, 1998), 24-25.

2. Ibid., 27, 32.

3. Ibid., 32-34.

4. Ibid., 34-35.

5. Ibid.

6. Ibid., 35-37.

7. Jonathan M. House, *Toward Combined Arms Warfare: A Survey of 20th-Century Tactics, Doctrine, and Organization.* Combat Studies Institute Research Survey Number 2 (Fort Leavenworth, KS: US Army Command and General Staff College, 1984), 39-42; Wilson, 48. The British division was three brigades, but the subordinate units to the brigade were battalion-sized, so the French and German divisions actually came to resemble the British one in terms of number of infantry battalions.

8. Historical Resources Branch, US Army Center of Military History (CMH), *The American Division in World War I*, undated document.

9. Glen R. Hawkins and James Jay Carafano, *Prelude to Army XXI: US Army Division Design Initiatives and Experiments 1917-1995* (Washington, DC: CMH, 1997), 5.; House, 42.

10. Virgil Ney, *Evolution of the US Army Infantry Battalion: 1939-1968* (Fort Belvoir, VA: US Army Combat Developments Command, 1968), 7-8; Wilson, 67.

11. As an exception, the 4th Brigade was actually a US Marine Corps organization attached to the Army. The 185th Brigade is numbered as a National Army brigade because it was composed of segregated Guard units assigned to one of the segregated National Army units. The missing higher numbered National Army brigades were being formed when the war ended.

12. Wilson, 73.

13. Wilson, 60; *Order of Battle of the United States Land Forces in the World War, Zone of the Interior: Directory of Troops*, Vol. 3, Art 3 (Washington, DC: CMH, 1988), 1277-308.

14. House, 42.

15. Corps here is used in the sense of an administrative organization and should not be confused with the large tactical unit, the corps, or more properly, the army corps.

16. Ibid., 1543. James Sawicki, *Tank Battalions of the US Army* (Dumfries, VA; Wyvern, 1983), 4-6.

17. Dale E. Wilson, *Treat 'Em Rough: The Birth of American Armor 1917-20* (Novato, CA: Presidio, 1989), 96.

18. Ibid., 163, 181.

19. *Order of Battle, AEF*, Volume 2, 259, 301-3; *Report of the Assistant Inspector General*, First Army, Subject: 77th Division, cutting off of seven companies and one machine gun company, 3 October 1918, dated 8 October 1918, found in the papers of Major H.A. Drum, *Papers Relating to Lost Battalion, 77th Division,* Document 12, Military History Institute, 25 March 2003, <http://carlisle-www.army.mil/cgi-bin/usamhi/DL/showdoc.pl?docnum =12>,(hereafter referred to as Drum Papers). The 77th Division had served in the trenches in Lorraine in July and August 1918 and participated in the Aisne-Marne Offensive in September right before moving to the Argonne.

20. *Report of the Assistant Inspector General,* Drum Papers. CMH, 1992, reprint of 1938), 176; Thomas M. Johnson and Fletcher Pratt, *The Lost Battalion* (New York: Bobbs-Merrill, 1938), 27; David D. Lee, *Sergeant York: An American Hero* (Lexington, KY: University Press of Kentucky, 1985), 33

22. *Report of the Assistant Inspector General,* Drum Papers; *Supplementary Report of Operations of the 308th Infantry Covering Period from October 2 to October 8, 1918*, Drum Papers.

23. Johnson and Pratt, 61.

24. Ibid., 41-44, 52-53.

25. Ibid., 43-44.

26. Ibid., 81-82, 86-88.

27. *Report of the Assistant Inspector General,* Drum Papers; *Supplementary Report of Operations of the 308th Infantry Covering Period from October 2 to October 8, 1918*, Drum Papers.

28. Ibid. *Extract from Report of Operations, 77th Division, Covering Period from November 1 to November 8, 1918*, Drum Papers.

29. Ibid.

30. Ibid. L. Wardlaw Miles, *History of the 308th Infantry*, "Chapter 7 The Lost Battalion." <http://longwood.k12.ny.us/history/upton.miles7.htm">, 24 Mar 2003.

31. York captured Germans from the 45th Reserve Division's 210th Reserve Infantry Regiment and the 2d *Landwehr* Division's 120th *Landwehr* Infantry Regiment. Lee, 33-38.

32. The relief medals were awarded to two airmen who died after their plane was shot down and to a first sergeant in the 307th Infantry who destroyed a machine gun nest on 4 October 1918. *The Lost Battalion of World War I*, <http://www.homestead.com/prosites-johnrcotter/lost_battalion_heroes.html>,, and, <http://www.homestead.com/prosites-johnrcotter/lost_battalion_heroes.html>, 28 March 2003

33. *Order of Battle*, 296; Johnson and Pratt, 290.

Chapter 5

INTERWAR AND GLOBAL WAR: DEATH OF THE BRIGADE

The Interwar Years: Square and Mechanized Brigades

The square brigade organization survived the demobilization of the Army after World War I. For the first time ever, the Army retained units larger than the regiment after demobilizing from a war. Despite several studies urging a smaller, triangular division based on three regiments, the four-regiment-, two-brigade division structure was retained throughout the interwar period. The Regular Army, though reduced in size, kept the brigade and divisional structure used in the war. The tidy numerical structure instituted in the war was soon disrupted by the shuffling of the brigades three times, twice in the 1920s, and later in 1933. Additionally, brigades that had formerly belonged to the 10th, 11th, and 12th Divisions were reassigned to the Panama Canal, Hawaiian, and Philippine divisions. In the force structure, seven brigades remained in an active status, while the other divisional brigade was retained in an inactive status. The National Guard was demobilized back under state control, and after a brief period of organizational turmoil, also retained the brigade and divisional designations and structure used in the war, though some designations were shuffled around and eight new brigades were created. The National Army was demobilized unit by unit, but its unit designations were used to form a new Federal Reserve component, the Organized Reserve Corps (ORC). Twenty new infantry brigades were formed in the ORC, as the ORC created 10 new divisions in the interwar period.

During the war, the Army had briefly organized the 15th Cavalry Division, consisting of the 1st, 2d, and 3d Cavalry Brigades. The brigades continued separately after the division's inactivation until 1919. In 1921, a new 1st Cavalry Division was created, using a variation of the two-brigade square division format, with the 1st and 2d Cavalry Brigades replacing the infantry brigades.[1]

European experimentation made Army leaders relook at the mechanization of cavalry and the employment of tanks as an item of interest in the late 1920s. In 1928, the Army assembled a group of units, the Experimental Force, at Fort Meade, Maryland. The force, a combination of an infantry battalion, two tank battalions, and a field artillery battalion, under the command of a colonel, would be the first combined arms maneuver brigade in the modern era. A board replaced the Experimental Force in 1928. The Mechanized Force Board report recommended the organization of a combined arms mechanized brigade in 1930. However, the organization barely got off the ground when fiscal restraints caused by the Great Depression reduced it to battalion strength. Under the new Chief of Staff, General Douglas MacArthur, the project was cancelled all together in 1931. MacArthur preferred a branch-specific approach to mechanization and both the cavalry and infantry branches therefore developed mechanized units separate from each other.[2]

Accordingly, cavalry branch organized the 7th Cavalry Brigade (Mechanized) in 1932 to be its experimental mechanized force. The brigade became the first combined arms maneuver brigade organized in the US Army since Washington had attached artillery directly to his brigades in 1777. The brigade's organization grew over time from the arrival of the 1st Cavalry Regiment at Fort Knox, Kentucky, in 1933, to the assignment of the 13th Cavalry Regiment and a battalion of the 68th Field Artillery in 1938. The cavalry regiments became mechanized by using "combat cars," the cavalry branch euphemism for tanks, in place of horses. While the brigade was formally organized without infantry (see Figure 13), the 6th Infantry was transferred to Fort Knox and mechanized in 1936 to support the brigade. The 7th Cavalry Brigade remained in the force structure until 1940, participating in numerous major exercises to validate the mechanized concept. In 1940, it was reorganized into the 1st Armored Division with the formal addition of the 6th Infantry Regiment. A provisional tank brigade, which had been formed early in 1940 from the infantry's tank units, was converted later the same year into the 2d Armored Division.

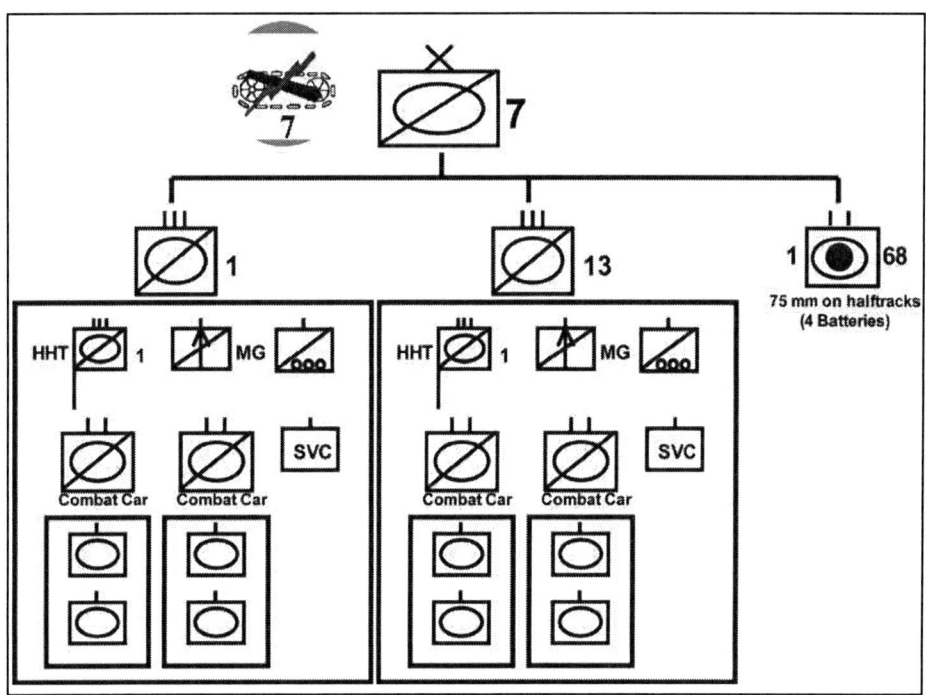

Figure 13. 7th Cavalry Brigade (Mechanized), 1938

Triangularized Divisions

As was previously discussed, after World War I, the Army retained the square division with its two brigades of two infantry regiments. However, since the end of the war, there had been a long-standing debate in the Army over the organization of the infantry division. Finally, between 1936 and 1939, the 2d Infantry Division experimented with a new triangularized infantry division structure, which was ultimately adopted Armywide starting in 1939. In this structure, one infantry regiment and the brigade level of command were removed from the division. The remaining three infantry regiments, commanded by colonels, were directly subordinate to the division commander. The conversion process took several years, with the National Guard, which was mobilized *in toto* in 1940-1941, gradually losing its brigades, until the last was gone in 1942. While some Regular Army units simply disbanded their brigades, the two brigades of some Regular and all of the National Guard and ORC divisions, the latter being reactivated from scratch starting in 1942, were converted to form the new divisional headquarters company and either all or part of the new divisional reconnaissance troop.[3]

As an exception, one brigade, the 51st Infantry Brigade from the Massachusetts National Guard, did, however, manage to get into combat even while its parent division, the 26th, was being converted to the triangular structure. The 51st headquarters, having become excess by the new table of organization, was available to command the American force sent to garrison the French island of New Caledoniain the South Pacific in early 1942. As Task Force (TF) 6814, the brigade headquarters left New York in January 1942, arriving in New Caledonia, after a stop in Australia on 6 March 1942. Initially, the task force controlled two infantry regiments, two artillery regiments, and two engineer regiments. Upon arrival in New Caledonia, a major general assumed command of the augmented force. A third infantry regiment and two more field artillery battalions were added in April 1942, with the whole force being designated as the Americal Division on 24 May 1942. HHC, 51st Infantry Brigade, was retained as the division headquarters company, being redesignated so in May 1943. The division fought on Guadalcanal from October 1942 to February 1943, and later fought on Bougainville and in the Southern Philippines.[4]

During World War II, the 1st Cavalry Division was the only division to retain the two-brigade, square division structure. The Army ultimately dismounted the division and sent it to the Pacific to fight as infantry, with the tag "Special" added to its designation, while retaining the square structure throughout the war and even up to 1949, when the triangular structure was finally adopted. The wartime division's cavalry regiments, after being dismounted, were smaller in size than a standard infantry regiment, and were reorganized partially under infantry and partially under cavalry organizational tables.[5]

After the conversion to the triangular division, only two brigades were organized in the Army during World War II. The 1st Parachute Infantry Brigade was organized at Fort Benning, Georgia, in 1942. In 1943, the brigade was redesignated as the 1st Airborne Infantry Brigade and the 2d Airborne Infantry Brigade was also organized at Fort Benning. Both brigades supported airborne training, but after most nondivisional airborne units deployed overseas in 1944, the 1st Brigade was disbanded. The 2d Brigade deployed to the United Kingdom to support airborne training there and was disbanded in early 1945.[6]

The US Army fought in World War II with three commands at roughly the same level as the former brigade: the regiment, the group, and the brigade, which was still sparingly used as an administrative headquarters for pooled separate battalions, were still sparingly used. Both groups and regiments were commanded by colonels. While the regiment was composed of its own organic battalions and regimental-level companies, the group was merely a headquarters to which subordinate General Headquarters (GHQ) battalions could be assigned.[7] Table 5 illustrates the differences and similarities.

Apart from in the Americal and 1st Cavalry Divisions, for all intents and purposes, the maneuver brigade as a tactical command did not exist in the US Army in World War II. However, two organizations widely used in the war bear mentioning as the future history of the brigade later in the century was clearly descended from these two units: the armored division combat command and the regimental combat team.

Table 5. Regiment versus Brigade versus Group

	Commanded by	Subordinate Units	Type	Primary Use
Regiment	Colonel	Organic Battalions	Tactical and administrative headquarters	Tactical (except in old style armored divisions)
Group	Colonel	Nonorganic battalions	Administrative headquarters (except in the cavalry)	To control GHQ units
Brigade	Brigadier General	Nonorganic groups and/or battalions	Tactical and administrative headquarters	Administrative or to control a force tactically smaller than a division

The Combat Command of the Armored Division

The organization of a new type of combat division, the armored division, led to experiments with unit structure. The basic difficulty with the employment of armor was its inherent combined arms nature. An organizational structure of pure tank and infantry regiments would not be organized in the manner in which early war experience had shown armor was fought best: a combination of tanks, mechanized or armored infantry, and self-propelled artillery.

The armored division was reorganized numerous times during the early part of the World War II. Most revisions involved the ratio of tanks to infantry and the use of brigade and regimental headquarters. Additionally, the formation of combat teams of tanks and infantry at the battalion and brigade level was an operational imperative for the new armored force. Early versions of the division contained an armored brigade consisting of three subordinate armored regiments. An infantry regiment, which reported directly to the division commander, was also part of the organization.[8]

Eventually, two different armored division organizations were used in World War II. Both no longer had brigade headquarters, but employed a small brigade-equivalent headquarters, a combat command, to control the combat teams in which the division was supposed to operate. The "heavy" structure retained branch-specific regimental headquarters, as well as two combat commands, A and B, which were command and control headquarters without any organic units assigned to them. The two armored regiments consisted of six tank battalions. The armored infantry regiment in the heavydivision provided three infantry battalions. These battalions were then used to form combat teams and the teams were assigned on a mission basis to the two combat commands, one of which was commanded by a brigadier general, the other by a colonel. The regimental headquarters were, therefore, basically administrative and in combat practice, the armored ones were used to create task forces, as were tank battalions, and the infantry regimental headquarters was used to form an ad hoc third combat command headquarters. The 2d and 3d Armored Divisions fought the war under this organization, retaining it as they were already in combat when a new, "lighter" organization was adopted in 1943.[9]

The majority of the armored divisions in the US Army in World War II, 13 out of 15, fought utilizing the light division structure. This organization eliminated the regiment in the division. Three separate tank and three separate armored infantry battalions replaced the two

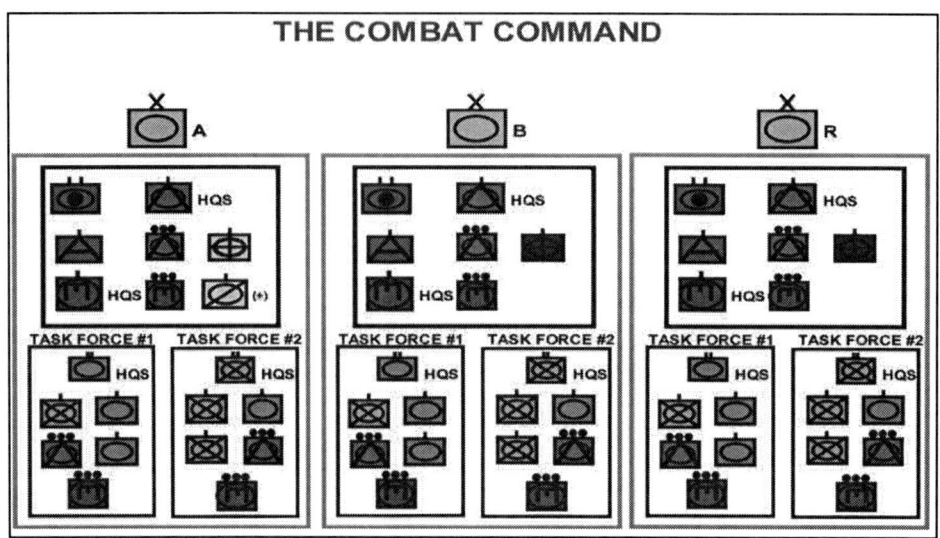

Figure 14. Typical Organization of a Light Armored Division Combat Command

tank regiments and infantry regiment. An A and a B Combat Command headquarters were part of the division, with a brigadier general and colonel commanding each respectively. A smaller headquarters, Combat Command Reserve (CCR), under an infantry colonel, was organized to command the divisional reserve or rear area. In practice, the many armored group headquarters which had been controlling the GHQ tank battalions before they were assigned to armies and corps, were then used to augment the small combat command headquarters and to make CCR into a full-sized headquarters equal with the other two. In some cases, combat commands fought separate from their parent division, either in support of infantry divisions or under a corps headquarters.[10]

The combat command was a unique organization. With no forces assigned to it, habitual attachments in the light division usually included a tank battalion, an armored infantry battalion and an armored field artillery battalion. With these, the commander usually formed two task forces by having each battalion swap a company. One task force would consist of two tank and one armored infantry companies and the other of two armored infantry and one tank company. The armored infantry usually was equipped with, and rode into battle on the M2 half track.[11]

The mission-oriented/task organized structure of the combat command often did not survive the crucible of combat. Many divisions retained the same organization for combat commands throughout the war. The detachment of combat commands to support infantry divisions or to otherwise fight independent of their parent divisions encouraged this. Nevertheless, some divisions did task organize, particularly those that used the reserve command as a reserve or rear area command. Some of these divisions rotated combat battalions through the reserve command as they got worn out in combat.[12]

Throughout World War II, there was a great debate over the ratio of infantry to tanks in the armored division. In the light division, the ratio was 1:1. In the heavy division, the ratio was

1:2. The heavy division, in particular, preferred to operate with an attached infantry regiment supported by truck companies to bring its ratio closer to that of the light division.

The European Theater of Operations General Board, which convened in 1945 to analyze combat operations and organization, recommended that the combat command be scrapped and replaced by a combined arms regiment. Despite, this, the postwar Army retained the combat command. After the war, a modified version of the light armored division structure was adopted Armywide, with an additional tank and infantry battalion assigned to the division, with the infantry battalions increased by one company each, and the combat command headquarters plussed up. Combat Commands A and B were now both commanded by brigadier generals. In 1954, the reserve command was redesignated as Combat Command C, and elevated to equal status with the other two commands, though it was still commanded by a colonel. Despite many proposed and tested changes in organization, the combat command remained the major maneuver element within the armored division up to 1963, with only the battalion designations changing in 1957 when the Army adopted the Combat Arms Regimental System (CARS), which discarded the separate battalion designation system used in the armored division up to that point, replacing it with a system based on battalions belonging to nontactical regiments.[13]

Figure 15. Remagen Bridgehead. *Army in Action Series, DA Poster 21-32*

Combat Command B, 9th Armored Division, at Remagen, Germany

In early March 1945, the US III Corps, consisting of the 1st, 9th, and 78th Infantry Divisions and the 9th Armored Division, was fighting in the Rhineland as part of the First Army. The corps' objective was to advance to the Rhine River and link up with elements of the US Third Army advancing from the south, in the process trapping as many German units as possible on the west bank of the Rhine.

On 6 March 1945, the 9th Armored Division ripped a big hole in the German line and ended the day at Stadt Meckenheim, 10 miles west of the major river obstacle, the Rhine. The German forces in the Rhineland, the 15th and 7th Armies, were in disarray, both trying to put on a show of defending every inch, to comply with Hitler's instructions, and at the same time retreat across the Rhine in good order before getting trapped on the wrong side of the wide river. Trapping the Germans was just what the Americans had in mind.

For 7 March 1945 the 9th Armored Division had the mission closing up to the Rhine and securing the key crossings of the Ahr River near where it met the Rhine. This would prevent the Germans from reaching the Rhine and set up a subsequent advance to the south to join up with units of Patton's Third Army near Coblenz, thus cutting off any Germans left on the wrong side of the Rhine. Combat Command A (CCA), with the 78th Division on its right, would cross the Ahr River at Bad Neuenahr to cut the Ahr Valley escape route of the German LXVII Corps. Combat Command B (CCB), commanded by Brigadier General William Hoge, would advance to the Rhine on the left of CCA, securing the west bank at the town of Remagen and taking easternmost crossings over the Ahr River for a follow on advance to link up with Third Army forces. Even though Remagen contained a large railroad bridge across the Rhine, planners gave little consideration to capturing the bridge intact.

Hoge divided his CCB into two task forces even though he had an extra armored infantry battalion. Attrition had given him only two seasoned commanders at the battalion/task force

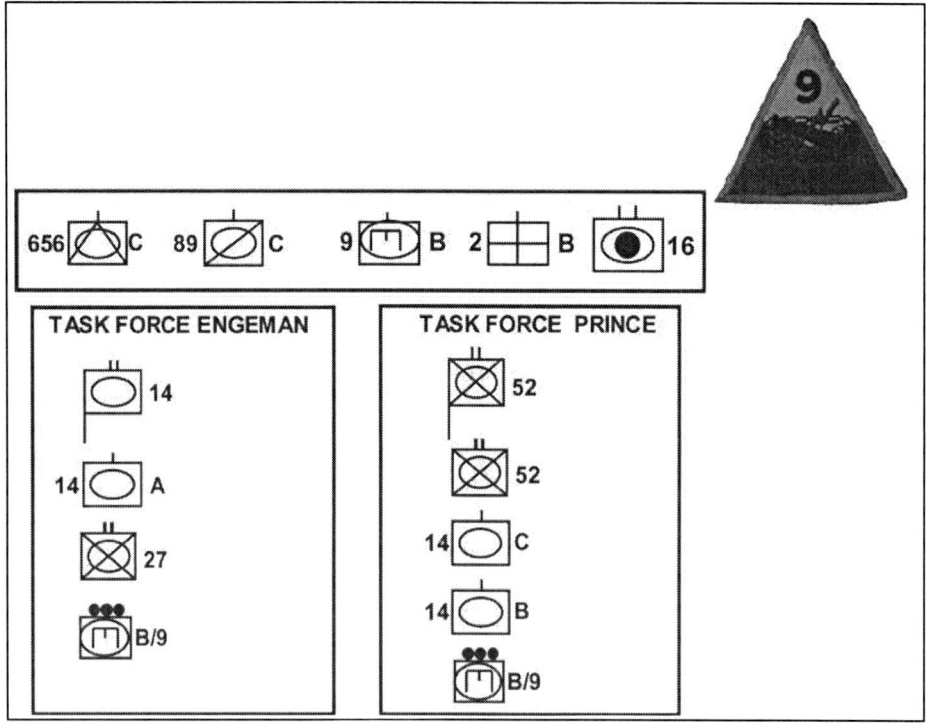

Figure 16. Combat Command B, 9th Armored Division, 7 March 1945

level. Lieutenant Colonel William R. Prince, commander, 52d Armored Infantry Battalion, led a task force consisting of his own battalion, two tank companies from the 14th Tank Battalion, and an armored engineer platoon. TF Prince was the combat command's main effort, advancing to the Ahr River on the left flank of CCA. Lieutenant Colonel Leonard Engeman, the commander of the 14th Tank Battalion, headed the other task force. TF Engeman consisted of Engeman's battalion headquarters and his Company A, and the 27th Armored Infantry Battalion and an armored engineer platoon from Company B, 9th Armored Engineer Battalion. On Prince's left, Engeman was to advance to the Rhine at Remagen, then advance south along the riverbank. The combat command's reconnaissance troop would screen CCB's left flank.

As mentioned previously, Hoge and Engeman gave little thought to capturing the railroad bridge at Remagen intact: the Germans had proven to be masters at blowing Rhine bridges up in the faces of advancing Americans. Therefore, Hoge was much more concerned with preventing the Germans from using the bridge to escape than he was about seizing it for his own use.

In Remagen, however, the rapid American advance over the previous week had left the Germans in disarray. Their LXVII Corps, whose main forces, the 89th Infantry Division and the 277th *Volksgrenadier* Division, were about to be trapped between the III Corps and the Third Army, had received responsibility for the bridge at Remagen from the German rear area authorities only on 6 March. The corps adjutant, Major Hans Scheller, assumed command of the bridgehead, but only arrived at Remagen minutes before the lead American elements arrived at the outskirts of the town. The explosives for the demolition of the bridge had only come 15 minutes before Scheller arrived and were half the required amount and of inferior quality. Scheller found a small infantry company at Remagen made up of a mix of seasoned veterans and local, overage residents, a small engineer company responsible for the demolition of the bridge, and part of an antiaircraft artillery battery. Planned reinforcements of two battalions were no longer available. Other German troops continued to stream across the bridge in a panic, making them unavailable for its defense. Neither Scheller nor the other officers at Remagen received any further instructions from German higher headquarters, even though reports from the troops crossing the bridge indicated that the Americans had broken through and would be at the river that day. Scheller alone would determine when to blow the bridge.[14]

CCB's advance on 7 March started off against only sporadic and uneven German defenses. Both task forces advanced rapidly throughout the morning. TF Prince captured the bridge over the Ahr River at Sinzig by noon. Meanwhile, TF Engeman, lead by Company A, 27th Armored Infantry Battalion, with a platoon of the newly fielded Pershing tanks from Company A, 14th Tank Battalion attached, arrived at the outskirts of Remagen around the same time Scheller arrived in the town to assume command. Second Lieutenant Karl Timmerman, commander of Company A, was amazed to see the bridge still standing and Germans streaming across it.

In short order, Engeman, Hoge, and Major Murray Deevers, commander, 27th Armored Infantry Battalion, joined Timmerman. A German prisoner captured at Sinzig had indicated, incorrectly as it was later to be shown, that the Remagen Bridge was scheduled to be destroyed at 1600, less than 5 hours away. Hoge seeing an opportunity to capture the bridge, ordered Engeman to make a try. Engeman, in turn, ordered the entire 27th Armored Infantry Battalion to advance to the bridge. The tanks and artillery would support in boldly attempting to seize the bridge. Hoge was blatantly ignoring new orders to advance south along the river toward Coblenz.[15]

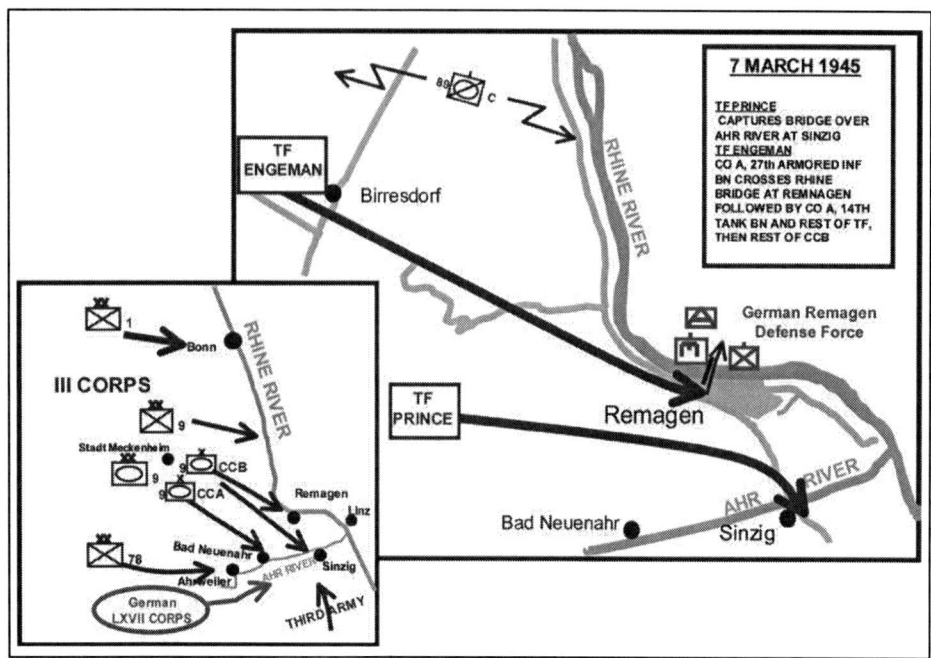

Figure 17. The Advance of CCB, 9th Armored Division, 7 March 1945

The three companies of the 27th Armored Infantry Battalion, led by Timmerman's Company A, and supported directly by Company A, 14th Tank Battalion, methodically advanced through Remagen, approaching the bridge before the 1600 deadline. The Germans responded to the American approach: Captain Karl Friesenhahn, the bridge demolitions commander, immediately, on his own initiative, blew a large antitank crater into the bridge's approach road. He then crossed the bridge to look for Scheller, losing 15 minutes when a tank round exploded near him, knocking him unconscious. Friesenhahn immediately requested and received permission to blow the bridge. However, even though the system had been tested several times, in the clinch it failed. The electrical firing circuit had been damaged. By this time the American forces had the bridge under small arms and machine gun fire. Nevertheless a German sergeant volunteered to go out onto the bridge and manually fire the emergency backup charges. He did so successfully, but when the smoke cleared from the explosion, the bridge still stood. Before the Germans could try a second charge, Timmerman's company was crossing the bridge, supported by Pershing tanks firing to suppress Germans shooting from the towers on each end of the bridge. The armored infantrymen crossed the bridge, clearing the towers as they went and the lead elements soon had a toehold on the opposite bank, capturing most of Scheller's men, who meekly surrendered when prompted from their shelter in a railroad tunnel next to the bridge.[16]

After the first troops crossed the river, Hoge immediately, on his own authority, ordered the whole 27th Battalion across. He also had some of his engineers go to the bridge and remove all traces of demolitions and set the wheel in motion for the erection of pontoon bridges to augment the damaged railroad bridge. Then he contacted the division commander, Major General John Leonard, who sent the news up higher and relieved CCB of its mission on the Ahr River so that Hoge could get the whole combat command onto the far bank. After dark the tanks of the 14th Battalion crossed, followed by the rest of the combat command and elements of the 78th and 9th Infantry Divisions. The rest of the 9th Armored Division soon followed, then the whole III Corps. Hoge was the bridgehead commander until the first follow-on division commander arrived.[17]

The Germans committed sizeable forces to eliminate the bridgehead and utilized frogmen, V-2 rocket volleys, and newly fielded jet bombers. The bridge ultimately collapsed on its own 10 days after its capture. By then, pontoon bridges had replaced it and there was an extensive bridgehead was on the west bank. The German attempts to destroy the bridgehead failed. As a sign of the low state the German armed forces had reached in early 1945, Scheller was executed by a flying court-martial on 12 March 1945. Also executed for their roles at Remagen were the commanders of the engineer regiment and the battalion responsible for the bridge and an air defense officer who could not prove he had destroyed some of his experimental weapons before they could fall into American hands. The commander of the infantry company at Remagen was found guilty in absentia, he already being a prisoner of war (POW), while, ironically, the engineer company commander, Friesenhahn, who was directly responsible for the demolition, also already a POW, was found innocent, probably because of his status as a longtime member of the Nazi Party. Scheller had commanded at Remagen less than 4 hours when the bridge was crossed and had no control over the supply of demolitions, the American advance, or the troops assigned to him. He also had no means of counterattacking or communicating with higher headquarters except through personal contact. The only decision he had made was to delay the demolition of the bridge a few minutes to let a field artillery battalion cross.[18] Portions of the German LXVII Corps headquarters escaped across the Rhine south of Remagen, only to be committed and depleted in counterattacks against the bridgehead.

The capture of the bridge at Remagen was essential in speeding the end of the war. The depleted Germans were soon surrounded in the Ruhr pocket and American armored forces, including the 9th Armored Division advanced far to the east. The 9th itself ended the war in upper Bavaria near Weiden. CCB was later awarded the Presidential Unit Citation for its actions at Remagen. Hoge went on to command the 4th Armored Division and higher units. His flexibility in the use of his combat command validated the concept of its employment in a mobile, fluid combat environment. The lesson would not be lost on Army planners later when they were seeking a flexible organization below the division level to facilitate and execute combat operations on the modern battlefield in all kinds of units, not just armored ones. But that would not be until the early 1960s.

The Regimental Combat Team

With the adoption of the triangular infantry division, the regiment replaced the brigade as the basic subordinate maneuver command in the division. When a separate force of infantry smaller than a division was required for operations, the Army formed a new organization based on an infantry regimental headquarters. This was the regimental combat team (RCT). By the end of the war, almost all infantry regiments not assigned to a division were RCTs.

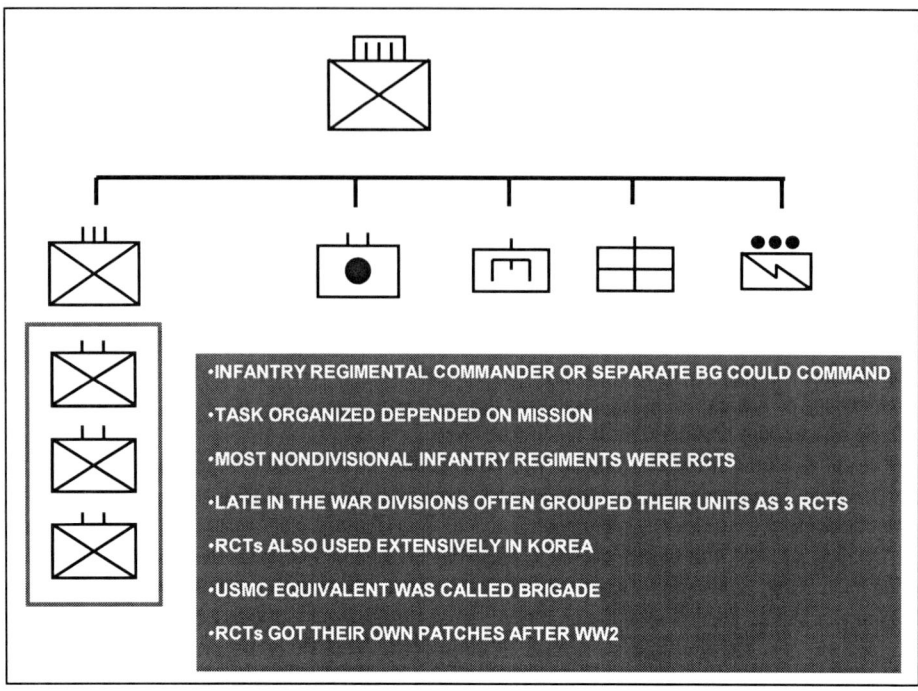

Figure 18. Typical Organization of a Regimental Combat Team

The RCT was an infantry regiment augmented with the support and combat support elements usually allocated within the division to support the regiment. With such augmentation, the RCT was capable of independent action and operations. Most of the time the colonel who commanded the infantry regiment commanded the RCT. Occasionally a brigadier general was sent to command an RCT. Typically an RCT consisted of, in addition to the infantry regiment, a field artillery battalion, engineer and medical companies, and a signal platoon. The organization was tailored for its particular mission, so different elements, such as antiaircraft artillery and tanks, could be added to groom the RCT for its particular assignment. The US Marine Corps also employed the RCT concept in World War II and after, but called their RCTs brigades.[19]

In the later stages of World War II, division commanders began organizing their three infantry regiments as RCTs within the division, giving them an appropriate slice of the division's combat and combat service support assets. This made it easier to detach regiments to other divisions or to attach additional regiments.

As with the combat command, the RCT concept lasted after World War II. RCTs were even authorized their own shoulder patches in the postwar era and were used extensively in the Korean War. The 187th Airborne RCT, consisting of parachute units detached from the 11th Airborne Division to fight in Korea, executed two combat airdrops during the war. The 5th RCT's structure, as of mid-1950, is given in Figure 18, to illustrate a typical RCT organization of the Korean War era. The RCT concept was retained until the Pentomic reorganization in 1957 (see Figure 19).

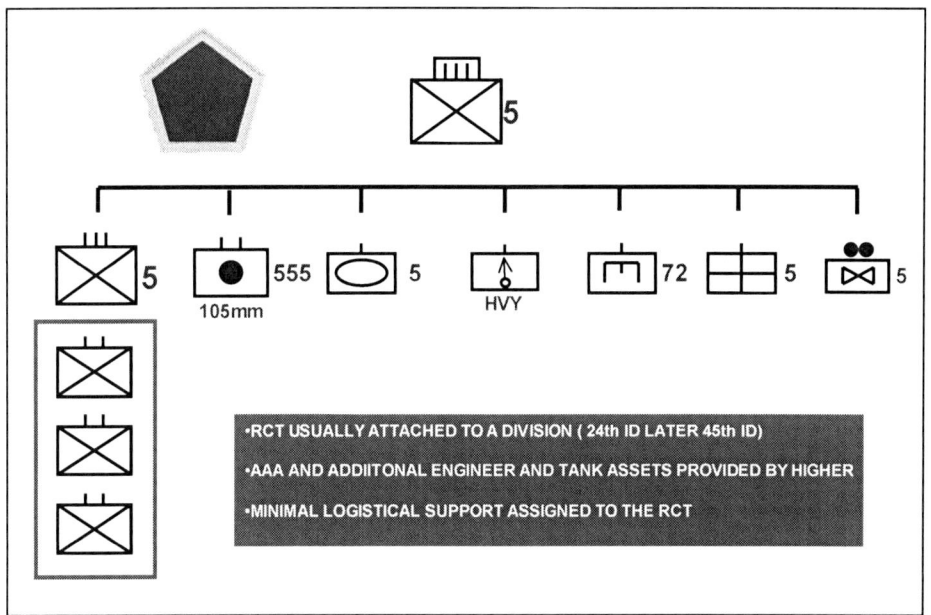

Figure 19. Organization of 5th RCT, Korea, 1950

NOTES

1. John B. Wilson, *Maneuver and Firepower: The Evolution of Divisions and Separate Brigades.* Army Lineage Series (Washington, DC: Government Printing Office, 1998), 64, 98.

2. Ibid., 122-23.

3. The Regular Army divisions converted to the new structure before 1941 were the ones that disbanded their brigades.

4. Shelby Stanton, *Order of Battle: US Army, World War II* (Novato, CA: Presidio, 1984), 184-85.

5. Ibid., 71-72; Wilson, *Maneuver and Firepower*, 191; John Wilson, *Armies, Corps, Divisions and Separate Brigades* (Washington, DC: US Army Center of Military History, 1999), 123, 125.

6. Wilson, *Firepower and Maneuver*, 169, 190-91; Wilson, *Armies, Corps, Divisions and Separate Brigades*, 135-36.

7. GHQ was the designation for units, usually battalions not assigned to a division or corps, but assigned as needed by the theater commander and his subordinates.

8. Glen R. Hawkins and James Jay Carafano, *Prelude to Army XXI: US Army Division Design Initiatives and Experiments 1917-1995* (Washington, DC: CMH, 1997), 8; *Sixty Years of Reorganizing for Combat: A Historical Trend Analysis.* Combat Studies Institute (CSI) Report No. 14 (Fort Leavenworth, KS: CSI, 1999), 9.

9. Wilson, *Maneuver and Firepower*, 184-85, 198; The General Board, United States Forces, European Theater, *Organization, Equipment and Tactical Employment of the Armored Division*, Number 48, 3, A-2, A-3 (hereafter referred to as General Board.)

10. Ibid.

11. General Board, Appendix 1.

12. Ibid.

13. Wilson, *Maneuver and Firepower*, 227-28; General Board, 24.

14. Ken Hechler, *The Bridge at Remagen* (New York: Ballantine, 1957), 112-15.

15. Hechler, 125; US Army Corps of Engineers History Office, *Engineer Memoirs: General William M. Hoge*, EP 870-1-25 (Fort Belvoir, VA: US Army Corps of Engineers, 1993), 143-45.

16. Hechler, 135-39, 151-52. There are many theories as to why the bridge remained standing. Most likely a tank round damaged the connection to the main charge. See Hechler, 219-20.

17. *Engineer Memoirs*, 145-46.

18. Hechler, 130, 196-212.

19. In the 1990s, the USMC began referring to their reinforced regiments as RCTs.

Chapter 6

THE EARLY MODERN BRIGADE, 1958-1972

Pentomic Era

Following World War II, the US Army retained the organizational structures, with minor modifications, which had won that war. This organization—which did not include a maneuver unit called the brigade after the two brigades in the 1st Cavalry Division were eliminated in 1949—was also used to fight the Korean War in 1950-1953. Despite the success of the triangular infantry division in two wars, the Army radically changed the structure in 1958 by converting the infantry division to what became known as the Pentomic Division. Ostensively, the Pentomic structure was designed to allow infantry units to survive and fight on an atomic battlefield. Structurally it eliminated the regiment and battalion, replacing both with five self-contained "battlegroups," each of which were larger than an old style battalion, but smaller than a regiment. A full colonel commanded the battlegroup and his captains commanded four, later five, subordinate rifle companies.

The Pentomic Division structurally reflected that of the World War II European theater airborne divisions. This was no surprise since three European airborne commanders dominated the Army's strategic thinking after the Korean War: Army Chief of Staff General Matthew Ridgway, Eighth Army commander General Maxwell Taylor, and VII Corps commander Lieutenant General James Gavin. Though theoretically triangular in design, the two airborne divisions Ridgway, Taylor, and Gavin commanded in the war, the 82d and 101st, fought as division task forces reinforced with additional parachute regiments and separate battalions. For most of the Northern European campaign, both divisions had two additional parachute regiments attached to them, giving them five subordinate regiments, each commanded by colonels. Parachute regiments were smaller than standard infantry regiments by organization and attrition often made them even smaller, giving the 82d or 101st commander a perfect prototype of the structure that later became the Pentomic Division.[1]

The Pentomic organization, officially known as the Reorganization of the Current Infantry Division (ROCID) went through frequent modifications from its conception in 1954 to 1958 when it was finally adopted, and even after adoption. The original tables of organization (TOE) which were implemented included a small brigade headquarters commanded by the brigadier general assistant division commander. This headquarters was designed to provide command and control of attached units from the division as directed by the division commander, and to act as an alternate division command post. The concept was not really used in practice and when Pentomic TOEs were modified in February 1960, the brigade was eliminated.[2]

Except for minor structural modifications, the armored division, with its three combat commands, was unaffected by the Pentomic changes. The division was considered already well suited for atomic operations and senior armor commanders favored the flexible combat command structure.[3]

As part of the Pentomic reorganization, the regiment and separate battalion were eliminated as tactical units in the infantry, field artillery, and tank units. The battle group, and later the battalion, became the basic maneuver unit. These units were, however, designated as components of historic regiments that became notional units. The new system, CARS, and a later variation of it, the Army Regimental System, is still in use by the US Army today. In this designation system, battalions in the infantry, armor, cavalry, and artillery, later field and air defense, were designated as numbered battalions belonging to a particular regiment. Separate companies would be lettered companies of a specific regiment. The regiments themselves were administrative entities, except in certain units, like armored cavalry, where the regiment was retained as a combined arms unit commanded by a colonel. This will be discussed in greater detail later in this work.

With the adoption of the new Pentomic divisional structure and the elimination of the regiment as a tactical unit, the force structure required a replacement for the now defunct RCT. The brigade was revived to fill this role. Accordingly, two brigades, numbered 1st and 2d, stationed at Fort Benning, and Fort Devens, Massachusetts, respectively, were established in the active Army force structure. The Army created three additional brigades. The 29th in Hawaii, the 92d in Puerto Rico, and the 258th in Arizona, were created in the Army National Guard to replace existing RCTs.

When established, the new nondivisional Pentomic brigade became the first permanently organized combined arms brigade in Army history. The brigade commander was a brigadier general and the brigade had two subordinate battlegroups commanded by full colonels, as well as a field artillery battalion and a support element, the brigade trains. Each battlegroup contained four rifle companies and a 4.2-inch mortar battery. While brigade organization varied in other units, the brigade established at Fort Devens in 1958, the 2d Infantry Brigade,

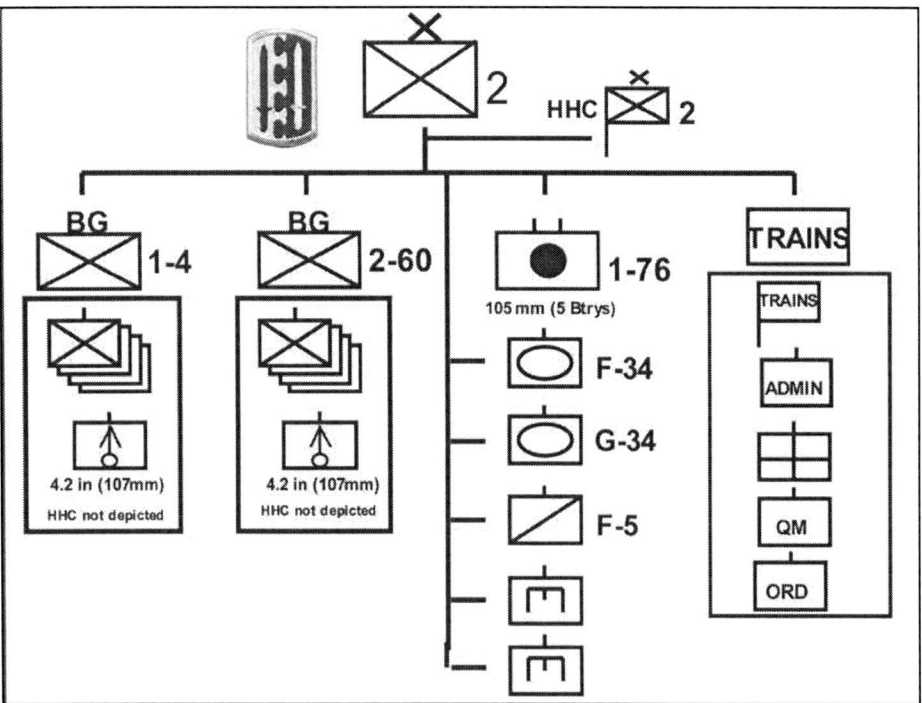

Figure 20. The Pentomic Brigade

60

also included two tank companies, two engineer companies, and a reconnaissance company. Its organization is illustrated in Figure 20.

ROAD Brigades and Airmobile Brigades

There were concerns about the Pentomic concept almost immediately. The span of control for the division commander was great and not compensated by advances in communications technology. Armored personnel carriers (APCs) were centralized in a transportation unit and assigned with drivers to infantry units as needed, though only one battle group at a time could be so mechanized. The command structure jumped from captain to colonel without any intermediate levels of command in between. And the infantry and armored divisions remained in two completely different organizational structures.

While the Army adopted the inventive Pentomic structure, most of the rest of the world's armies retained or adopted more traditional organizations. In the British army, the brigade had traditionally contained subordinate battalion-sized units, called regiments in the armored force, cavalry, and artillery branches, and called battalions in the infantry. During World War II, brigades were augmented with support elements and called brigade groups. To the present day, the British have maintained this concept. Brigades and brigade groups have, since 1945, become the basic operational unit in the British army in lieu of the division.[4]

When the new West German army, the *Bundeswehr*, was established in the mid-1950s, it, like the French army of the same era, used the combat command structure of the US armored division. However, starting in 1957, the Germans reorganized into a brigade structure. The brigades were combined arms organizations and fixed in structure, with permanently assigned combat battalions and support elements. While brigades still belonged to divisions, the brigade here too replaced the division as the *Bundeswehr*'s basic tactical unit at the operational level.[5]

The US Army's Continental Army Command (CONARC) began formal studies for a new divisional structure in December 1960, only two years after the adoption of the Pentomic structure. In 1961, President John F. Kennedy approved CONARC's proposal, the Reorganization Objective Army Divisions (ROAD), for immediate implementation. The Army was reorganized between 1961 and 1963.[6] With later modifications, the ROAD structure is basically still in use in the Army today.

Unlike the previous organizational structure, ROAD created a universal divisional structure, which depending on the mix of combat battalions, could be armored, mechanized infantry, infantry, or airborne. ROAD restored the brigade as a command, both in divisions and separately. ROAD established three brigade headquarters in each division, the 1st, 2d, and 3d. The new brigade combined features of the former divisional regiments and the armored division's combat commands. Like the former regiments, the new divisional brigades controlled battalions, were commanded by colonels, and reported directly to the division commander. Like the combat command, the ROAD brigade was a headquarters with no organic troops, being task organized by the division commander for particular missions. The brigade was not to be part of the division's administrative or logistical chains of command. Maneuver combat battalions (infantry, mechanized infantry, armor) would be assigned to the brigade in a mix of from two to five battalions, to complete specific missions. One of three divisional direct support field artillery battalions would normally be assigned to support each brigade. A slice of combat support and combat service support elements assigned to the division would be placed in support of the brigade.[7]

A new type of infantry, mechanized, was established with the ROAD reorganization. This type of infantry was the lineal descendent of the armored infantry formerly found in the armored divisions. Unlike the old armored infantry, mechanized infantry battalions could now be part of organizations other than armored divisions. And unlike the APC-mounted infantry in the Pentomic division, the new mechanized infantry had its APCs assigned directly to the unit, with one per infantry squad. In brigades with a mix of tank and mechanized infantry battalions, the old task force concept was codified into battalion task forces and company teams. A battalion task force was a tank or mechanized infantry battalion with one or more companies of the battalion cross-attached to an equivalent battalion of the other branch. Therefore, a battalion task force could consist of a mix of tank and mechanized infantry companies. Once formed, a battalion task force could in turn combine mixes of tank and mechanized infantry platoons under its companies, the resulting unit being referred to as a company team.[8]

In armored divisions, lineages for the new brigades were created by the redesignation of the former combat commands. In infantry, mechanized, and airborne divisions, the third brigade was created from scratch or from the former divisional headquarters company, which had been eliminated in the Pentomic division. The 1st and 2d brigades were created based on the lineages of the old square division brigades. While some of these had been disbanded, many had been converted to all or part of the divisional reconnaissance troop in the triangular division. Some Army National Guard divisional brigades were given special numbers, to reflect historical designations. This was done particularly in divisions that were formed of contingents from multiple states. Active Army separate brigades were named using the designations of former Organized Reserve/Army Reserve divisional brigades no longer in the force structure.

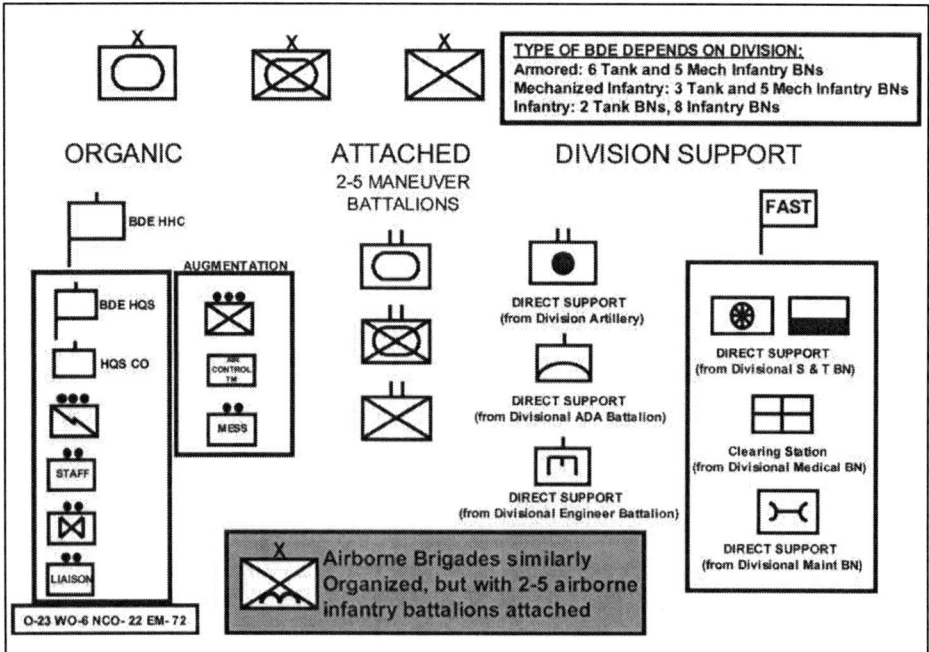

Figure 21. The ROAD Divisional Brigade

Four separate infantry brigades were also created from inactivating Army Reserve divisions, designating them with the lower brigade number formerly associated with the division under the square organization (before 1942). In both cases this was done so as to give the brigades numerical designations high enough not to be confused with the numbers used in divisional brigades. ARNG separate brigades were designated either with old square division brigade designations or, if they were replacing an inactivated ARNG division, by using the former division number. Several ARNG brigades were designated with the number of former infantry regiments that had been replaced in the force structure. Army Reserve training divisions, which formerly had training regiments directly under the division headquarters, concurrently converted these regiments to sequentially numbered brigades. A complete listing of all brigades since 1958 may be found in Appendix 4.

Separate, nondivisional brigades were part of the ROAD concept from the start for missions requiring less than a division or for the reserve components. Unlike divisional brigades, which were commanded by colonels, the separate brigade retained the tradition of being commanded by a brigadier general. While planners envisioned these brigades to be like divisional ROAD brigades, a bare bones headquarters with two to five attached maneuver battalions, and support provided either by a corps or a division to which the brigade would be attached, one brigade, the 173d Airborne Brigade on Okinawa, was established from the start with organic support troops. This was because Army planners envisioned the airborne brigade as a special task force that could deploy rapidly and act independently. Within a year similar support elements were applied to all separate brigades. As with the earlier RCTs, the separate brigades were also given their own unique shoulder patches.[9]

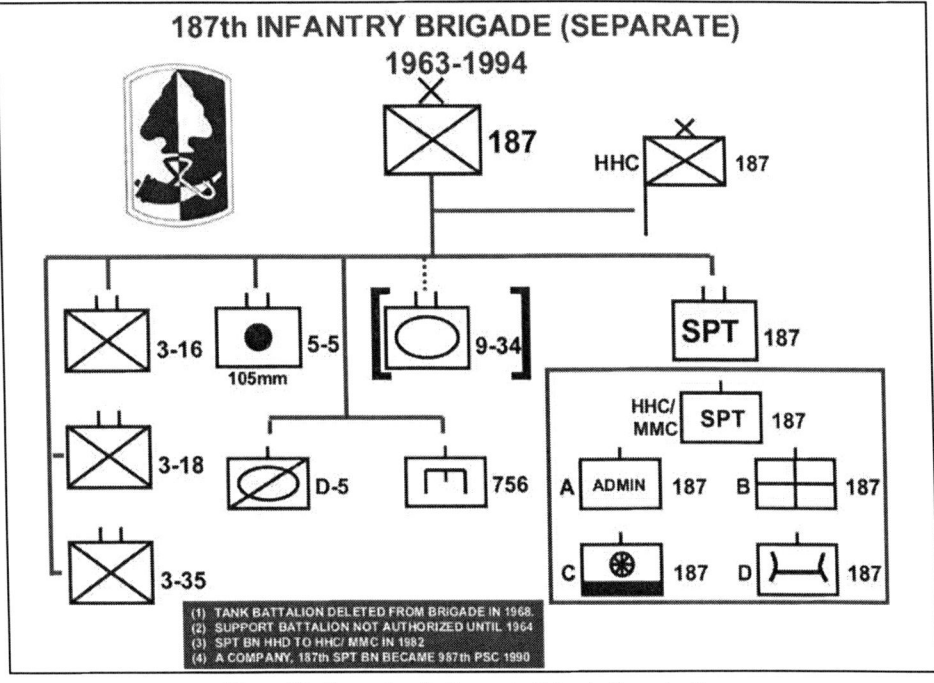

Figure 22. Example of a Separate Brigade Organization

63

The standard separate ROAD brigade, thereafter, in addition of having between two and five maneuver battalions, consisted of a small headquarters company, an armored cavalry troop, an engineer company, a direct support field artillery battalion, and a support battalion. The support battalion consisted of a small headquarters and administrative, medical, maintenance, and supply and transportation companies. The 173d Airborne Brigade additionally contained a separate tank company. An example of a typical brigade organization is found in Figure 22. The brigade illustrated was a US Army Reserve (USAR) brigade located in New England.

While the Army reorganized under ROAD at Fort Benning, an experimental organization was formed to test the incorporation of the helicopter directly into the divisional structure. This test unit, designated the 11th Air Assault Division, was ultimately redesignated as the 1st Cavalry Division (Airmobile) in mid-1965, becoming an additional type of ROAD division: the airmobile division. The airmobile division was designed with helicopter, and originally fixed wing, assets to provide operational troop movements and fire support. Two aspects of the organization and employment of the 1st Cavalry Division (Airmobile) relates specifically to the employment of brigades. One brigade of the division, including a brigade headquarters and three of the infantry battalions, was qualified additionally as paratroopers, along with one of the field artillery battalion and slices of the division's support command. This unique composition of one brigade within a division lasted only until 1968, when the paratrooper qualification was dropped.[10] The second brigade-specific feature of the airmobile division was in its inherent structure. Assigned to the division was an aviation group which consisted of two assault

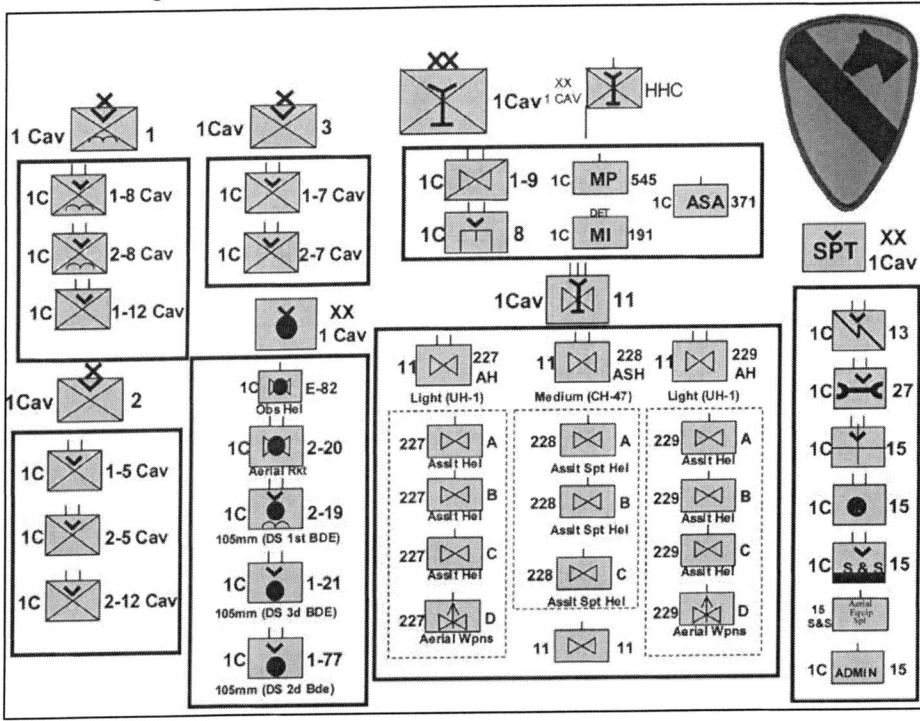

Figure 23. The First Cavalry Division (Airmobile), 1965

64

helicopter battalions equipped with the UH-1 Huey light transport helicopter and one assault support helicopter battalion equipped with the medium CH-47 Chinook transport helicopter. Each aviation battalion could carry a comparable sized infantry or artillery unit. Accordingly, the airmobile division was designed so that the aviation assets could move only one brigade at a time. The division, therefore, was naturally fought by maneuvering brigades. One brigade was in contact, one was in reserve, and one was reequipping and guarding the division's large base camp. The 1st Cavalry Division's organizational structure upon its deployment to Vietnam in 1965 is illustrated in 23.[11] In 1968 the 101st Airborne Division became the second Army airmobile division, a role it continues to the present day, with the tag "airmobile" being changed to "air assault" in 1974.[12]

Figure 24. The 196th Infantry Brigade Ships Out to Vietnam, Boston, 1966

The Brigade in Vietnam

The ROAD reorganization had barely been effected when it was given its first test in Vietnam. Earlier units that arrived were either separate brigades or brigade elements of deploying divisions. The first Army unit deployed was the 173d Airborne Brigade in May 1965, followed closely by the 1st Brigade, 101st Airborne Division, and 2d Brigade, 1st Infantry Division. From then until the end of the US ground involvement in the war in 1972, 18 divisional brigades, including one detached from its division for a long period of time, five separate brigades, including three later made part of the American Division, and two brigades detached from their parent division served in Vietnam at one time or another. In June 1972, the 196th Infantry Brigade departed Vietnam as the last brigade in country.

In many ways Vietnam was a war of brigades. Brigades, especially in the early days, were moved from one part of the country to another or from one mission to another with a flexibility and celerity that quickly validated the ROAD concept. The flexibility of the ROAD brigade with its subordinate, self-contained battalions, greatly facilitated the use of the helicopter to transport infantry. Several times in the course of the war, brigade elements operated far from their parent unit for extended periods. In one case, in August 1967, the 4th and 25th Infantry Divisions swapped brigades including subordinate infantry, armor, and field artillery battalions, with the brigades changing designations.[13] One division was created in Vietnam by assigning three separate brigades, the 11th, 196th, and 198th Light Infantry, to a single new command. The new division so cobbled together, was given the designation of the Americal Division, as that division had been created in World War II under similar circumstances. The early organization of the Americal, whose official designation was 23d Infantry Division, is illustrated in Figure 24. The division was later reorganized as a standard ROAD division, except that its brigades retained the 11th, 196th, and 198th designations. The Americal Division also retained an attached aviation group throughout its stay in Vietnam.[14]

For duty in Vietnam, both separate and divisional brigades were modified, either prior to deployment or in country. A new type of brigade, the light infantry brigade, was created specifically for service in the counterinsurgency environment of Vietnam. The brigade contained less than half of the number of vehicles found in the standard infantry brigade. The infantry battalions were organized with a structure similar to the airmobile infantry battalions of the First Cavalry Division, to facilitate the conduct of airmobile operations.[15] Most light brigades had four assigned infantry battalions, instead of the more typical three.

There were additional attachments found in Vietnam. Early on brigades acquired provisionally organized long-range patrol companies. These were later standardized and then redesigned as ranger companies. The 173d Airborne Brigade received its own aviation company in

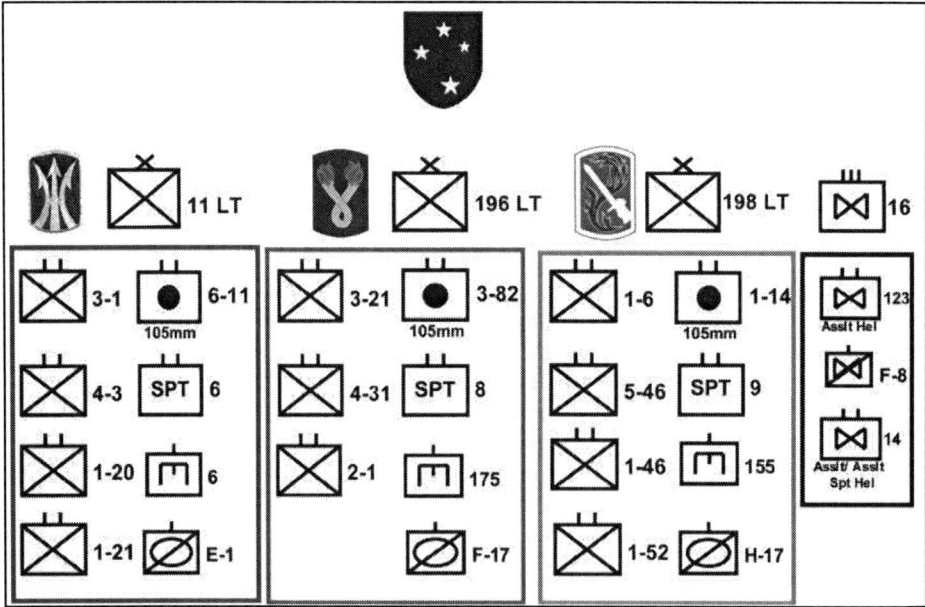

Figure 25. The Americal (23d Infantry) Division as Originally Organized in 1967

1966, making the brigade a de facto airmobile brigade. During the course of the war, several divisional brigades were detached from their parent divisions and deployed to Vietnam. These separate divisional brigades were given a slice of division support elements, typically a direct support field artillery battalion, an engineer and a signal company, and an armored cavalry troop. For these geographically separate brigades, the parent divisions also organized a provisional support battalion made up of companies from the division support battalion, similar to those found in the support battalion of the separate nondivisional brigades, i.e., an administrative, medical, maintenance, and supply and transportation company.[16]

The ubiquitous use of the helicopter and the area, rather than linear, nature of warfare in Vietnam gave brigade operations a unique flavor. Typically a brigade in counterinsurgency mode would be given a geographically based tactical area of operations (TAOR). In its TAOR, a brigade would defend any fire support bases (firebases or FSBs) established in the TAOR, as well as any helicopter landing zones (LZs) and any other larger bases located in the TAOR. A brigade would also secure any land supply routes between the bases and to sources of supply outside the TAOR. Aside from these defensive missions, the brigade conducted offensive operations within its TAOR to destroy any Communist forces and assisted in the internal development and defense of the civilian populace and infrastructure in the TAOR.[17] In Vietnam, the brigade usually fought from a series of LZs and FSBs. Initial operations were designed to find and fix the enemy. FSBs would be established within artillery range of probable or known enemy positions and artillery batteries would be airlifted into the FSBs. Follow-on operations would air assault troops into LZs whose locations were designed to surround the enemy. Then the brigade commander would coordinate the maneuver of the battalions toward the enemy positions. Once the exact positions were found, the battalions would either assault them directly or attack them by fire support assets followed by an assault, usually from two directions. A good example of this type of operation can be found in the actions of the 3d Brigade, 101st Airborne Division (Airmobile), in the A Shau Valley in May 1969, this action codenamed Operation APACHE SNOW, culminated in the Battle of Hamburger Hill, which is highlighted in the next section of this chapter.

Sometimes combat operations in Vietnam consisted of multiple brigades and a combination of air assault and ground assault operations. A good example of this was the first phase of Operation JUNCTION CITY, conducted by the 1st and 25th Infantry Divisions in War Zone C, Tay Ninh province, in February and March 1967. Executed over two years earlier than Operation APACHE SNOW and several hundred miles to the south, Operation JUNCTION CITY was a much larger operation in both concept and execution. In fact, its initial air assault, which utilized 249 helicopters to insert eight battalions, with a ninth parachuted in by Air Force aircraft, was the largest airmobile operation of the Vietnam War. The nine battalions were under the control of three brigade headquarters. The three brigades, plus another in the southwest which had deployed via ground transportation, were maneuvered to set up a massive cordon around War Zone C, the sparsely settled, heavily vegetated area of Tay Ninh province directly adjacent to the Cambodian border. In 1967 the major headquarters controlling Communist operations in the south, Central Office for South Vietnam (COSVN), was believed to be in War Zone C. The 9th Viet Cong (VC) Division also operated out of War Zone C, though the 1st Infantry Division had, in 1966, kept the division's two subordinate regiments away from the heavily populated areas to the south and east.[18] Two additional

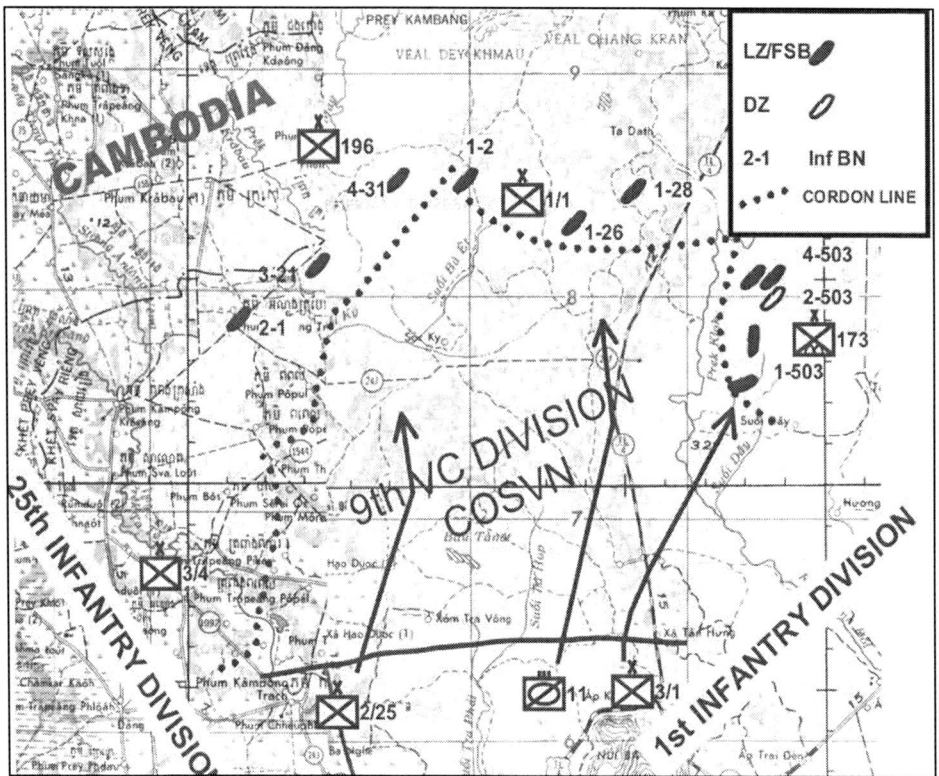

Figure 26. Phase 1 of Operation JUNCTION City, February 1967

brigades, along with an armored cavalry regiment (ACR), executed a ground attack the next day from the south into the area previously cordoned off. Two divisions, the 1st Infantry and 25th Infantry, controlled the six brigades and one ACR assigned to the operation under the overall command of the corps-equivalent headquarters, II Field Force Vietnam. The brigades included a separate infantry, a separate airborne brigade, and a brigade from the 4th Infantry Division attached to the 25th Division.[19]

While only traces of COSVN were found, the operation battered the 9th VC Division, whose response, aside from fleeing, was a series of small scale assaults on US positions that appeared to be isolated, but in fact were not. Operation JUNCTION CITY validated the flexibility of the ROAD brigade concept with its mix of forces, ground and air assaults, and paratrooper drops. This flexibility was the hallmark of US brigade operations in the Vietnam War.

Foreshadowing postwar plans for brigades of different capabilities in the same division, the Army organized one brigade of the 9th Infantry Division as a special amphibious force to operate in the densely populated and enemy infested Mekong River Delta area south of Saigon. The 2d Brigade, 9th Infantry Division, referred to as the Mobile Riverine Force (MRF), consisted of the 3d Battalion, 47th Infantry; 4th Battalion, 47th Infantry; 3d Battalion, 60th Infantry; and the 3d Battalion, 34th Artillery; along with slices of divisional support elements.

The MRF was specially organized for its mission in the United States prior to deployment and served on the Mekong River from 1967 to 1969. The Army selected a brigade-sized unit for the mission because experience had taught that the brigade was the smallest unit capable of operating independently in the Delta. The force worked out of a base on an island in the river at Dong Tam. The Navy directly supported the brigade with five self-propelled barracks ships, two landing ship, tank (LST) landing craft, two large harbor tugboats, and two landing craft repair ships. Additionally, two Navy river assault groups, each capable of transporting a battalion at a time, provided mobility for the force. The river assault groups, which were redesignated later as river assault squadrons, were each equipped with 52 LCM-6 armored landing craft, for use as troop carriers.[20]

The operations of the MRF were highly successful. Viet Cong forces were pushed away from the populated areas of the Delta and the main roads were kept open, allowing farm produce to reach markets in Saigon. The brigade was so successful, that the 9th Division's headquarters eventually moved to Dong Tam as the brigade shifted operations farther south. During the 1968 Tet Offensive, the MRF successively ejected communist forces from the cities of My Tho, Vinh Long, and Can Tho, effectively saving the Delta area from enemy takeover. The brigade was a unique organization in the Army and in Vietnam.[21]

Operation APACHE SNOW: Brigade Employment in Vietnam

The 101st Airborne Division (Airmobile) executed Operation APACHE SNOW in the northern portion of the A Shau Valley in Thua Thien province between 10 May and 7 June 1969 with its 3d Brigade and elements of two regiments from the Army of the Republic of Vietnam's (ARVN) First Infantry Division. This was the middle of three operations that the 101st conducted in different sections of the narrow, 30-mile long valley in 1969.

In May 1969, the A Shau Valley, located on the Laotian border west of Hue, had been a North Vietnamese-controlled sanctuary since a Special Forces camp had been driven out of the valley in 1966.[22] Since then, the valley and its adjoining jungle-covered ridgelines had become a major Communist base area and supply route into the coastal regions of Thua Thien province, Hue, and Quang Tri province to the north. The enemy forces that attacked Hue city during the Tet Offensive in 1968 had assembled in the A Shau Valley and infiltrated out of there. The valley's location next to the safe haven of Laos and the Ho Chi Minh Trail made it of great importance to the North Vietnamese. Later in 1968, the 1st Cavalry Division (Airmobile) had conducted operations in the valley, but did not establish a permanent presence there. After the air cavalry's departure, the Communists restored their infrastructure, which included a main supply route running down the middle of the valley on an improved road, Route 548. Jungle-covered mountains surrounded the valley itself. One of these, the 937-meter high Dong Ap Bia, would become the focus of the 3d Brigade's activities during Operation APACHE SNOW.

The 3d Brigade, commanded by Colonel Joseph Conmy, consisted of three airmobile infantry battalions: 1-506th Infantry, 2-506th Infantry, and 3-187th Infantry. Each battalion had one or more companies detached for FSB security or in a reserve role during the operation. One field artillery battalion, 2-319th Artillery, was in direct support of the brigade, with an additional three batteries in general support, reinforcing. The divisional aerial rocket artillery battalion was also in direct support of the brigade. In addition, an engineer company and two assault helicopter companies from the division's 160th Aviation Group were supporting the brigade.

Troop A, 2-17th Cavalry, from the divisional air cavalry squadron, support the brigade with air reconnaissance and related activities. Companies from the division medical, maintenance, and supply and service battalions were assembled to support the brigade as Forward Service Support Element (FSSE) 3. Supporting brigade operations to the north was the 1st ARVN Infantry Regiment of the 1st ARVN Infantry Division.[23]

The objective of Operation APACHE SNOW was to locate and destroy any enemy found in each battalion's assigned sector, destroy any enemy infrastructure, and, if necessary, fix the enemy in place until reinforcements could arrive. The operation was called a reconnaissance in force (RIF), as the North Vietnamese locations, bases, camps, and defensive positions, would have to be found as the operation progressed. Battalions normally separated into company-sized elements to conduct RIF operations, massing as a battalion as necessary. At the brigade level, airmobile assets would be used to shift battalions to large enemy locations. LZs for the battalions were selected in the hilly area west of the A Shau Valley on the Laotian border, the theory being to get US forces between the Communists and their Laotian sanctuary area, to which, upon contact, they would naturally tend to try to move. All operations were conducted within the range of preemplaced field artillery located at FSBs established in the hills on the eastern side of the valley and at one FSB, Currahee, built on the valley floor south of the area where the battalions were to operate.[24]

Unidentified enemy forces were known to be located in the northern A Shau Valley. The large troop concentration near Dong Ap Bia turned out to be the 29th North Vietnamese Army (NVA) Regiment, a well-trained and reconstituted unit that had not been located since 1968. Two battalions, the 7th and 8th, plus part of the regimental headquarters, defended a hilltop fortified area with extensive bunker and trench line complexes. Farther to the northwest in the A Shau Valley were elements of the 6th NVA Regiment's 806th Battalion and the separate K10 Sapper Battalion.[25]

In preparation for the operation, the infantry battalions were shifted from LZs and FSBs near Hue to FSBs Blaze and Cannon, located on hilltops east of the A Shau Valley near the main ground supply route into the area, Route 547. The brigade command post moved from its large base camp near Hue, Camp Evans, to FSB Berchtesgaden. Three new or formerly abandoned FSBs were quickly built to support the operation: FSB Bradley, located to the north and to be primarily used by the ARVN 1st Regiment; FSB Airborne, located in the hills overlooking the valley from the east, north of FSB Berchtesgaden; and FSB Currahee, built on the valley floor itself at its broadest section, 3,000 meters wide near the village of Ta Bat, . The new FSBs, plus FSBs Cannon and Berchtesgaden, were designed to be mutually supporting and allow the entire area of operations to be within the range of field artillery. On 9 May (D-1), 10 batteries were shifted to these FSBs to support the initial insertions of the infantry.

As mentioned above, the brigade command post was located at FSB Berchtesgaden during the operation. The brigade commander controlled the overall operations of the brigade through the extensive use of nonsecure and secure FM radio, with VHF radio being used between the brigade and division. He augmented radio communication with personal observation from a command and control light observation helicopter and personal visits to unit locations.

Logistics support for the brigade in Operation APACHE SNOW was tailored for the operation. While most logistics assets remained back in the division support command base camp near Hue, medical support and ammunition resupply was brought forward to FSB Blaze. Route 547, the improved road built by Army engineers from Hue to the A Shau Valley, provided a ground main supply route up to FSB Bastogne, several miles short of FSB Blaze. From FSB Bastogne forward, almost all supplies were airlifted, primarily by medium cargo helicopters, the CH-47 Chinook.[26]

On D-Day, 10 May, 65 UH-1H Huey helicopters airlifted the four battalions in consecutive company-sized lifts from FSBs Blaze and Cannon into new LZs on the Laotian border in the jungle area west of the A Shau Valley proper. An extensive 70-minute artillery, aerial rocket, and air support preparation preceded the combat assaults.[27] The battalions all landed without contact and immediately commenced company-sized RIF operations to find the enemy forces known to be in the area. While all four battalions received sporadic contact of one kind or another, one of the companies of 3-187 was stung by contact with entrenched North Vietnamese troops below the summit of Dong Ap Bia, a 937-meter high mountain that dominated the northern A Shau Valley from the west.

Lieutenant Colonel Weldon Honeycutt, 3-187, had a tiger by the tail. But it took him and his brigade commander, Conmy, several days to realize the extent of the enemy force atop Dong Ap Bia. Honeycutt initially continued RIF operations with his other companies and had a single company assault the hilltop on 11 May. When this failed, he went with a two-company assault on 12 May. The terrain and the enemy hindered coordination and this attack also failed.

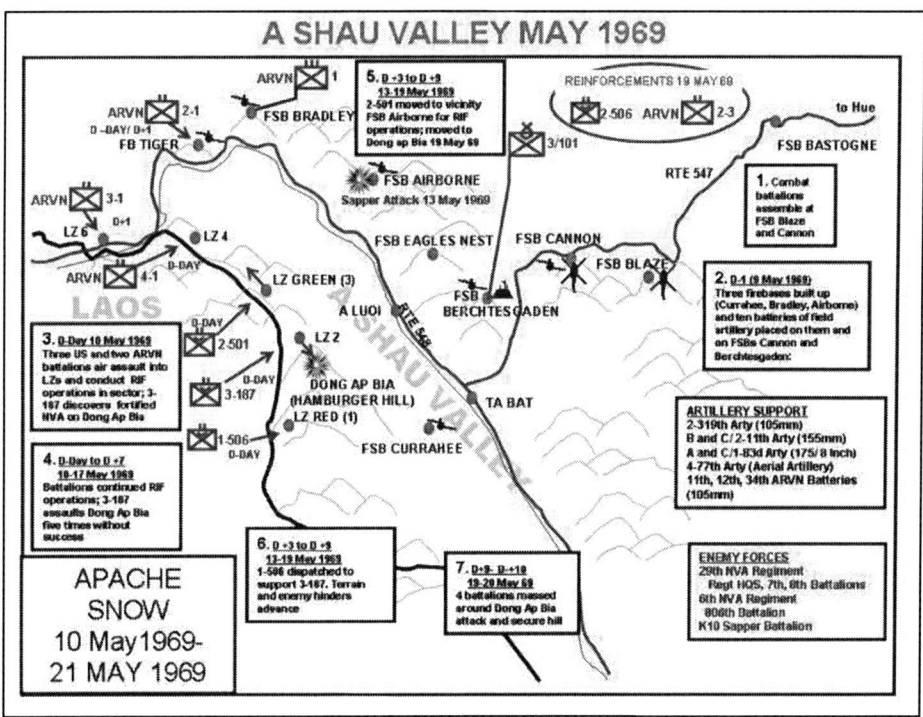

Figure 27. Operation APACHE SNOW, May 1969

A three-company advance the next day also got bogged down, with the third company, advancing to the left of the other two, getting pinned down by heavy enemy fire. A day later, on 14 May, Honeycutt again tried with three companies. Two squads of one company actually reached the summit, but with the other two stopped cold, had to withdraw. The next day the advance began again with three companies. A combination of stiff resistance from NVA soldiers in bunker complexes and a friendly-fire incident with aerial rockets stopped the attack. Honeycutt's original estimate of two companies on the hill was now raised to two battalions. The enemy also seemed to be reinforced nightly from additional forces across the border in Laos. For five days the 3-187th Infantry had attacked Dong Ap Bia without success and against stiff resistance.[28]

Elsewhere in the brigade operational area, early in the morning on D+ 3, 13 March 1969, two company-sized elements of the enemy's 806th NVA Battalion and K12 Sapper Battalion infiltrated FSB Airborne, supported by mortar and rocket propelled grenade fire. Stationed at the firebase were three field artillery batteries: C/2-11th Artillery, four 155 mm howitzers; C/2-319th Artillery, four 105mm howitzers; and a composite battery from B and C/2-319th Artillery, four 105mm howitzers. The firebase was defended by Company A, 2-501st Infantry. The defenders drove off the attack with the attacking force suffering heavy casualties, but five howitzers were damaged and 22 American soldiers were killed and another 61 wounded.[29] With enemy forces obviously in the area of FSB Airborne, the brigade commander pulled the rest of the 2-501st out of its area on the Laotian border and airlifted it to FSB Airborne to commence RIF operations near the firebase.

After the heavy repulses of the 3-187th on Dong Ap Bia, clearly a larger enemy force held the hilltop than could be ejected or destroyed by a single battalion. As early as noontime on 13 May, the brigade S3 (operations) staff alerted Lieutenant Colonel J.M. Bowers that his battalion, the 1-506th infantry, then conducting RIF operations south of Dong Ap Bia, was to plan for immediate movement overland to attack the hill from the southwest in conjunction with 3-187th's attacks from the northwest. Bower's movement commenced on 14 May for a projected two-battalion attack on the 16th.[30] At first, the 1-506th advanced with little contact, while the 3-187th paused to await its arrival. But soon Bower's advance was stopped by a large NVA bunker complex on Hill 916, a peak on the same ridgeline as Dong Ap Bia's 937-meter summit, roughly 1,500 meters to the southwest. This delayed the combined two-battalion attack until the 17th, as the 506th soldiers cleared Hill 916 and then began advancing up Hill 937 itself.[31]

The concept of the 17 May attack was for the companies of the 3-187th to hold blocking positions to the northwest of the fortified enemy position and support by fire the 1-506th's three-company, on-line advance from the southwest. Extensive artillery, rocket, and air strike preparation would precede the attack. As part of this prep, about 200 105mm artillery rounds of CS gas (tear gas) would be used to force the NVA troops out of their bunkers before the conventional high-explosive artillery barrage. Despite the preparatory fires, the attack met stiff resistance near a small knoll on the ridge, Hill 900. The intense enemy fire prevented the 1-506th from advancing farther than 300 meters.[32]

The renewed attack the next day, 18 May, used both battalions with six companies advancing. Bowers' three companies advanced slowly against heavy fire. Honeycutt's three companies advanced anyway and one company took over 50-percent casualties in short order.

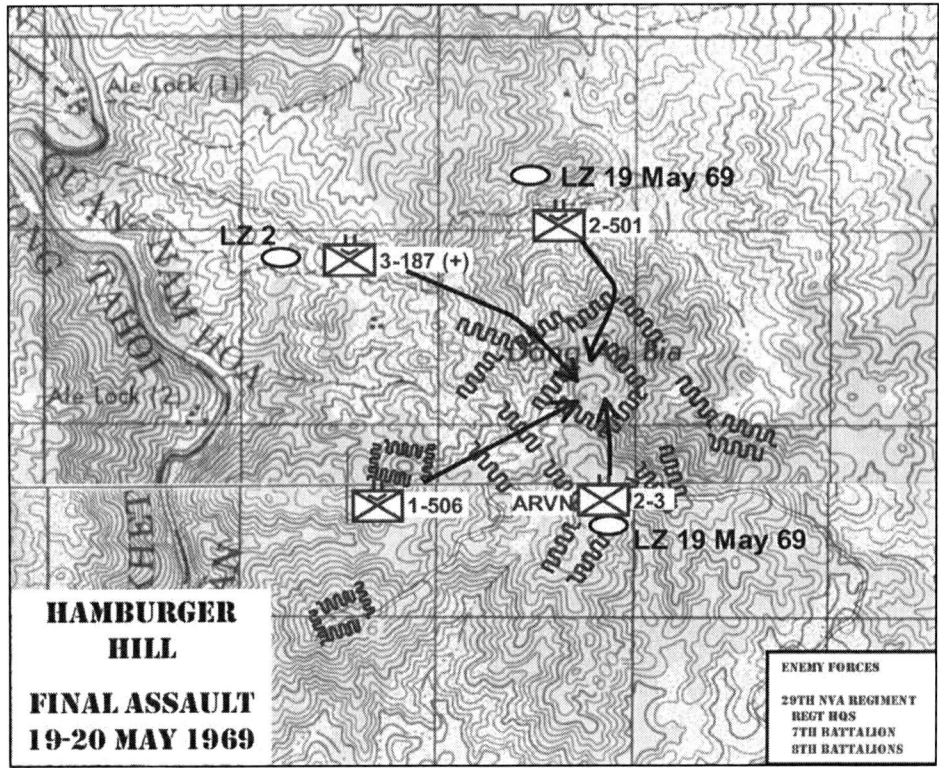

Figure 28. Final Assault on Hamburger Hill, 19-20 May 1969

Nevertheless two companies of the 187th were on the hilltop, while part of the 506th was just below the top on the opposite side. At this point, torrential rain started to pour hindering operations and forcing Honeycutt to withdraw his two unsupported companies from the top to more defensible positions.[33]

The enemy force and the terrain indicated that two reduced battalions would need reinforcement to take Dong Ap Bia. Accordingly, the division commander gave the 2d Brigade's 2d Battalion, 506th Infantry, to the 3d Brigade for use in the operation. The battalion moved to FSB Blaze and its A Company was airlifted into LZ 2 for attachment to the 3-187th on 19 May. The 1st ARVN Division supplied its 2d Battalion, 3d Infantry Regiment, which was airlifted to FSB Currahee the same day for use by the 3d Brigade. The 2-501st, which had been conducting RIF operations near FSB Airborne, in the wake of the sapper attack, was also added to the ong Ap Bia force for the 20th. Both battalions were airlifted into LZs around the hill on the 19th, the 2/3 ARVN on south and the 2-501st on the north side of what was now being referred to as "Hamburger Hill."

The combined force of four battalions was in its attack positions at nightfall on the 19th and attacked after preparatory fires from all sides on 20 May, destroying the remaining enemy forces on the hilltop and securing the position 11 days after the start of the operation.[34]

APACHE SNOW officially continued until 7 June 1969. After the conclusion of the Battle of Hamburger Hill, most enemy contacts, except for several additional sapper attacks on firebases, consisted of much smaller contacts than was had on Dong Ap Bia.[33] During the operation, the 2d Brigade showed its flexibility and, once the size of the enemy force was appreciated, its capability to mass multiple battalions against a large, well-dug in enemy force. The operation was typical of many of the airmobile brigade operations conducted in Vietnam between 1965 and 1972.

NOTES

1. Lalev I. Sepp, "The Pentomic Puzzle: The Influence of Personality and Nuclear Weapons on U.S. Army Organization 1952-1958," *Army History* 51 (Winter 2001), 8-11. The organic regiments in the 82d were the 504th and 505th Parachute Infantry Regiments and the 325th Glider Infantry Regiment. For most of 1944 and 1945, the nondivisional 507th and 508th Parachute Infantry Regiments were attached to the division. The 507th was later assigned to the 17th Airborne Division. The 101st originally had as organic the 502d Parachute and 401st and 327th Glider Infantry Regiments. The 401st was later broken up to provide third battalions for the 325th and 327th as glider regiments originally only had two battalions. The 501st and 506th Parachute Infantry Regiments were attached to the 101st for most of the war, with the 506th becoming organic in March 1945. See *Order of Battle, United States Army, World War II, European Theater of Operations: Divisions* (Paris: Office of the Theater Historian, European Theater, 1945), 283-84, 383-85.

2. Glen R. Hawkins and James Jay Carafano, *Prelude to Army XXI: US Army Division Design Initiatives and Experiments 1917-1995* (Washington, DC: US Army Center of Military History (CMH), 1997), 14.

3. Sepp, 11.

4. Ibid., 5; Jonathan M. House, *Combined Arms Warfare in the Twentieth Century* (Lawrence, KS: University Press of Kansas, 2001), 223

5. Sepp, 6.

6. *Sixty Years of Reorganizing for Combat: A Historical Trend Analysis.* Combat Studies Institute (CSI) Report No. 14 (Fort Leavenworth, KS: CSI, 1999), 23.

7. John B. Wilson, *Maneuver and Firepower: The Evolution of Divisions and Separate Brigades.* Army Lineage Series (Washington, DC: Government Printing Office (GPO), 1998), 169, 190-91; Wilson, *Armies, Corps, Divisions and Separate Brigades,* 297.

8. House, *Combined Arms Warfare,* 213.

9. Wilson, *Firepower and Maneuver,* 300-303; John J. McGrath, *History of the 187th Support Battalion.* Brochure created for the inactivation of the battalion, Brockton, Massachusetts, 1994.

10. Shelby Stanton, *Vietnam Order of Battle* (Washington, DC: US News Books, 1981), 71-72, 101.

11. Shelby Stanton, *Anatomy of a Division: The First Cav in Vietnam* (Novato, CA: Presidio, 1987), 195-201. Despite its organization, original employment plans for the division in Vietnam was to split it up by brigade and send it to different parts of the country. To retain a limited airmobile capability in each brigade, the aviation group would have had to provide a slice to each brigade. See Stanton, *Anatomy of a Division,* 39.

12. Wilson, *Firepower and Maneuver,* 356.

13. Stanton, *Vietnam Order of Battle,* 75-77, 81-82. The battalions were transferred back to their original divisions after the war, as these divisions were considered their "traditional" assignment.

14. Ibid., 79-80.

15. Wilson, *Maneuver and Firepower,* 325.

16. Stanton, *Vietnam Order of Battle,* 77-78, 82-83, 85.

17. Duquesne A. Wolf, *The Infantry Brigade in Combat: First Brigade, 25th Infantry Division ("Tropic Lightning") in the Third Viet Cong/North Vietnamese Army Offensive, August 1968* (Manhattan, KS: Sunflower University Press, 1984), 3.

18. Romie L. Brownlee and William J. Mullen III, *Changing an Army: An Oral History of General William E. DePuy, USA Retired* (Washington, DC: CMH, 1985), 163.

19. George L. MacGarrigle, *Taking The Offensive: October 1966 to October 1967.* The United States Army in Vietnam (Washington, DC: CMH, 1998), 115-17.

20. Major General William B. Fulton, *Riverine Operations 1966-1969.* Vietnam Studies (Washington, DC: Department of the Army, 1985), 31-33; Stanton, *Vietnam Order of Battle,* 77-78.

21. Fulton, 190-93.

22. As a major, Colin Powell served as an advisor to the ARVN forces which evacuated the A Shau Valley in 1966.

23. 22d Military History Detachment, *Narrative Operation "Apache Snow" 101st Airborne Division,* 1969, 8 (hereafter referred to as *Apache Snow*).

24. 101st Airborne Division (Airmobile), *Operational Report—Lessons Learned, 101st Airborne Division (Airmobile) for Period 31 July 1969, RCS CSFOR-65 (R1) (U),* dated 9 December 1969, 4 (hereafter referred to as *101st ORLL*).

25. *3d Brigade, 101st Airborne Division (Airmobile),Combat Operations After Action Report—Summary APACHE SNOW*, dated 25 June 1969, (hereafter referred to as *3d Bde AAR*), Enclosure 2, Intelligence, 2.

26. *3d Bde AAR*, 2, and Enclosure 4, Logistical Support.

27. *Apache Snow*, 2.

28. Ibid., 4-12; 3d Battalion, 187th Airborne Infantry, *Combat Operations After Action Report, Operation Apache Snow*, dated 20 June 1969, 30, 32-33 (hereafter referred to as *3-187th AAR*).

29. *101st ORLL*, 8-9.

30. 1st Battalion, 506th Airborne Infantry, *Combat Operations After Action Report, Operation Apache Snow*, dated 18 June 1969, 6 (hereafter referred to as *1-506th AAR*).

31. *Apache Snow*, 12-15.

32. *1-506th AAR*, 9; *Apache Snow*, 16; *3-187th AAR*, 36.

33. *Apache Snow*, 18.

34. *Apache Snow*, 19-20.

35. 3d Brigade commander, Colonel Joseph Conmy, considered one of the sapper attacks, which was aimed at the brigade headquarters at FSB Berchtesgaden on 13-14 June 1969 to be an attempt to personally kill him in revenge for Hamburger Hill. See Joseph B. Conmy, Jr., "Crouching Beast Cornered," *Vietnam* (December 1990), 36.

Chapter 7

COLD WAR AND POST-COLD WAR

Table 6. Reserve Component Roundout Brigades, 1973-1996

Unit	Location/ Component	Roundout to	Years
27th Infantry Brigade	NY ARNG	10th Mountain Division (Light Infantry)	1986-92
29th Infantry Brigade	HI ARNG/USAR	25th Infantry Division	1973-85
41st Infantry Brigade	OR ARNG	7th Infantry Division	1977-84
48th Infantry Brigade (Mech)	GA ARNG	24th Infantry Division (Mech)	1975-92
81st Infantry Brigade (Mech)	WA ARNG	9th Infantry Division	1988-91
116th Cavalry Brigade	ID ARNG	4th Infantry Division	1989-96
155th Armored Brigade	MS ARNG	1st Cavalry Division	1984-91
205th Infantry Brigade	MN/IA USAR	6th Infantry Division (Light)	1985-94
218th Infantry Brigade (Mech)	SC ARNG	1st Infantry Division (Mech)	1991-96
256th Infantry Brigade (Mech)	LA ARNG	5th Infantry Division (Mech)	1975-92
		2d Armored Division	1992-93

Roundout Brigades

After the withdrawal of the major US Army units from Vietnam in 1972, the Army shifted its attention back to the Cold War and the European battlefield. While the ROAD brigade had vindicated its adoption, its design as a tailored task organized maneuver command often seemed endangered. Many Army initiatives, in both force development and unit stationing ,seemed to solidify the brigade as a specific combat command containing certain units. These initiatives, most prompted by the smaller size of the All-Volunteer Army, adopted in 1973, included the creation of divisions with brigades of different capabilities, the stationing of divisional brigades overseas away from their parent unit, and the use of separate reserve component brigades to "round-out" active divisions staffed to only two-thirds strength by providing a third brigade with its slice of support and combat elements.

The latter organizational concept, officially known as the Reserve Component Roundout Brigade Program, commenced in 1973 when the Hawaii Army National Guard's 29th Infantry Brigade rounded out the 25th Infantry Division, which had never reestablished its 3d Brigade upon return from Vietnam. The program had a precedent during the Vietnam War when several ARNG separate brigades were mobilized to augment active Army divisions in the strategic reserve.[1] The roundout concept lasted, in one form or other, until 1996, when the ARNG enhanced brigade concept supplanted it. At its height from 1986 to 1991, Reserve Component brigades rounded out five Army divisions. The roundout program ebbed and flowed with other Army force structure issues.

When the program began in 1973, the Army was a 13-division force and the 25th Division was left at two brigades because of environmental concerns at Schofield Barracks, Oahu,

Hawaii. In 1974 the Army added two mechanized divisions, the 5th and 24th, and an infantry division, the 7th. Each were eventually organized with only two brigades, being rounded out with Army National Guard separate brigades.[2] This force structure remained basically intact until the mid-1980s, when the 7th and 25th Divisions were reorganized as new style light infantry divisions, each gaining an active third brigade in the process. At the same time, the Army organized two new light infantry divisions, the 6th in Alaska and the 10th Mountain Division, split between Fort Drum and Fort Benning (the brigade at Fort Benning later relocated to Fort Drum). The new divisions were organized by design with only two brigades. One of the three USAR separate infantry brigades, the 205th from Fort Snelling, Minnesota, rounded out the 6th. The Army removed the 27th Brigade, a component of the New York Army National Guard's 42d Infantry Division, from its parent division and reorganized it as a separate light infantry brigade to round out the 10th Mountain Division.[3]

The roundout concept was extended even to units expected to deploy early as contingency forces under the Rapid Deployment Joint Task Force (RDJTF), created in 1980 and redesignated as the US Central Command (CENTCOM) in 1983. The RDJTF's early deploying heavy division, the 24th Infantry Division (Mechanized), remained at two brigades, being rounded out by the Georgia Army National Guard's 48th Infantry Brigade (Mechanized). In 1990, the roundout concept was tested when Army forces were quickly deployed to Saudi Arabia to forestall an Iraqi attack after the invasion of Kuwait. The 24th, followed by the 1st Cavalry Division, deployed without their roundout brigades, using instead the separate 197th Infantry Brigade (Mechanized) and a brigade from the 2d Armored Division, respectively.[4] The reasons for not using the ARNG brigades were complicated and still controversial years later, but the

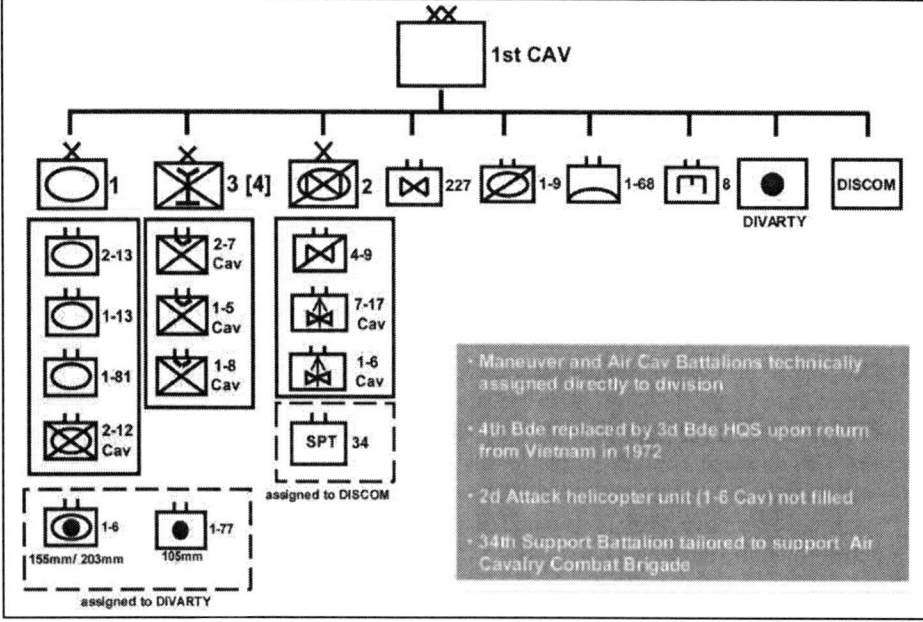

Figure 29. The TRICAP Division, 1971-1974

78

net effect was to discredit the roundout program. After 1991, units expected to deploy early in contingencies were removed from the roundout program. In 1996 the Army replaced the program completely with the ARNG Enhanced Brigade Program, which will be discussed later in this work. Table 6 lists the roundout brigades, as they existed throughout the duration of the program.[5]

The TRICAP Division and the Air Cavalry Combat Brigade

Even before the end of the Vietnam War, the Army was experimenting with the ROAD force structure, proposing a division where the three maneuver brigades each had a different structure or function. This division, the TRICAP division, for triple capability, essentially would consist of an armored brigade, an airmobile brigade, and a new type of unit which had been experimented with in Vietnam, an air cavalry combat brigade (ACCB). The plan was on the drawing board in 1970 for the 1st Armored Division. But when the 1st Cavalry Division returned from Vietnam to Fort Hood, Texas, in 1971 with two brigades, one remaining in Vietnam until 1972, it fell in on the personnel and equipment and mission of the 1st Armored Division, which had, in turn, fallen in on the personnel and equipment of the 4th Armored Division in Germany, which was inactivated in turn.[6]

The resulting experimental division design included a brigade of three tank and one mechanized infantry battalions, supported by a battalion of self-propelled field artillery; a brigade of three airmobile infantry battalions supported by a divisional aviation battalion and a towed field artillery battalion; an air cavalry combat brigade, consisting of an air cavalry squadron like the one fielded by the airmobile 1st Cavalry and 101st Airborne Divisions in Vietnam; and one, two on paper, new attack helicopter battalion, equipped with Cobra attack helicopters.[7]

Even though technically all the maneuver and aviation battalions belonged to the division directly, the three brigade headquarters, with three distinct organizational structures and missions, actually controlled the battalions, with division support elements equally organized to specifically support specific brigades. For example, the division support command (DISCOM) organized a special support battalion tailored for supporting the ACCB. The TRICAP experiment lasted until 1974, when Army planners, concerned with a new emphasis on armored combat in Europe, converted the division into a standard armored division and made the ACCB into the separate 6th Cavalry Brigade (Air Combat).[8] It's organization is depicted in Figure 30.

Forward Deployed and Rotating Brigades in Europe

While the Army was involved in Vietnam, the Soviet Union had been building up its forces in Central Europe, and in 1968, used military force to put down a reform movement in Czechoslovakia. Accordingly, the Army turned its focus back to Europe in the early 1970s. As part of this focus, the brigade again was tailored as a separate force, despite division affiliations.

The 24th Infantry Division (Mechanized) had returned from Germany in 1968, leaving its 3d Brigade behind. In 1970, the 1st Infantry Division returned from Vietnam and replaced the 24th Division at Fort Riley and in Germany. The original concept for the brigade remaining in Germany was that the rest of the division would return to Germany for periodic training exercises, called the Return of Forces to Germany (REFORGER), and swap brigades. While

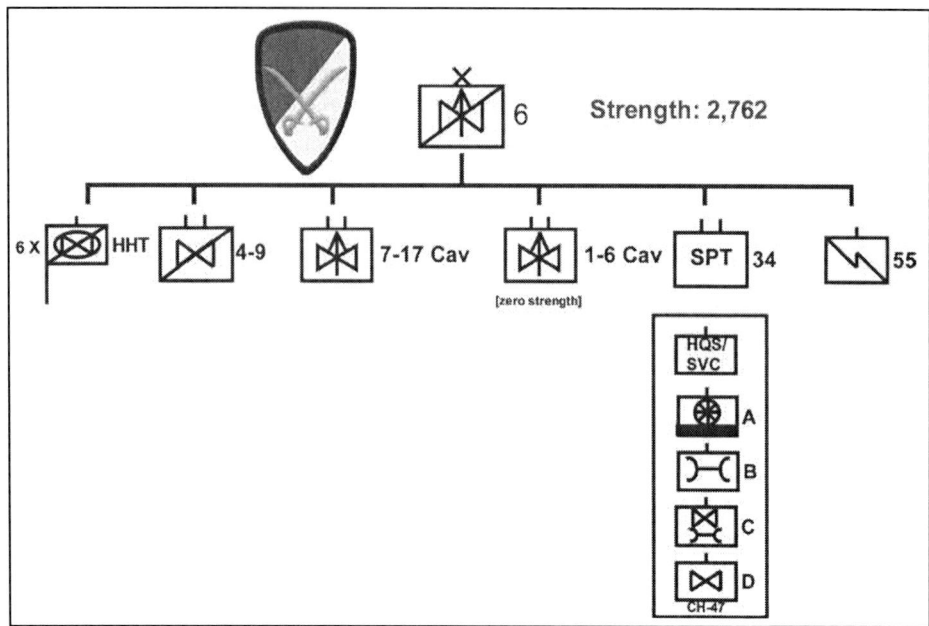

Figure 30. Air Cavalry Combat Brigade

the swap never took place, except for the change in unit designation from 24th to 1st, the brigade was upgraded with support elements and a brigadier general commander and redesignated as the 1st Infantry Division (Forward) in 1975.[9]

The idea of brigade swaps was revived several years later. Congress passed the Nunn Amendment in 1974, which called for an increase of combat troops in Europe at the expense of support troops. The Army sought to meet the conditions of the amendment by placing two brigades in Europe on continuous six-month rotations. The headquarters and support elements would be permanently assigned to Germany, but the combat troops would rotate over six-month periods, not bringing dependents or requiring on or off-post quarters. The brigades would be stationed at the Army training areas of Grafenwöhr, Wildflecken, and Hohenfels, Germany, as well as at the former Air Force base in Wiesbaden. The two brigades chosen were the 3d Brigade, 2d Armored Division, from Fort Hood, designated Brigade 75, and a newly raised 4th Brigade, 4th Infantry Division (Mechanized), from Fort Carson, as Brigade 76. Each division raised an additional brigade to replace the rotating one, the 2d Armored Division raising its 4th Brigade. Some units for the rotating brigades came from the 1st Cavalry Division and 1st Infantry Division (Mechanized). Brigade 75 moved to Germany between March and June 1975. Brigade 76 followed a year later. Army studies quickly decided that the rotation of combat battalions did not enhance readiness and both brigades were designated for permanent assignment to Germany. The 4th Brigade, 4th Infantry Division (Mechanized), was permanently assigned to Wiesbaden Air Base in the fall 1976. Though considered a V Corps asset, the brigade was operationally attached to the 8th Infantry Division (Mechanized), while that division's 2d Brigade, located at Baumholder, the farthest major unit from the East

German border and on the wrong side of the Rhine, was detached operationally as the V Corps operational reserve. The 3d Brigade, 2d Armored Division, did not become a permanent European brigade for two more years. In 1978, the brigade moved into a new kaserne built for it in northern Germany at Garlstedt near the port of Bremerhaven, becoming the only US Army unit in northern Germany. As with the 1st Infantry Division's forward brigade, this brigade received a brigadier general commander, a support slice, and was called the 2d Armored Division (Forward). The 2d Armored Division then inactivated its now extra 4th Brigade. The 4th Division retained its extra brigade, as, operationally, its 4th Brigade was no longer part of the division.[10]

1970s and 1980s Brigade Redesign Initiatives

The original Army concept after Vietnam was for a 13-division active force. As part of this force, the Army retained separate brigades for special missions or as theater defense forces, and in the reserve components. Brigades were stationed in Alaska, Panama, Berlin, and to support the Infantry and Armor Schools. The Army National Guard and Army Reserve still maintained a large number of separate armor and infantry brigades. The use of separate brigades made up of troops from one state often simplified the force structure in the state-specific Army National Guard. In the mid-1970s, the Army increased its force structure gradually by three divisions, each with only two brigades and a roundout brigade, but no new separate brigades were added to the force.[11]

In the decade between 1976 and 1988, the Army conducted major consecutive or simultaneous studies of organizational structure (listed in Table 7). For the maneuver brigade, the culminative effect of these studies was the adoption of modified brigade organizations, the creation of divisional aviation brigades, and a revision of the divisional brigade service support organization. The new organization retained the ROAD concept of brigades as unfixed task forces.

Table 7. Army Organizational Redesign Initiatives, 1975-1988

Program	Dates	Scope	Test Unit/Remarks
Division Restructuring Study (DRS)	1975-1979	armored and mechanized infantry divisions	2d Brigade, 1st Cavalry Division; proposed fixed brigade and divisional air cavalry attack brigade
Division 86	1978-1980	armored and mechanized infantry divisions	expanded on DRS; unfixed brigade; Division 86 Restructuring Study 1982; began implementation 1983
Army 86	1980-1983	light divisions and larger units and their elements	expansion of Division 86 to rest of the Army
High Technology Test Bed (HTTB)/High Technology Light Division (HTLD)/High Technology Motorized Division (HTMD)	1980-1988	new light division/new motorized division	9th Infantry Division; expansion of Army 86 to test light infantry division organizations
Army of Excellence (AOE)	1983-1986	Whole Army; specifically tested new light infantry division concept	7th Infantry Division (Light); revision and expansion of Army 86; 1988 was the Army's "Year of Excellence." implemented 1983-1986

General William DePuy, the first commander of the Army's new Training and Doctrine Command (TRADOC), which was established in 1973, commenced many organizational and doctrinal initiatives during his tenure (1973-1977). DePuy's focus was based on a combination of the Soviet buildup in Europe, the Army's placing of Europe on the back burner during the Vietnam War, the impact of modern weapons demonstrated in the 1973 Arab-Israeli War, and the projected introduction of new weapons systems and equipment into the Army in the early 1980s. This new equipment included a utility/transport helicopter (UH-60 Blackhawk), a tank (M1 Abrams), an infantry/cavalry fighting vehicle (M2/M3 Bradley), and an attack helicopter (AH-64 Apache). In May 1976 DePuy initiated a study of the divisional and brigade operational structure, again using the 1st Cavalry Division as the test unit. The study, known as the Division Restructuring Study (DRS), proposed a divisional organization which included a fixed brigade structure for the armored and mechanized infantry divisions. Each brigade would consist of three tank battalions and two mechanized infantry battalions. Only the 2d Brigade, 1st Cavalry Division, implemented the structure in a test mode and the fixed brigade, as it was called, was ultimately nixed by DePuy's successor, General Donn Starry and the then Army Chief of Staff, General Edward Meyer, in 1979.[12]

Meyer and Starry transformed DePuy's DRS study into a more wide-ranging one, called Division 86, which eventually was expanded into the Army 86 and, under Meyer's successor, General John Wickham, the Army of Excellence (AOE) programs. The revised Army organizational schemes were adopted both as the new equipment was fielded and as a matter of course. Army armored and mechanized units began implementing the Division 86 structure in 1983, with AOE changes. In 1986, the armored and mechanized divisions completed the AOE conversion by forming the divisional aviation brigades.

The new organization, while changing the structure of the maneuver battalions, basically retained the nonfixed brigade standard of the ROAD configuration. The tank and mechanized battalions were standardized in structure, with a fourth line company added to each and supporting elements, such as mortars and scouts, moved to the battalion headquarters company from the now deleted combat support company. Doctrinally, the old ROAD standard of cross attaching platoons to make combined arms company teams, was discouraged, with the lowest level for such actions now to be the battalion.[13] Forward support battalions, which consisted of a slice of division service support elements to support each brigade, also came into being.

When Meyer expanded Division 86 to include other types of units, he set up the High Technology Test Bed (HTTB) in 1980 at Fort Lewis. Using the 9th Infantry Division, the HTTB tested organizational structure and equipment to try to produce a lighter version of the armored or mechanized division which could be deployed easily by aircraft, while maintaining more firepower than the standard infantry division. Meyer's successor, Wickham, branched the project off into two directions in 1983: a lighter infantry division and a motorized infantry division equipped with enhanced technology to give it deployablity and firepower. The 9th Division continued with the motorized mission and the 7th Infantry Division, at Fort Ord, California, assumed the light infantry test mission.

At Fort Lewis, the 9th Infantry Division continued to develop a motorized divisional structure, using available wheeled equipment to stand in for projected technological developments. The organizational structure was tweaked and changed numerous times until a final structure was adopted in 1988, which included two motorized brigades and a roundout mechanized infantry brigade from the Washington state Army National Guard and an air cavalry attack brigade. As subordinate units to the two motorized brigades, the division developed three new types of combat battalions: a light combined arms battalion CAB (L), a heavy combined arms battalion CAB (L), and a light attack battalion (LAB). The types are listed in Table 8.[14]

Table 8. Combined Arms Battalions in the Motorized Division, 1988

Type	Designation	Composition	Projected Equipment	Actual Equipment
Light Combined Arms Battalion	Infantry	2 Assault Gun Cos 1 Light Motorized Infantry Co 1 CSC		TOW-HMMWVs, M551 Sheridans (briefly) Motorized infantry squads ride in M998 HMMWV/Mk 19 Grenade Machine Guns (GMGs)
Heavy Combined Arms Battalion	Infantry	1 Assault Gun Co 2 Light Motorized Infantry Cos 1 CSC	Assault Gun System	TOW-HMMWVs, M551 Sheridans (briefly) Motorized infantry squads ride in M998 HMMWV/Mk 19 GMGs
Light Attack Battalion	Armored Cavalry	3 Light Attack Cos 1 CSC	83 Fast Attack Vehicles (FAV); dune buggies equipped with TOWs or 50 cal machineguns (MG s)	One battalion equipped as a standard M60A3 tank battalion; other equipped with M966 HMMWV/TOW 2 and M1025 HMMWV/Mk 19 40mm GMGs
Combat Support Company (CSC)	Organic to each of above battalion types	1 Scout Plt 1 AT Plt 1 107 mm Mortar Plt	AT Plt Ground-launched Hellfire missile system mounted on HMMWVs	AT Plt M966 HMMWV/TOW 2

The motorized division was predicated on the fielding of new equipment. In the interim, it was equipped, except in the case of the LAB, with substitute items. The projection was for the LAB to be equipped with three companies of fast attack vehicles (FAV), dune buggies armed with TOW missile systems or .50 caliber machine guns. Replacing the dune buggies, which were still in the developmental stage, were armored high-mobility multipurpose wheeled vehicles (HMMWV) equipped with TOW missiles and the new Mark 19 40mm grenade machine gun (GMG). The combined arms battalions were organized as a mix of assault gun companies and motorized infantry companies. The heavy CAB had two assault gun companies and one motorized infantry company, while the ratio was reversed in the light CAB. The assault gun was a proposed system (AGS) being developed as a lightly armored tracked vehicle armed with a low-velocity 105mm gun. In place of the AGS, the M551 Sheridan light tank was initially used, later replaced with the ubiquitous TOW or Mk 109 GMG HMMWV. Each CAB and the LAB also had an organic combat support company containing, along with mortars and scouts, an antiarmor platoon slated to be equipped by 1989 with HMMWVs mounting a specially designed ground version of the Hellfire missile. In lieu of this system, which was ultimately never fielded, the TOW was again used. The motorized infantry companies rode in specially modified M998 cargo HMMWVs, mounting GMGs.[15]

The end of the Cold War and budget considerations doomed the motorized division experiment. A standard mechanized infantry roundout brigade had already replaced the 2d Brigade in 1988. The 1st Brigade was inactivated in 1990 and the division headquarters and support elements followed in 1991, while the 3d Brigade was converted into the separate 199th Infantry Brigade. The 199th was then redesignated as the 2d Armored Cavalry Regiment in 1992.

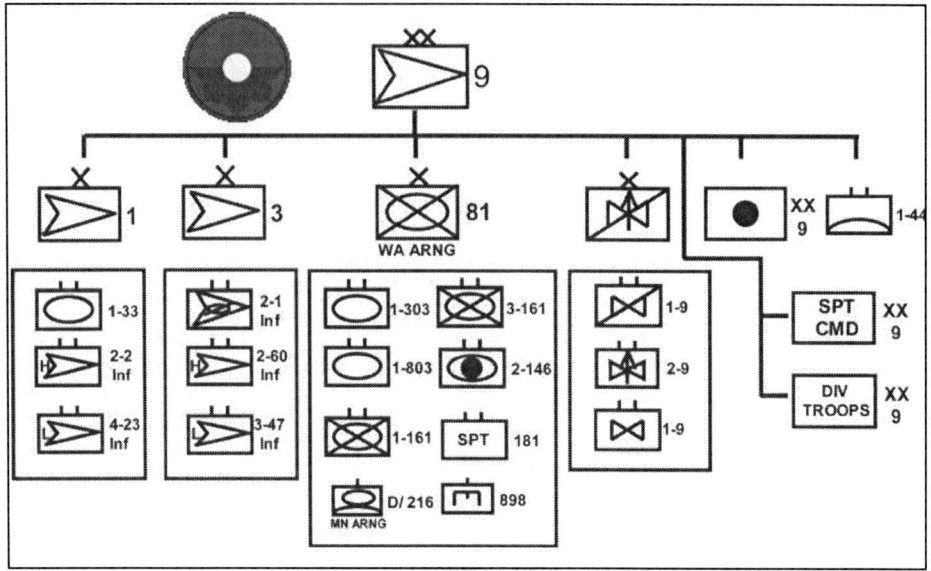

Figure 31. 9th Infantry Division (Motorized), 1988

At Fort Ord, the 7th Infantry Division developed a new, lighter infantry division structure. After some modifications and adjustments, the new light infantry division resembled the heavier Division 86 in general structure, with less heavy equipment. The nine light infantry battalions were parceled out between the standard three brigade headquarters. The division also contained a modified aviation brigade, with less attack and more utility helicopters than found in the armored or mechanized division. In addition to the 7th Infantry Division, the 25th Infantry Division also converted to the light design. Three new divisions, the 10th Mountain, the 6th Infantry, and the Army National Guard, of Virginia and Maryland's, 29th Infantry were activated, the former two with reserve component roundout brigades.[16]

In the 1980s, the Army also experimented with modifications of the unit manning system. Since the end of World War II, with a few exceptions, the Army had manned units based on individual replacements. Meyer proposed to rotate personnel as units. To execute this, in the mid 1980s, he modified the CARS unit designation system, which had been used to identify units in the combat arms since 1957. The new US Army Regimental System (USARS) applied the regimental system to the entire Army, making many of the noncombat branches into single branch regiments and attempting to make the regiments into the avenue along which the unit replacement system would run. Battalions belonging to the same regiment would rotate between Continental United States posts and overseas sites. Accordingly, the system required large-scale unit redesignations and the loss of many regimental designations made excess. An additional component of this system was the Cohesion, Operational Readiness and Training (COHORT) project, which trained a company-sized unit of combat arms soldiers from basic training and then kept them together for an overseas and Continental US tour of duty.

84

Both COHORT and the unit replacement system were eventually abandoned after a period of experimentation. However the redesignations remained and in divisions with nine infantry battalions and only three regimental affiliations, like the 101st and 82d Airborne, the battalions ended up grouped in the same brigade by regiment and the brigades are often referred to, informally, and confusingly, as regiments. In the 82d, the informal usage includes reversion to a mixing of World War II and Korean War era designations.

After several years of rotating units and downsizing, when the rotation program ended, many Army battalions ended up under divisions to which they did not traditionally belong. In 1995 the Army, as the final act of the 1980s flirtation with unit replacement, redesignated battalions to return these traditional designations to their long-established divisions.

However, vestiges of the regiment as a tactical unit roughly equivalent to the brigade still remained. AOE planners had sought to turn the Army's ACRs into brigades, but after resistance from the cavalry community, the ACRs were retained. The trend was taken further with the creation of several other regiments including the 75th Ranger Regiment in 1985, as a controlling and planning headquarters for the Army's three Ranger battalions. Originally a special task force, then a battalion and a group, the 160th Aviation Regiment (Special Operations) was activated in 1990 and controls various elements including four organic battalions. The regiment is equipped with specialized helicopters and trains to conduct special operations worldwide.

Table 9. Informal Regimental Designations 82d and 101st Airborne Divisions

Designation	Informal Designation	Battalions
1st Brigade, 82d Airborne Division	504th Parachute Infantry Regiment	1-504th Infantry 2-504th Infantry 3-504th Infantry
2d Brigade, 82d Airborne Division	325th Airborne Infantry Regiment	1-325th Infantry 2-325th Infantry 3-325th Infantry
3d Brigade, 82d Airborne Division	505th Parachute Infantry Regiment	1-505th Infantry 2-505th Infantry 3-505th Infantry
Division Artillery, 82d Airborne Division	319th Airborne Field Artillery Regiment	1-319th Field Artillery 2-319th Field Artillery 3-319th Field Artillery
1st Brigade, 101st Airborne Division (Air Assault)	327th Infantry Regiment	1-327th Infantry 2-327th Infantry 3-327th Infantry
2d Brigade, 101st Airborne Division (Air Assault)	502d Infantry Regiment	1-502d Infantry 2-502d Infantry 3-502d Infantry
3d Brigade, 101st Airborne Division (Air Assault)	187th Infantry Regiment	1-187th Infantry 2-187th infantry 3-187th Infantry
Division Artillery, 101st Airborne Division (Air Assault)	320th Field Artillery Regiment	1-320th Field Artillery 2-320th Field Artillery 3-320th Field Artillery

As in the case of the 82d and 101st Divisions' combat brigades, often units that are not regiments have been informally referred to as such, even in official or semiofficial correspondence. A good example of this is the 11th Aviation Group, which had served in Germany since 1993 as a group, although it had formerly been an aviation brigade. The group was often referred to in the 2003 Iraqi War as the "11th Aviation Regiment" or the "11th Attack Helicopter Regiment." However, the name was officially incorrect and the organization had no organic battalions assigned to it.[17] Some Army brigades have official special designations or nicknames, the most famous being the 1st Brigade, 2d Armored Division, which in the 1991 Gulf War was much more widely known as the Tiger Brigade. These designations are found in the brigade listing located in Appendix 4.

Aviation Brigades

One of the novel concepts of Division 86 and its follow on, the AOE, was the inclusion of an aviation brigade in the divisional structure. The amount and placement of aviation in the division structure had gone up and down since the adoption of ROAD in 1963. ROAD initially included an aviation battalion in each division, a unit basically responsible for providing command and control helicopters, and limited troop and supply transportation. The battalion was reduced to a company in the ROAD armored and mechanized divisions, and then had been removed entirely during Vietnam, only to return in 1970.[18] In Vietnam itself, each deployed division retained the organic aviation battalion, some even receiving additional companies or battalions for extended periods.[19]

An aviation brigade was used in Vietnam, but in a far different way from the projected use of the new aviation brigades. The 1st Aviation Brigade, which stood up in 1966, essentially controlled administratively all aviation assets not assigned to divisions and at one time or another had seven aviation group headquarters, 20 aviation battalions, and four air cavalry squadrons under its control. For operations, the aviation groups with attached battalions, were assigned or attached to divisions or higher headquarters. The 1st Aviation Brigade's legacy would be found in the corps and theater aviation brigades deployed in the 1980s and 1990s. These brigades provided aviation assets to subordinate units, while not usually being used as operational headquarters.[20]

Originally the divisional aviation brigade was called the air cavalry combat brigade. As mentioned previously in this work, the ACCB was a concept experimented with in the TRICAP division, resulting in the creation of the separate 6th Cavalry Brigade (Air Combat) in 1975.[21] The new brigade was initially the simple addition of the ACCB to the division structure, with other divisional aviation assets added. The divisional ACCB included the divisional cavalry squadron, which was reorganized to include air cavalry elements; an attack helicopter battalion or two; and the former divisional aviation battalion, which was originally designated as a general support aviation battalion and later as an assault helicopter battalion.

The brigade was an anomaly in that its structure contained aspects of an administrative and of a tactical organization. Many aviation proponents and the Army itself, considered the brigade, with its attack helicopter battalions, to be a fourth maneuver brigade in the division. The brigade also consisted of an assault helicopter battalion, used to carry troops and supplies, and the divisional cavalry squadron. The latter, with its mix of air cavalry and armored cavalry troops, normally worked directly for the division commander, while the former generally served in a combat support role, moving troops and supplies.[22]

To reflect the notion of the brigade as a combat organization, in spite of its possession of units it only controlled administratively or in a supporting capacity, the organization has often been referred to in doctrinal literature as the divisional combat aviation brigade and in the field as the 4th Brigade. However, its actual designation is simply "Aviation Brigade, XX Division."[23]

As with all AOE organizational structures, the aviation brigade evolved from its original structure into a more robust organization. The modern brigade consists of one or two attack helicopter battalions, an assault helicopter battalion, and the divisional cavalry squadron.

After much debate over whether tanks should be included in the cavalry squadron in the heavy division (i.e., armored and mechanized), the tanks remained in the ground cavalry troops, which consisted of a mix of M1 Abrams tanks and M3 Bradley Fighting Vehicles. In the light infantry division, the ground cavalry troops used the HMMWV. Each squadron also contains two or three air cavalry troops, equipped primarily with the OH-58D Kiowa observation helicopter.

The assault helicopter battalion provided helicopters for small-scale (up to a battalion) air assault operations, aerial resupply, casualty evacuation, and command and control and special mission helicopters.

In the DISCOM was found an aviation maintenance battalion, which was essentially the support battalion for the aviation brigade. This battalion provided centralized maintenance for the division's aviation, though each aviation battalion also had limited maintenance assets of its own.

The attack helicopter battalions contained the AH-64 Apache in the heavy division and modified OH-58Ds in the light and airborne divisions. The attack units of the aviation brigade provided the basis for its consideration as a maneuver brigade. The original air assault division had the forerunner of the attack helicopter battalion in its aerial surveillance and escort battalion. The battalion was equipped with armed Mohawk planes and designed to support airmobile operations. It was scrapped from the final division design, though rocket-firing helicopters were found in a battalion that was part of the division artillery. The new attack helicopter battalions, equipped primarily with antiarmor weaponry, were designed to destroy enemy forces at decisive points throughout the depth of the battlefield.

Aviation units in the new aviation brigades suffered from a long-term identity crisis concerning unit designations in the 1970s and 1980s. There was debate in the 1970s over whether attack helicopter units should be considered attack helicopter aviation battalions or air cavalry squadrons. The air cavalry won that round, but in 1983 the Army made aviation a separate branch and attack helicopter aviation battalions were organic components of the new aviation brigades, though air cavalry attack battalions still existed as well in some nondivisional units.

Adding to the confusion, aviation units were formerly labeled with separate battalion designations, but in the late 1980s the branch adopted a regimental system, causing the renaming of all aviation units, including the maintenance battalion in the DISCOM. Since

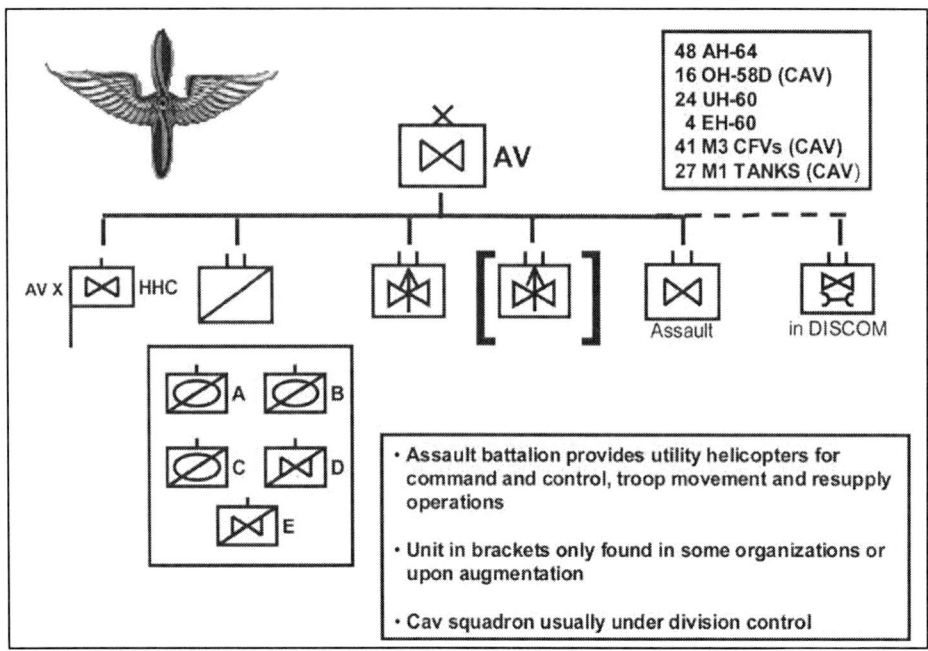

Figure 32. Armored/Mechanized Division Aviation Brigade, 2003

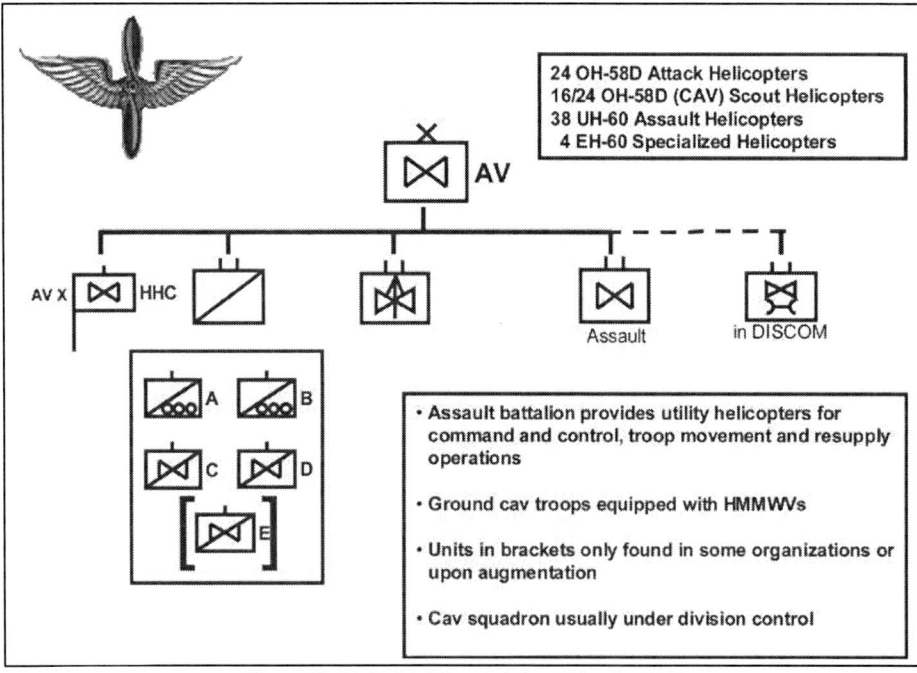

Figure 33. Light Division Aviation Brigade, 2003

aviation did not possess a history of regimental organization, most divisional battalions became elements of a regiment created from the former division aviation battalion.

At one point during the TRICAP experiment, an air cavalry combat brigade was designed to consist of one airmobile infantry battalion and two attack helicopter squadrons, without any support elements. This plan, which would have provided a truly combined arms aviation brigade, was scrapped and when the aviation brigade eventually joined the division, ostensively as a maneuver brigade, it was as an entirely aviation entity, including combat support aviation elements used to support the division as a whole.[24]

The Air Assault Division

The Army left Vietnam with two airmobile divisions. As we have seen, the 1st Cavalry Division was promptly converted into the TRICAP division, and then later into a standard armored division. The other airmobile division was the 101st Airborne, which had been converted from airborne to airmobile division status while in Vietnam in 1968. The 101st returned to Fort Campbell, Kentucky, in 1972. Awaiting it there was the 173d Airborne Brigade, which the Army had retained after Vietnam as a quick deploying contingency brigade. Later in 1972, the 173d merged with the 101st, which had to be rebuilt after its Vietnam service as part of the new all-volunteer Army. The 173d was resdesignated as the division's 3d Brigade, paratrooper qualified, a revived status that had been dropped from the airmobile division in Vietnam. In 1974, the Army again dropped the paratrooper status. However, the 101st commander, Major General Sidney Berry, capitalized on the division's unique organization, getting the division redesignated as an air assault division and receiving authorization to award its members the newly created air assault badge.[25]

With the adoption of the AOE program, the air assault division was modified. To standardize the division's unique aviation group with the terminology used by the other divisions, the group was upgraded to become the 101st Aviation Brigade. The new AOE brigade contained the divisional air cavalry squadron, a general support, or command, aviation battalion; two combat assault aviation battalions, one medium, one light; and four attack helicopter battalions.[26] The structure was, however, again modified, even as it was being implemented. The 101st retained the second light assault battalion the division already had under the earlier tables of organization and never activated the fourth attack helicopter battalion, while, in turn inactivating the third battalion.[27]

Robust modifications to the air assault division, initially done ad hoc and later officially sanctioned, provided the 101st with eight aviation battalions in its aviation brigade at the start of the 1991 Gulf War. With an additional attached attack battalion added to the division after the war, this provided a unique aviation force of three attack battalions, three assault battalions, a medium assault battalion, and the divisional cavalry squadron and a battalion, which provided command and control and special operations helicopters. This organization permitted the forming of air assault brigade combat teams, each consisting of three infantry battalions, a field artillery battalion, an assault aviation battalion, and an attack aviation battalion. When so organized, the divisional brigades could conduct separate air assault operations. When not so organized, the attack battalions provided a separate strike force available to the division commander. The division was truly an air assault organization in that each brigade could conduct such operations simultaneously, unlike the Vietnam era airmobile divisions.

However, placing nine battalions under one brigade headquarters was difficult, both administratively and for command and control purposes. Accordingly, in 1997, a reorganization divided the aviation assets of the Aviation Brigade, 101st Airborne Division (Air Assault), into two brigades: the 101st Aviation Brigade and the 159th Aviation Brigade. The attack assets, along with the command battalion and air cavalry squadron, were under the control of the 101st Brigade. The one Chinook medium and three Blackhawk assault battalions were placed under the 159th Brigade.[28] The revived number 159 was one of the original brigades of the 101st Division under the square division. Number 101, used as the divisional aviation brigade, was the organizational descendent of the ROAD-era 101st Aviation Group.

Two systems developed in the late 1970s and early 1980s drove the force structure of the air assault division: the UH-60 Blackhawk transport helicopter and the AH-64 Apache attack helicopter. The Blackhawk was issued to the division starting in 1979. The AH-64 replaced older AH-1 Cobras as the division embraced the attack helicopter concept in the early 1980s. Additionally, the 101st contained the only divisional battalion equipped with the CH-47 Chinook. The Chinook, technically a medium cargo helicopter, was capable of heavy duty carrying troops, supplies, equipment, and even sling-loading towed howitzers. The helicopter, around since Vietnam, was refitted in the 1980s and 1990s, allowing it to keep up with the times in military technology.

In the 1990s, for the first time, air assault infantry battalions were deployed outside the 101st Airborne Division, with two battalions in the 2d Infantry Division in Korea and an additional battalion in the Alaska-based 172d Infantry Brigade. The 2d Division, therefore, had the capability to organize one of its brigades as a small air assault brigade.

Combat Service Support and the Brigade[29]

Since the adoption of ROAD in 1963, with its task organized brigade structure and consolidated logistical units in the DISCOM, brigade commanders depended on a slice of support from the division's assets. This support typically included a supply and truck company from the division supply and transportation battalion, which provided fuel, rations, ammunition, and trucks; a medical company from the medical battalion of the division, to provide a medical clearing station complete with ambulances; and a maintenance company from the divisional maintenance battalion, to provide direct support maintenance and repair parts supply.

The separate brigade, though originally configured with no service support elements, was quickly given an organic support battalion containing all of the above elements and an administration company to augment the brigade headquarters with support normally provided by the divisional adjutant general section.

In Vietnam, brigade combat service support usually consisted of a large base camp that contained the brigade rear elements including the field train elements of the combat battalions (unit supply and maintenance) and the brigade's slice of the division support command assets. This slice, the FSSE, usually consisted of a company from the medical battalion, a company from the maintenance battalion and platoon- or company-sized elements from the division's supply and services or supply and transportation company. Sometimes the FSSE echeloned

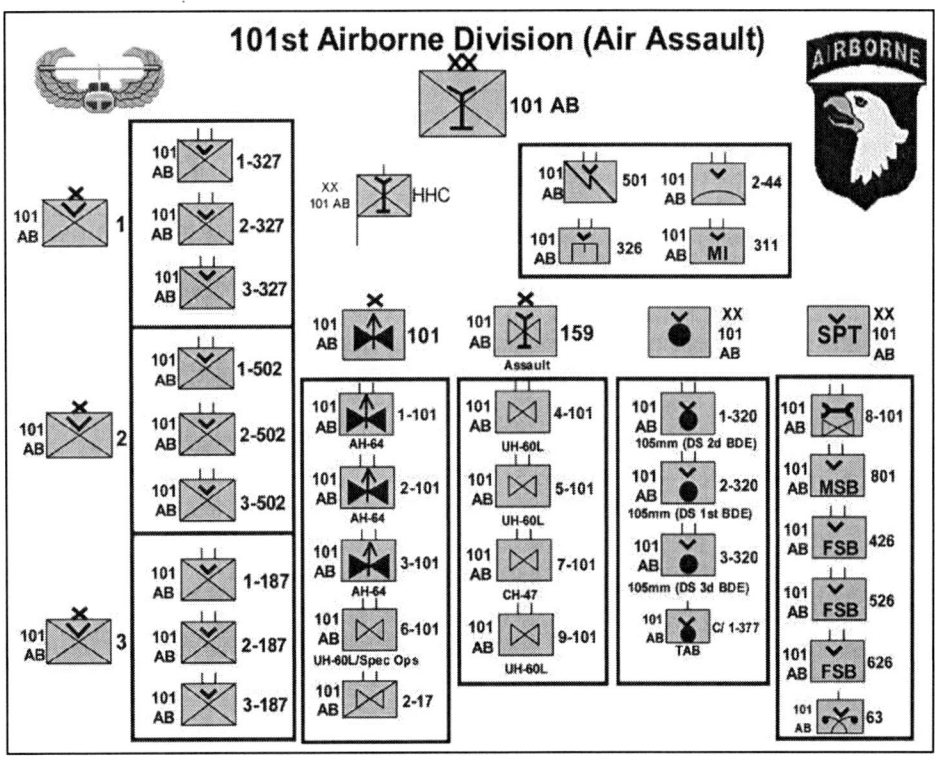

Figure 34. Air Assault Division Structure, 2003

itself with a forward element located at a forward support base, usually collocated with the brigade command post.[30]

After Vietnam, the armored and mechanized divisions developed a logistical support concept similar to the FSSE. This was the Forward Area Support Team (FAST), which provided similar slices of the DISCOM, as were found in the FSSE, to support the divisional brigades logistically. The FAST Team was headed by a Forward Area Support Coordinator (FASCO), who was usually the executive officer of one of the DISCOM's functional battalions. By the early 1980s, the FASCO was permanently detailed to that job.[31]

Almost from its inception, the separate ROAD brigade had its own logistical element, a multifunctional support battalion. This battalion provided most of the same type of support found in the FAST Team. However, the organization was permanent and under its own commander. The separate brigade support battalion also included an administrative company, which was later made a separate element. In the transformation from ROAD to AOE structures, the separate brigade's logistical structure remained basically as under ROAD, with the additional of a Brigade Materiel Management Center (BMMC) in the support battalion's headquarters company. The BMMC matched a similar organization added to the divisional DISCOM in the 1970s to provided automated management of logistics.

Division 86 and AOE transformed brigade logistics from depending on ad hoc task forces from the DISCOM's functional battalions to permanent, tailored multifunctional FSB. The new FSBs were organized with a headquarters company, supply company, maintenance company, and medical company. The FSB commander also commanded the brigade rear area or brigade support area (BSA) and had an organic support operations section to plan and execute the logistics mission for the brigade. The emphasis was now on forward support, typified by the placing of an ammunition transfer point (ATP) at the brigade level. The ATP was essentially the brigade's own mini-ammo dump. AOE organization also provided a tailored support battalion for the aviation brigade.[32]

With the AOE adjustments, brigade logistics were organized in the late 20th and early 21st centuries as follows: each unit echeloned its logistics assets to provide for their survivability and responsiveness.

At the lowest level, the company, the company first sergeant, or sometimes the executive officer, oversaw the company trains, which generally consisted of only the logistic elements the company would most need, but would not survive well in the frontline. This typically was a recovery vehicle with several mechanics, the company armorer, and medics from the battalion headquarters company with an ambulance. The company trains normally located themselves one terrain feature behind the company, less than a kilometer from the frontline.

The next level was the battalion or task force's combat trains. The battalion executive officer located the combat trains in the battalion sector, within 5 kilometers of the frontline

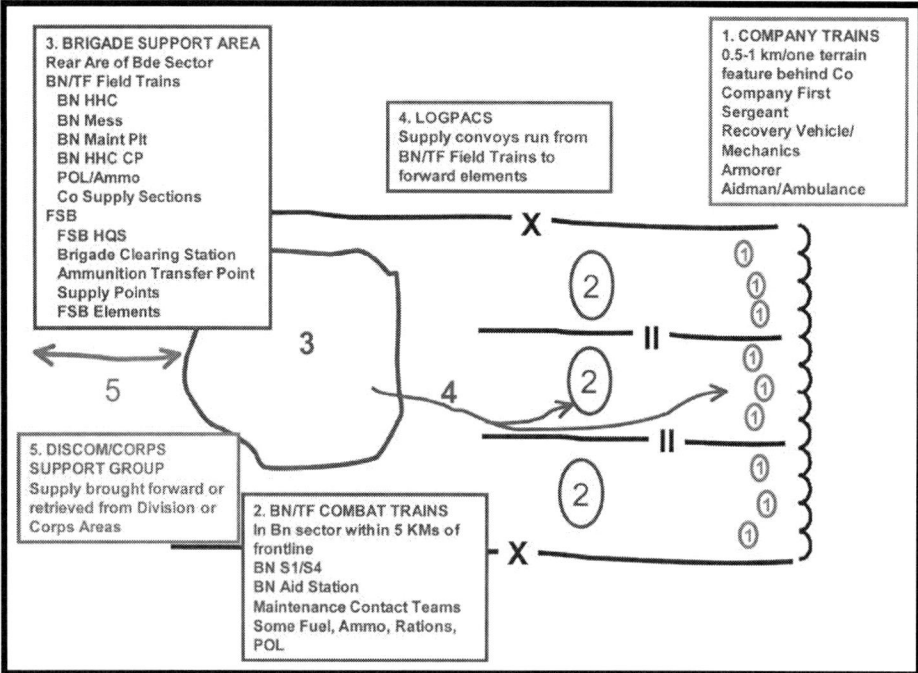

Figure 35. Brigade Tactical Logistics Organization

units. These trains typically consisted of the battalion's S1 (personnel) and S4 (logistics) officers with part of their respective sections. The battalion medical platoon established the battalion aid station at the combat trains. There would also be some ammunition, fuel, and rations loaded into trucks or into packets for resupply.

The brigade support area would be located in the brigade sector behind the battalion sectors on a defensible terrain feature with a good road network. The BSA contained the brigade's forward support battalion, battalion/task force field trains, and, in some cases, elements from higher echelon logistical units. Battalion/task force field trains, normally headed by the battalion headquarters company commander, included the elements of the Headquarters and Headquarters Company (HHC) not already deployed forward, such as the battalion mess section, maintenance platoon, and fuel and ammunition stockpiles. The line company supply sections would also be located in the field trains. FSB elements in the BSA included the brigade medical clearing station and ammunition transfer point, as well as various types of supply points and direct support maintenance activities. The BSA would be organized either as one large base camp or a series of smaller positions, each of which could mutually support each other if attacked. In each case, the overall commander of the BSA was the FSB commander.[33]

As part of the support forward philosophy, resupply from the BSA was executed through the use of Logistical Packages (LOGPACS), specially tailored supply convoys which would move forward and link up with the battalion field trains or company trains at predetermined logistical release points. LOGPACS would also bring forward mechanics, mail, and personnel replacements.

Above the BSA level was the division support area, where various DISCOM and corps support group (CSG) elements would be found. Resupply above the brigade worked both ways, with supplies being brought forward from higher or retrieved, if necessary, by brigade logistical elements.

The Brigade in Panama and in the Gulf War

The 1980s were a turbulent decade for the US Army and its brigades. By the end of the decade, however, the AOE organizational changes were implemented, the light divisions fielded, and the Cold War was virtually over—symbolized by the fall of the Berlin Wall in November 1989.[34] This portended an Army downsizing, which would have a great impact on the brigade and its role.

But first, two foreign threats needed to be dealt with. The initial one, December 1989's Operation JUST CAUSE, the invasion of Panama to remove the regime of Manuel Noriega, highlighted both the flexibility inherent in the ROAD/AOE brigade concept and the utility of the new light divisions. Brigades from the 7th Infantry Division (Light), the 82d Airborne Division, and the separate, Panama-based, 193d Infantry Brigade task organized to complete specific operational missions. The operation commenced on 20 December 1989, and employed six brigades, including three in the initial phase: the 1st Brigade, 82d Airborne Division, the division's contingency brigade, called by the designation division ready brigade-1 (DRB-1), parachuted and airlanded into Panama and conducted immediate air assault operations; the 193d Brigade moved from its garrison locations to neutralize key Panamanian Defense Force (PDF) positions on the Pacific side of the Canal Zone; and the 3d Brigade, 7th Infantry Division

(Light), forces placed in Panama prior to the operation, neutralized key PDF positions on the Atlantic side of the Canal Zone. Elements of the 7th Division's aviation brigade supported the operation and the bulk of the 7th Division, two brigades and part of the aviation brigade, arrived in follow-on echelons. The successful operation's tactical phase lasted until the end of January 1990. Brigades that participated in Operation JUST CAUSE are listed in Table 10.

The August 1990 Iraqi invasion of Kuwait set the stage for the largest overseas deployment of US Army forces since Vietnam, culminating in a brief, highly successful ground campaign in March 1991.[35] In total, the Army deployed 21 maneuver brigades, excluding divisional aviation brigades, under seven divisional headquarters. But the deployment of brigades is not

Table 10. Brigades in Panama, December 1989-January 1990

Brigade	Composition
1st Brigade, 7th Infantry Division	3 light infantry battalions 1 air defense artillery battery 1 engineer company 1 ad hoc support battalion
2d Brigade, 7th Infantry Division	3 light infantry battalions 1 field artillery battalion 1 air defense artillery battery 1 engineer company 1 ad hoc support battalion
3d Brigade, 7th Infantry Division	1 light infantry battalion 1 airborne infantry battalion 1 military police company 1 field artillery battery 1 air defense artillery battery 1 engineer company 1 ad hoc support battalion
Aviation Brigade, 7th Infantry Division	2 attack helicopter battalions 1 assault aviation battalion 1 general support aviation battalion 1 air cavalry troop
1st Brigade, 82d Airborne Division	3 airborne infantry battalions 1 field artillery battery 1 air defense artillery battery 1 tank company 1 engineer company 1 Military intelligence company 1 ad hoc support battalion
193d Infantry Brigade	1 mechanized infantry battalion 1 light infantry battalion 1 airborne infantry battalion 2 tank platoons 1 Military police battalion 1 support battalion

94

as clear-cut as the 21 to 7 ratio would seem to indicate. The drawdown, which had commenced with the end of the Cold War, was in full swing when forces were needed to defend Saudi Arabia and restore Kuwait. As previously mentioned, several divisions deployed without their ARNG roundout brigades. Additionally, the 1st Infantry Division's forward deployed 3d Brigade was in the middle of drawing down. Filler brigades were used to replace the missing ones. The separate 197th Infantry Brigade (Mechanized) at Fort Benning, was assigned to the 24th Infantry Division (Mechanized) and two brigades of the partially inactivated 2d Armored Division were used to fill out the 1st Infantry and 1st Cavalry Divisions. Additionally, US Army Europe (USAREUR) substituted one of the brigades of the 3d Infantry Division (Mechanized) for the 1st Brigade, 1st Armored Division. The equipmentless 3d Brigade, 1st Infantry Division (Mechanized), used its personnel at the port of Dammam, Saudi Arabia as a badly needed port support activity, supervising and conducting the unloading of ships during the deployment. The 1st Brigade, 2d Armored Division, originally deployed as a filler brigade for the 1st Cavalry Division, was detached and assigned to support the US Marine forces south of Kuwait City, providing an armored force to augment the Marines in their drive on the Kuwait airport. The assignment of brigades during the deployment and ground campaign are listed in Table 11.

Gulf War Brigade Assignments, 1990-1991

Table 11. Gulf War Brigade Assignments, 1990-1991

Division	Organic Brigades	Filler Brigades	Remarks
1st ID (Mech)	1, 2	3d Bde, 2d AD (2d AD FWD)	3d Bde (1st ID FWD) used at Dammam as port support activity
1st AD	2, 3	3d Bde, 3d ID (Mech)	
1st Cav Div	1, 2	1st Bde, 2d AD	Filler bde detached to US Marine Corps, Central Command (MARCENT); 155th Armored Bde (MS ARNG), originally slated as roundout
3d AD	1, 2, 3		
24th ID (Mech)	1, 2	197th Inf Bde (Mech)	48th Inf Bde (Mech), (GA ARNG) originally slated as roundout
82d AB Div	1, 2, 3		
101st AB Div	1, 2, 3		

The Gulf War was the first large-scale deployment utilizing the new AOE brigade and logistical organizations, as well as the new equipment and weapons ushered into the force in the 1980s. The speedy deployment of two corps worth of brigades, the execution of a rapid, decisive campaign, and the subsequent redeployment, were feats unique in US military

95

history. The fast ground campaign generally did not allow for extensive independent brigade maneuvers and was over quickly as the Iraqi Republican Guard and Army forces were swiftly destroyed in an uneven clash of arms, facilitated by the six-week air campaign and by air and artillery support on the ground.

In Operation DESERT STORM, brigades were components of larger forces and were seldom used for independent maneuver. The flexible organizational structure of the AOE division and the use of brigades as intermediate headquarters and task forces ratified the AOE force structure. When US forces returned to Iraq in 2003, the flexible organization would allow for the more independent use of the brigade in combat. In the next section, the operations of the 24th Infantry Division (Mechanized) will be examined to illustrate brigade operations in 1991.

24th Mechanized Division Brigades in Operation DESERT STORM

The mission of the 24th Infantry Division (Mechanized) in the ground campaign phase of Operation DESERT STORM was to attack northeast from Saudi Arabia on the right flank of the XVIII Airborne Corps and advance almost 200 miles to the Euphrates River valley, block this key escape route for the Iraqi forces trying to escape from the Kuwaiti Theater of Operations (KTO), then wheel to the right and advance 70 miles to the east toward Basra to help complete the destruction of the Iraqi Republican Guard.[36]

To control the operation, the division commander used graphic control devices. Each brigade was given a sector. Movement was keyed to perpendicular phaselines, battle positions, areas of operation (AO), and objectives. The division planned and executed the operation in five phases. The phases were as follows:[37]

Each brigade contained three battalions. The 1st and 197th had two mechanized infantry battalions and a tank battalion and the 2d Brigade the reverse, two tank battalions and a mechanized battalion. The brigades were supported by from two to five artillery battalions at any given time. An engineer battalion was also in direct support of each brigade.

Table 12. 24th Mechanized Division Five-Phased Attack, 1991

Phase 1	Three brigades abreast attack across the border for 27 miles to Phaseline Colt
Phase 2	Two brigade attack roughly 100 miles to Objectives Brown (west), Grey (east), and the third brigade to pass through the rightmost brigade (at Objective Grey) and advance an additional 60 miles to Objective Red
Phase 3	Attack into Euphrates Valley to seize battle positions facing east and west to block reinforcement to and escape from KTO
Phase 4	Attack to Jalibah and Tallil Airbases
Phase 5	Attack eastward toward Basrah

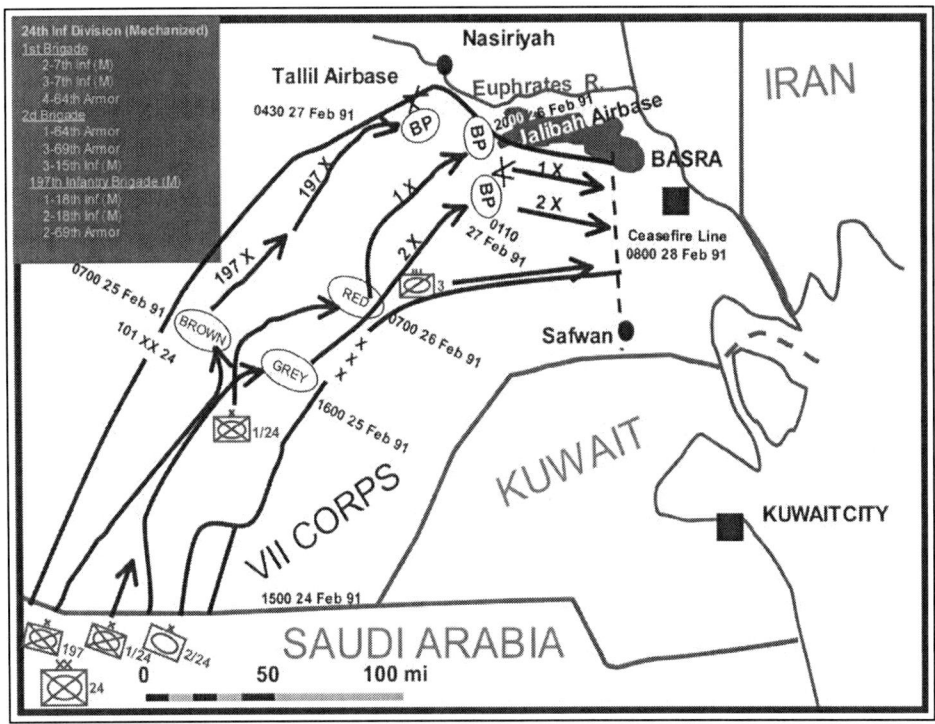

Figure 36. 24th Mechanized Division Brigade Operations in the Gulf War, 1991

Initial coordination for the attack required that the 24th not initiate offensive operations for over 24 hours after the Marines south of Kuwait and the rest of the XVIIII Corps had done so. However, the rapidity of the Iraqi collapse in other sectors pushed the attack ahead 15 hours and the three division brigades crossed the line of departure at 1500 on 24 February 1991, with the 197th on the left, the 1st in the center, and the tank-heavy 2d on the right. Upon reaching Phaseline Colt, 27 miles inside Iraq, Phase 1 ended and the 197th and 2d Brigades continued the advance, while the 1st followed the 2d Brigade. Opposition was light and spotty. The aviation brigade conducted aerial reconnaissance forward of each brigade and the brigade's armored cavalry troop preceded the 197th, with the divisional squadron scouting forward for the 2d Brigade. Throughout the afternoon and evening, the brigades advanced, even when sandstorms reduced visibility to zero. The terrain hindered the 2d Brigade's advance, when the unit had to negotiate a rugged escarpment. The 197th secured Objective Brown at 0700 25 February and linked up with elements of the 101st Airborne Division to its left. The 2d Brigade secured Objective Grey at 1600. By then, the 1st Brigade had already passed through the 2d Brigade and advanced an additional 60 miles to the north to secure Objective Red and establish east-facing blocking positions. The 1st Brigade secured Objective Red at 2230. In a little over a day and a half the three brigades had advanced 160 miles into Iraq and were preparing to close the back door on the KTO.[36]

As the 1st Brigade advanced on Objective Red, the 197th Brigade continued its advance from Objective Brown to the northeast to a battle position to launch Phase 3. Rain and rugged terrain slowed the advance, but the brigade was in its forward position at Objective Red. At 1400 on 26 February the 1st Brigade commenced Phase 3 as the division's main attack. Severe sand dunes hindered the brigade's advance, followed by defensive actions from the battalion-sized Iraqi 3d Commando Regiment, the first real opposition encountered by any of the brigades. After close in action where several small American units were briefly cut off, precision artillery strikes broke the Iraqi will to fight and they surrendered. The 197th Brigade secured its battle position overlooking the Tallil Airbase facing west at 0430 on 27 February. To the east, the 2d Brigade had already secured its eastward-facing battle position near the Jalibah Airbase at 0110. Phase 3 was over—the Euphrates Valley escape route was blocked.[37]

With the brigades in position, the division turned its attention to the key Tallil and Jalibah Airbases. At 0600 on 27 February, while the 1st Brigade fixed the enemy along east-west Highway 8 to the north and the 197th Brigade protected the western flank, the 2d Brigade, supported by an artillery barrage from five battalions, assaulted Jalibah with its two tank battalions supporting by fire, while the mechanized infantry battalion seized the airfield itself. Within 4 hours the facility was secured. The Iraqi tank battalion defending Jalibah was destroyed along with 80 antiaircraft guns. Over 200 prisoners were taken. On the afternoon of 27 February, after an air strike preparation, the 197th's TF 2-69 Armor raided Tallil to neutralize fire coming from the airbase. The raid ended the threat, but the 197th was not directed to secure the airfield, as the division was now turning east to execute the fifth and final phase of the operation. Tallil was left to the 101st Airborne Division.[38]

For Phase 5, the 24th Division reoriented to the east. Corps attached the 3d Armored Cavalry Regiment to the division, allowing the division commander, Major General Barry McCaffrey, to place the 197th Brigade in reserve. Phase 5 commenced at 1300 on 27 February. The division attacked with the 1st Brigade on the left as the main attack, 2d Brigade in the center, and the 3d ACR on the right. The 197th Brigade protected the division rear area and followed behind the 2d Brigade, ready to assume the main attack if necessary. The advance was steady, even though elements of the Republican Guard Al Faw, Adnan, Hammurabi, and Nebuchadnezzar Divisions opposed it, mostly with ineffective artillery fire. The swift drive captured a major Iraqi logistics hub, including 1,300 ammunition bunkers. The division had planned to continue the advance toward Basra on the 28th, but President George H.W. Bush issued orders for a ceasefire effective at 0800 on that day.[39]

Even though the war was technically over, elements of the 1st Brigade fought the Battle of Rumaylah on 28 March. Fleeing portions of the Hammurabi Division were discovered trying to fight their way across to the north on the causeway across marshy Lake Hawr Al Hammar, in the 1st Brigade's sector. The brigade, reinforced with an air cavalry troop and five artillery battalions, sealed off this northern escape route. As a coupe de grace, brigade received an Apache attack helicopter company which destroyed 102 enemy vehicles with Hellfire missiles from long range. To finish things, the brigade sent a reinforced armored battalion task force to attack the length of the enemy column from south to north. In the whole action the 1st Brigade destroyed over 187 Iraqi armored vehicles, 400 wheeled vehicles, 34 artillery pieces, and seven FROG missile systems, with the loss of one soldier wounded and one M-1 tank disabled when it caught fire from being too close to an exploding Iraqi T-72 tank.[40]

The 24th Division used its three maneuver brigades to both fight and maneuver. Flexible organization and teamwork with supporting elements enhanced the division's ability to accomplish its mission quickly and effectively, even though the operation was complex, the terrain daunting, and the enemy aggressive when cornered.

NOTES

1. The brigades were the 69th Infantry Brigade (Mechanized), Kansas ARNG, which filled in for the 5th Infantry Division's brigade in Vietnam at Fort Carson from 1968-1969, and the 29th Infantry Brigade, Hawaii Army National Guard, which served at Schofield Barracks, Hawaii, as Pacific strategic reserve in 1968-1969. Both units sent soldiers as individual replacements to Vietnam.

2. John B. Wilson, *Maneuver and Firepower: The Evolution of Divisions and Separate Brigades*. Army Lineage Series (Washington, DC: Government Printing Office, 1998), 355-65.

3. Ibid., 395.

4. Both of these units subsequently, after redeployment, were redesignated as the 3d Brigade of each division.

5. Ibid., 364-66, 421-22; RC combat battalions were also used to round out AC divisions.

6. Shelby Stanton, *Anatomy of a Division: The First Cav in Vietnam* (Novato, CA: Presidio, 1987), 246-50

7. There was controversy over the naming of the attack helicopter units between being designated as attack helicopter battalions (aviation battalions) or air cavalry squadrons. The cavalry designation won out in the TRICAP division. However, with the creation of a separate aviation branch in the 1980s, the designations were switched back to aviation ones.

8. Colonel Charles E. Canedy, "From ACCB to the 6th Cavalry Brigade (Air Combat)," *United States Army Aviation Digest*, 21 (May 1975), 1-4; Lieutenant Colonel Donald R. Martin, "First Cavalry Division Reorganization," *Armor*, 83 (July-August 1974), 51-52; Ivan H. Oleson, "TriCap: A New Logistics Challenge," *Army Logistician* 3 (September-October 1971), 5-7, 33. The 3d Brigade of the division (the airmobile brigade) was originally designated 4th Brigade, as the 3d Brigade was still in Vietnam. Upon that brigade's return from Vietnam, the 4th was redesignated the 3d, although the troop units in the brigade remained the same.

9. John Wilson, *Armies, Corps, Divisions and Separate Brigades* (Washington, DC: US Army Center of Military History (CMH), 1999), 137; Wilson, *Maneuver and Firepower*, 337.

10. Wilson, *Maneuver and Firepower*, 366-67.

11. Ibid., 353, 355-56, 361, 364-65.

12. John L. Romjue, *A History of Army 86. Volume I Division 86: The Development of the Heavy Division* (September 1978- October 1979), Headquarters, US Army Training and Doctrine Command (TRADOC), August 1980, 43, 66.

13. Romjue, 44.

14. John L. Romjue, *The Army of Excellence: The Development of the 1980s Army* (Fort Monroe, VA: TRADOC, 1993), 18, 20, 75, 179-86; The 2d Brigade with three combined arms battalions (CABs) was inactivated in 1988, replaced by the roundout brigade. The CABS were given infantry regimental designations, while the light attack battalions were given armor regimental designations, as there was no provision for CAB designations except within the existing branches. When Combat Arms Regimental System was first adopted in 1957, it initially merged the infantry and armor units into combined arms regiments. But it was soon dropped in favor of the traditional branch system.

15. Richard J. Dunn III, "Transformation: Let's Get It Right This Time, " *Parameters* (Spring 2001), 22-28; Romjue, *Army of Excellence*, 76; Lieutenant Colonel Stephen Bowman, "'The Old Reliables' One of a Kind," *Army* 38 (February 1988), 29-31.

16. Wilson, *Maneuver and Firepower*, 397.

17. A clarification of this point may be found on the CMH' website, written 31 January 2002, but current as of 24 April 2003, <http://www.army.mil/cmh-pg/lineage/branches/av/default.htm>.

18. Wilson, *Maneuver and Firepower*, 354.

19. Shelby Stanton, *Vietnam Order of Battle* (Washington, DC: US News Books, 1981), 109-23.

20. Ibid., 109.

21. In 1996, the 21st Cavalry Brigade (Air Combat) was created at Fort Hood, Texas, from the redesignation of the former US Army Combat Aviation Training Brigade. However this brigade is a purely training init, despite its designation.

22. Field Manual (FM) 71-100, *Division Operations*, 28 August 1996, states "the aviation brigade is a maneuver force... ," g. 1-9.

23. As an exception to this, the aviation brigade of the 1st Cavalry Division is officially called "Cavalry Brigade, 1st Cavalry Division."

24. Wilson, *Maneuver and Firepower*, 359.

25. Ibid., 356.

26. Romjue, *Army of Excellence*, 78.

27. Wilson, *Maneuver and Firepower*, 400.

28. Sometimes the command battalion, 6-101st Aviation, is placed under the 159th Bde.

29. This section is largely, but not exclusively, based on the author's experiences. Headquarters, Department of the Army. FM 71-123, *Tactics and Techniques for Combined Arms Heavy Forces: Armored Brigade, Battalion Task Force, and Company Team* (Washington, DC: US Army, 1992), and US Army Logistics Management College. *Support Operations Course (Phase 1)*. Lesson Book (Fort Lee, VA: US Army Logistics Management College, 1992).

30. *3d Brigade, 101st Airborne Division (Airmobile),Combat Operations After Action Report—Summary APACHE SNOW*, dated 25 June 1969, 1-2.

31. Romjue, *Division 86: The Development of the Heavy Division*, 87. In 1981, the FASCO had his own office in the headquarters, 2d Brigade, 8th Infantry Division (Mechanized), Smith Barracks, Baumholder, Germany.

32. Romjue, *Army of Excellence*, 49, 55, 91.Colonel John R. Landry and Lieutenant Colonel Bloomer D. Sullivan. "CSS: Resourcing and Sustaining the AirLand Battle: Forward Support Battalion," *Military Review* 67 (January 1987), 27-29.

33. Romjue, *Army of Excellence*, 10; Landry and Sullivan, 27; Major John E. Edwards, *Combat Service Support Guide*. Second Edition (Harrisburg, VA: Stackpole Books, 1993), 51.

34. Operation URGENT FURY, the invasion of the island of Grenada, October 1983, saw the use of three brigade headquarters and attached units from the 82d Airborne Division, still organized under the old ROAD tables of organization.

35. The deployment of US forces was actually two roughly 90-day deployments: XVIII Airborne Corps in August-November 1990, and VII Corps in November 1990- February 1991. See John J. McGrath. *Gulf War Build Up*, unpublished PowerPoint document, 2001, CMH, Washington, DC.

36. *The Victory Book: A Desert Storm Chronicle* (Fort Stewart, GA: Public Affairs Office, 24th Infantry Division (Mechanized), 1992), 70-71; Major Joseph C. Barto III, *Task Force 2-4 Cav-"First In, Last Out": The History of the 2d Squadron, 4th Cavalry Regiment, During Operation Desert Storm* (Fort Leavenworth, KS: Combat Studies Institute, 1993), 47.

37. *The Victory Book*, 76; Barto, 47-51.

38. *The Victory Book*, 82-91; Barto, 57-60, 62-71.

39. *The Victory Book*, 94-95; Barto, 72-76.

40. *The Victory Book*, 98, 100-1; Barto, 76-77, 79-81.

41. *The Victory Book*, 104-5; Barto, 80.

42. *The Victory Book*, 108-16; Barto, 96-99.

Chapter 8

THE MODERN BRIGADE, 1991-2003

Enhanced Brigades

In the early 1970s, the Army had embraced the "Total Army" concept, which made the reserve components, ARNG and USAR, full partners in the defense establishment with projected roles and missions upon mobilization. The Total Army concept had its ups and downs as the readiness of reserve component units fluctuated, based on recruitment, turnover, equipment, and training time factors. Various programs, such as the use of roundout brigades and the affiliation program, where Reserve Component (RC) units were made partners with similar active component units, were designed to enhance reserve readiness. After the Gulf War, where the roundout brigades remained nondeployed, the Army's drawdown required the continuation of the program. Once the Army reached its 10-division structure in 1996, however, the roundout program was replaced. The new program, ARNG Enhanced Brigades, utilized the acronyms eSB (enhanced separate brigade) and eHSb (enhanced heavy separate brigade). The Army selected 15 separate Army National Guard brigades, most of which had been part of the roundout program, for special (enhanced) status. The program was a comprehensive planning, training, and equipment package designed to enhance the ability of the brigades to mobilize and be combat ready within between 90 and 120 days. The selected brigades received special attention from active component soldiers, most of whom were assigned to regionally based readiness groups.

In 1999, the Army initiated two new organizational changes to increase the readiness status of the enhanced brigades. The first was the activation of two division headquarters without assigned brigades of their own. The 24th Infantry Division (Mechanized), activated at Fort Riley, Kansas, and the 7th Infantry Division, activated at Fort Carson, were designated as Active Component (AC)/RC integrated divisions: divisional headquarters staffed with active duty soldiers, but with subordinate units consisting of assigned Army National Guard separate brigades. The divisions were the first units to combine active duty and nonmobilized reserve soldiers under the same headquarters in US Army history. Additionally, all the support elements normally assigned to the division were assigned directly to each brigade in their separate brigade configurations. The only previous parallel to this, was the assembly of the Americal Division in Vietnam in 1967. The divisions were organized to enhance pre- and postmobilization training, war preparation, and facilitate rapid deployment. The division headquarters oversaw the planning, preparation, and coordination of training for the assigned enhanced brigades.[1]

The second change was the merging of the active component readiness groups with the Army Reserve exercise divisions into a new organization, the training support division. The readiness groups were regionally based active Army agencies designed to advise and support reserve component training. With the creation of the enhanced brigades in 1996, the readiness groups were the spearhead of the Army's effort at supporting the brigades. The Army Reserve exercise divisions had been created in the mid-1990s to prepare and run training exercises for RC units After 1999, the new training support division was specially tailored to support the enhanced brigades, containing a special eSB training support brigade for each enhanced brigade within its assigned region.

Enhanced brigades not assigned to an integrated division were given a status of "training association" with specified active component units, as well as being supported by eSB training support brigades in the AC/USAR training support divisions. A listing of the enhanced brigades follows in Table 13.

Table 13. National Guard Enhanced Brigades and AC/RC Divisions

Unit	Location	AC/RC Division (1999)
27th Infantry Brigade	Syracuse, New York	
29th Infantry Brigade	Honolulu, Hawaii	
30th Infantry Brigade (Mech)	Clinton, North Carolina	24th Infantry Division
39th Infantry Brigade	Little Rock, Arkansas	7th Infantry Division
41st Infantry Brigade	Portland, Oregon	7th Infantry Division
45th Infantry Brigade	Edmond, Oklahoma	7th Infantry Division
48th Infantry Brigade (Mech)	Macon, Georgia	24th Infantry Division
53rd Infantry Brigade	Tampa, Florida	
76th Infantry Brigade	Indianapolis, Indiana	
81st Infantry Brigade (Mech)	Seattle, Washington	
116th Cavalry Brigade (Mech)	Boise, Idaho	
155th Armored Brigade	Tupelo, Mississippi	
218th Infantry Brigade (Mech)	Newberry, South Carolina	24th Infantry Division
256th Infantry Brigade (Mech)	Lafayette, Louisiana	
278th Armored Cavalry Regiment	Knoxville, Tennessee	

From 1994-1995, the Army Reserve lost its three maneuver brigades to force cuts. However, the training divisions of the USAR still retained from three to nine training brigades in each division. Between 1994 and 1999, the training divisions were reorganized into two new types of divisions: institutional training divisions, which, in addition to conducting the traditional entry training missions of the former training divisions, also assumed the reserve component military occupational specialty and NCO and officer training missions formerly conducted by US Army Reserve Forces (USARF) school units; and the previously mentioned exercise divisions, which planned and executed both computer simulated and on-the-ground training exercises, in specially prepared training "lanes." Each of these divisions had subordinate training brigades, which carried the colors and traditions of brigades belonging to the divisions when they were tactical units. As mentioned above, the exercise divisions were merged with the active component readiness groups in 1999 to form new AC/RC training support divisions.

Force XXI and Other Tweaks

A combination of force reductions and an analysis of the 1991 Gulf War made the Army reanalyze its force structure. Technological advances promised to digitalize future Army organizations. Digitalization meant the linking of combat elements by computer, allowing for a higher situational awareness and a speedy transmission of reports and orders, easing command and control and logistics accordingly. The Army formally initiated its new organizational study, coined Force XXI, in March 1994. Planners developed a divisional structure, referred to as the Interim Division Design, in 1995. The 4th Infantry Division (Mechanized) became the test unit at Fort Hood, experimenting with the interim design in 1996-1997.[3]

In terms of the brigade, Force XXI had three structural changes: it added a small brigade reconnaissance troop in armored HMMWVs at the brigade level, made the brigade organizational structure fixed, and proposed the removal of all organic combat service support elements from the brigade's combat battalions to the forward support battalions of the DISCOM. The reconnaissance troop, which was implemented Armywide, separate from Force XXI, will be discussed below. The fixed brigade included a division of one armored and two mechanized brigades. The armored brigade would consist of two tank battalions and one mechanized infantry battalion, the mechanized brigades of one tank battalion and two mechanized battalions. Each battalion would consist of only three line companies instead of the four found under AOE. As of 2003, the fixed one armored, two mechanized brigade structure, had not been adopted even in the 4th Infantry Division, which fielded two armored and one mechanized brigade, despite its designation, as an armored division.[4] The combat service support modifications were based on the advantages of a centralized system of digitalized logistics, which allowed units to send logistics support requests quickly and accurately direct to the units responsible for providing the support. As of spring 2003, only the 4th Mechanized Division and parts of the 1st Cavalry Division were organized under Force XXI structure. The 4th ID was completely digitalized in Fiscal Year 2000, with the 1st Cavalry Division following. The rest of the Army retained modified AOE force structure organizations reflected in Limited Conversion Division XXI (LCD XXI), which reduced the line companies to three in each battalion and added a reconnaissance troop to the brigade.[5]

Even while the Force XXI study and test unit were being developed, tweaks and changes to Army brigade and division structure continued apart from Force XXI. Among these were the creation of divisional engineer brigades, the addition of an organic reconnaissance troop to the brigade, and the widespread adoption of the BCT concept.

In the Gulf War, virtually every brigade had a combat engineer battalion attached. Accordingly, the Army initiated a program called the Engineer Restructuring Initiative almost immediately after that war. The result was the addition of two engineer battalions and an engineer brigade headquarters to the heavy division. Unlike the aviation brigade, there was no pretense that the engineer brigade was a maneuver element. Instead, the brigade headquarters was considered much like the division's artillery (DIVARTY) headquarters, a specialty headquarters controlling troops usually placed in direct support of the division's maneuver brigades. Army thought flip-flopped back and forth about retaining the engineer brigade headquarters or simply assigning the battalions either directly to the division or the brigades. However, as of early 2003, the engineer brigade was still a basic component of the heavy divisions, though in most divisions the engineer battalions were attached directly to the brigades under the BCT concept. In 2004, as will be seen in the next chapter, the engineer brigade is to be converted into a fourth maneuver brigade headquarters in the division.

Separate brigades had long been authorized a brigade reconnaissance element, a troop of armored cavalry. Divisional brigades would normally receive similar support from the divisional cavalry squadron. However, after the Gulf War, and in studies promulgated under Force XXI, planners focused on the need for an organic reconnaissance troop in each armored and mechanized infantry brigade assigned to a division. The troop would provide the brigade commander with direct reconnaissance assets already found at both the battalion and division levels, but lacking at the brigade level. In 1998, under LCD XXI, the Army authorized the troop, commonly referred to as the brigade reconnaissance troop (BRT), but officially given a cavalry designation.[6] Troops were added to brigades over the next two years. This marked the first time since the creation of the brigades under ROAD in 1963 that the brigade had an organic combat element.

The brigade reconnaissance troop organization consisted of a troop headquarters and two scout platoons. The scout platoons were made up of six M1025 HMMWVs, divided into three squads. Each squad comprised two HMMWWVs, one with a MK19 GMG or M240B medium machine gun and the other with the M2 .50 caliber machine gun. The HMMWVs were manned by a three-scout crew. The troop was often augmented with other reconnaissance assets, particularly Combat Observation Laser Teams (COLT), to provide specialized indirect fire observers.[7] The troops as fielded and configured in 2003 are shown in Table 14.

Brigade/Cavalry Troops, 2003

Table 14. Brigade Reconnaissance Troops, 2003

Brigade	Cavalry Troop
1st Brigade, 1st Armored Division	Troop F, 1st Cavalry
2d Brigade, 1st Armored Division	Troop G, 1st Cavalry
3d Brigade, 1st Armored Division	Troop H, 1st Cavalry
1st Brigade, 1st Cavalry Division	Troop C, 10th Cavalry
2d Brigade, 1st Cavalry Division	Troop D, 9th Cavalry
3d Brigade, 1st Cavalry Division	Troop F, 9th Cavalry (2004)
1st Brigade, 1st Infantry Division	Troop D, 4th Cavalry
2d Brigade, 1st Infantry Division	Troop E, 4th Cavalry
3d Brigade, 1st Infantry Division	Troop D, 4th Cavalry
1st Brigade, 3d Infantry Division	Troop C, 1st Cavalry
2d Brigade, 3d Infantry Division	Troop E, 9th Cavalry
3d Brigade, 3d Infantry Division	Troop D, 10th Cavalry
1st Brigade, 4th Infantry Division	Troop G, 10th Cavalry
2d Brigade, 4th Infantry Division	Troop H, 10th Cavalry
3d Brigade, 4th Infantry Division	Troop B, 9th Cavalry

Despite many changes in Army organization, force strengths and the adoption of whole new generations of weapons systems and participation in conflicts as varied as Vietnam and Iraq, the brigade's basic design remained a flexible task force to which combat units were attached based on specific mission requirements. The reason the structure was retained was not institutional lethargy or resistance to change. It was retained because it worked. The brigade had proven to be a highly effective means of organizing to execute most aspects of modern warfare. Tweaks such as the reorganizing of the division support command to provide multifunctional support battalions for each brigade and the addition of an organic brigade reconnaissance troop were just fine-tuning an organizational concept that had repeatedly proven its value. But force drawdowns, stationing concerns, and the desire to create special types of forces in sizes smaller than division would impact on the brigade concept at the close of the century.

Stryker Brigades: Army Transformation Redux

In the modern era, the Army has suffered from the perennial problem of projecting forces to the far reaches of the globe quickly and with adequate firepower to deal with indigenous threats. Armored and mechanized units require a lot of shipping and extended periods of up to 30 days to arrive on the scene, unless propositioned equipment is used. Light units can arrive via parachute or aircraft relatively quickly, but are then often too light to successfully fight the heavy forces of the threat already there. The deployabilty versus survivability debate was not a new one. The testbed motorized division and light divisions formed in the 1980s were approaches to solving the same problem.

In October 1999, Army Chief of Staff Eric Shinseki announced the latest effort at providing a highly deployable and combat capable Army force with the creation of the Interim Brighade Combat Team (IBCT) project. Like the 9th Infantry Division motorization project from almost 20 years before, the IBCT project's goal was to use new technology to field lightweight motorized vehicles with adequate firepower. The program postulated the development of a family of wheeled armored vehicles to provide both troop carriers and assault guns.[8]

Instead of selecting a division to be the experimental force (EXFOR) for the IBCT, in April 2000, the Army selected two divisional brigades, which were stationed at Fort Lewis, away from their respective parent units in Korea and Hawaii. One brigade was a mechanized brigade, the other light. An additional four brigades were added to the program in July 2001, including a separate light brigade, a divisional light brigade, a light armored cavalry regiment, and a mechanized divisional brigade from the Army National Guard. The brigade package, once deployed, was designed to be used under a division or independently and be capable of deployment worldwide by air force transports within 96 hours. The brigade was to fill the deployment gap between early-entry units (light infantry and airborne) and the later deploying heavy forces.[9]

The centerpiece of the new brigade was a new light-armored wheeled vehicle. When the IBCT program commenced, the vehicle did not exist. The first brigade utilized a combination of Land Assault Vehicles (LAV-III) borrowed from the Canadian army and HMMWVs. General Dynamics and General Motors developed the new vehicle under a contract awarded in November 2000. The first models were delivered in March 2002. Initially called the Interim Armored Vehicle, the Army officially renamed the vehicle the Stryker after two unrelated Army Medal of Honor winners in February 2002. As developed, the Stryker is a 19-ton, 8-wheeled armored vehicle with eight different variants and capable of speeds up to 60 miles per hour. A single C-17 Air Force cargo airplane can carry three Strykers. The first Strykers delivered were infantry carriers, capable of carrying a nine-man infantry squad and armed with either a MK19 GMG or .50 caliber machine gun. Other models included the mobile gun system (MGS), the first of which were delivered as test systems in June 2002. The MGS mounts a stabilized 105mm gun. Until it is fully fielded in 2005, the MGS units of the brigade will substitute the Stryker antitank missile variant. The other variants are reconnaissance, mortar, command, fire support, engineer, medical, and nuclear, biological, chemical (NBC) reconnaissance vehicles. In addition to the Strykers, the brigade would also utilize digital technology to provide wireless communications and sensors to enhance the unit's ability to maintain situational awareness on the battlefield.[10]

The first Stryker brigade was projected to be operational by December 2001, with the second a year later and the remaining four over the course of the next few years. However, developmental problems with the Stryker and its production delayed the program. The first IBCT, the 3d Brigade, 2d Infantry Division, commenced its final two-month field training at the Army training centers at Fort Irwin, California, and Fort Polk, Louisiana, in late March 2003. Upon successful completion of the tests, the brigade was considered operational. It began deploying to Iraq for employment in contingency operations in late 2003. Stryker units are shown in Table 15.

Table 15. Projected Stryker Interim Brigade Combat Team Units

3d Brigade, 2d Infantry Division	Fort Lewis, Washington
1st Brigade, 25th Infantry Division	Fort Lewis, Washington
172d Infantry Brigade	Fort Richardson, Alaska
2d Armored Cavalry Regiment (Light)	Fort Polk, Louisiana
2d Brigade, 25th Infantry Division	Schofield Barracks, Hawaii
56th Brigade, 28th Infantry Division (Mech)	Pennsylvania ARNG

Stryker brigade organization contained 309 Strykers and over 700 other wheeled vehicles. The brigade consisted of three combined arms infantry battalions and a new type of cavalry squadron, the reconnaissance, surveillance, and target acquisition (RSTA) squadron. The brigade also included antiarmor and engineer companies, a field artillery battalion, military intelligence and signal companies, and a brigade support battalion. The organization is structured to allow it to readily fight as combined arms units down to the company level.[11]

The combined arms infantry battalions consisted of three companies, each organized with three infantry platoons (three Stryker infantry vehicles), a 81mm mortar section (three Stryker mortar carriers), and a MGS platoon (four Stryker MGS vehicles), as well as a sniper team. At the battalion level were also found reconnaissance and mortar platoons and a sniper squad.[12]

The RSTA squadron was organized with three reconnaissance troops and a surveillance troop. The reconnaissance troop was composed of three reconnaissance platoons and a mortar section. The surveillance troop consisted of a platoon of unmanned aerial vehicles (UAV), NBC reconnaissance platoon, and a multisensor platoon.

108

The rest of the Stryker brigade consisted of a towed M198 155mm field artillery howitzer battalion, an antitank company equipped with TOW missile mounted Strykers (to be ultimately replaced with a new "bunker-busting" TOW), an engineer company geared to clearing obstacles, a military intelligence company specially designed to facilitate the use of human intelligence assets, an organic signal company to provide command and control support, and a support battalion consisting of a medical company, a support company, and a headquarters/supply company. The support battalion was designed to provide self-sustaining combat service support to the brigade for the first 72 hours of combat operations.[13]

Figure 37. Stryker Vehicles. Infantry Carrier (left) and Mobile Gun System (right)

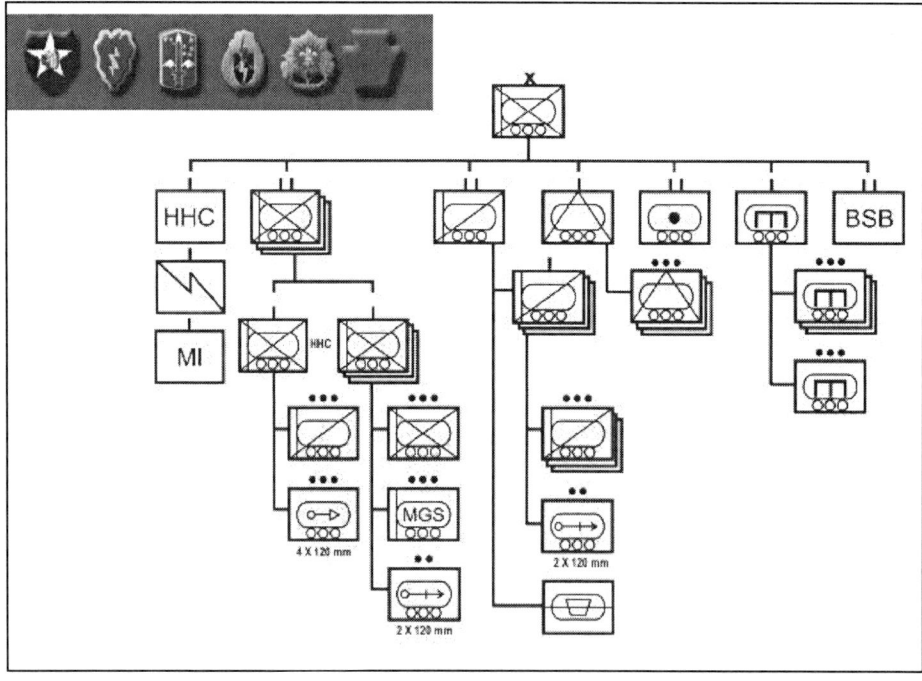

Figure 38. The Stryker Brigade

The Brigade Combat Team

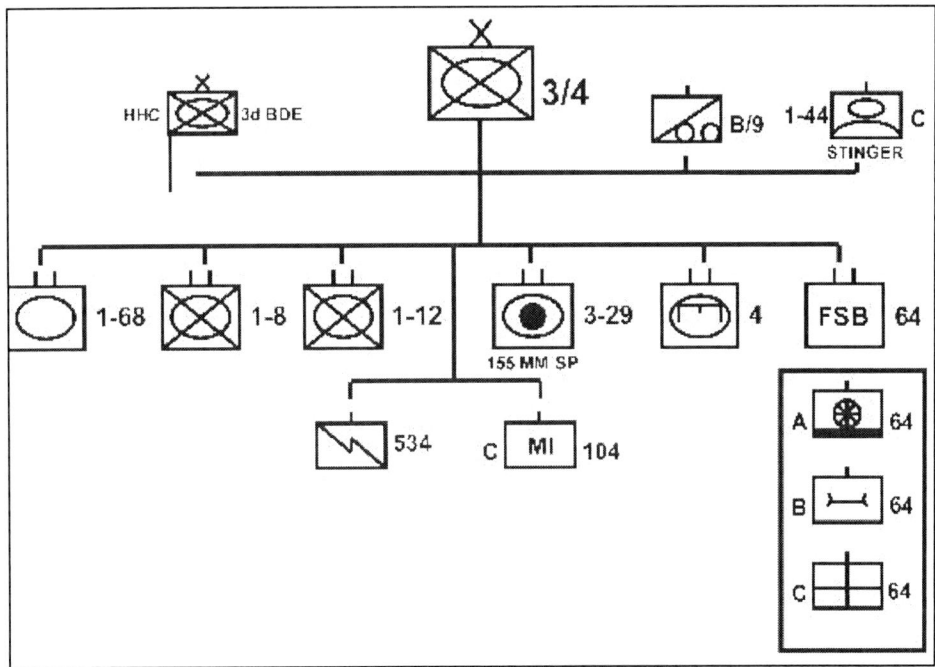

Figure 39. Brigade Combat Team, 2004

A combination of downsizing and stationing issues in the late 1990s affected the role of the brigade vis-à-vis the division. In 2003, there are more Army brigades stationed apart from their parent divisions then ever since the revival of the brigade in 1963. Ironically, at the same time, the Army's force of separate brigades, which at one point in the late 1990s was at zero, was now at only two: one theater defense brigade, the 172d Infantry, in Alaska and one special purpose brigade, the 173 Airborne, in Italy. In effect, the 21st century Army had replaced the self-contained separate brigade's role with divisional brigades, which had become self-contained through the use of the BCT concept.

The BCT is based on analogy with the pre-1957 RCT concept. It designates a brigade with, in addition to the 2-5 maneuver battalions typically attached to it, an attached slice of divisional support elements designated to support it. The terminology is a bit of a misnomer, as the brigade, unlike the old regiment, is a task force headquarters by design. Nevertheless the term BCT allows the Army to easily designate divisional brigades that are basically configured as self-contained units.

In 2003 almost all divisional brigades, whether collocated with their parent division or not, were organized as BCTs. Stationing considerations enhance the viability of the BCT, particularly when several large Army posts had two brigades from different divisions assigned to them without either divisional headquarters onsite. The designation of the test organization for the Stryker brigades as BCTs, with no divisional headquarters, and the selection of Stryker Brigade Combat Teams (SBCTs) from three different divisions, a separate brigade, and an armored cavalry regiment, clearly indicated that SBCTs were being packaged as independent entities, rather than divisional components, despite their designations. Brigades active in 2004 and their home stationing are listed in Table 16. (Those in boldface are not stationed with their parent divisions or are separate by organization.)

An example of the organization of a typical brigade combat team organization is shown in Figure 39.

Brigades in the War with Iraq, 2003

In the March-April 2003 war with Iraq, the Army deployed far fewer ground combat maneuver brigades than in the 1991 Gulf War: eight versus 21 in 1991. However, the results were far more decisive in a much shorter period of time: in 22 days the Iraqi army was destroyed as a viable combat force and the capital city of Baghdad occupied, versus in 1991, a six-week air campaign followed by a four-day ground campaign against only a portion of the Iraqi army, which left much of that army intact. Brigades deployed in the ground campaign phase of Operation IRAQI FREEDOM are included in Table 17.

The campaign once again proved the utility and flexibility of the maneuver brigade on the modern battlefield. The three heavy brigades of the 3d Infantry Division (Mechanized) spearheaded the advance on Baghdad, moving almost 200 miles in less than 40 hours, then, after a preplanned logistical halt, which coincided with bad weather conditions, completed the movement to the Iraqi capital, after a major river-crossing operation, in two days, and secured major portions of the city over the course of several more days.[14]

The air assault brigades of the 101st Airborne Division (Air Assault) and a paratrooper brigade of the 82d Airborne Division, both supported by elements of the heavy 3d Brigade, 1st Armored Division, advanced after the 3d Mechanized Division, relieved brigades of that division containing bypassed cities and protected the long supply and communications line, while destroying enemy resistance at Samawah, Najaf, Karbala, and Hillah. The 173d Airborne Brigade parachuted into key positions in northern Iraq to assist the Kurdish forces and complete the defeat of the demoralized Iraqi forces on that front. The use of the 173d as a component of a Special Operations task force was a unique first in US Army history.[15]

Aviation brigades, both divisional and the corps-level 11th Aviation Group and 12th Aviation Brigade, saw extensive service in the Iraqi War. However, use of these organizations as maneuver elements was limited at best. The 11th was an attack helicopter organization, while the 12th provided mostly lift assets for maneuver units. The 3d Infantry Division's Aviation Brigade was, however, used in the later stages of the campaign near Karbala to control reconnaissance and security operations, traditionally maneuver-type missions.[16]

Other future works will undoubtedly fully document the activities of these brigades and the Marine, air and naval forces involved in Operation IRAQI FREEDOM. This work will now offer a preliminary analysis of the operations of the three maneuver brigades of the 3d Infantry Division (Mechanized) as the final case study in this history of brigade development and operations in the US Army.

Table 16. Brigade Stationing, 2004

Brigade	Home Station	Parent Unit Location	Type
1st Brigade, 1st Armored Division	Germany	col ocated	armored
2d Brigade, 1st Armored Division	Germany	col ocated	mechanized
3d Brigade, 1st Armored Division	**Fort Riley, Kansas**	**not collocated**	**armored**
1st Brigade, 1st Cavalry Division	Fort Hood, Texas	col ocated	armored
2d Brigade, 1st Cavalry Division	Fort Hood, Texas	col ocated	armored
3d Brigade, 1st Cavalry Division	Fort Hood, Texas	col ocated	mechanized
1st Brigade, 1st Infantry Division	**Fort Riley, Kansas**	**not collocated**	**armored**
3d Brigade, 1st Infantry Division	Germany	col ocated	armored
2d Brigade, 1st Infantry Division	Germany	col ocated	mechanized
1st Brigade, 2d Infantry Division	Korea	col ocated	armored
2d Brigade, 2d Infantry Division	Korea	col ocated	mechanized/or scout
3d Brigade, 1st Infantry Division	Germany	col ocated	armored
3d Brigade, 2d Infantry Division	**Fort Lewis, Washington**	**not collocated**	**SBCT**
1st Brigade, 3d Infantry Division	Fort Stewart, Georgia	col ocated	mechanized
2d Brigade, 3d Infantry Division	Fort Stewart, Georgia	col ocated	armored
3d Brigade, 3d Infantry Division	**Fort Benning, Georgia**	**not collocated**	**mechanized**
1st Brigade, 4th Infantry Division	Fort Hood, Texas	col ocated	Force XXI/armored
2d Brigade, 4th Infantry Division	Fort Hood, Texas	col ocated	Force XXI/armored
3d Brigade, 4th Infantry Division	**Fort Carson, Colorado**	**not collocated**	**Force XXI/ mechanized**
1st Brigade, 10th Mountain Division	Fort Drum, New York	col ocated	light
2d Brigade, 10th Mountain Division	Fort Drum, New York	col ocated	light
1st Brigade, 25th Infantry Division	**Fort Lewis, Washington**	**not collocated**	**SBCT**
2d Brigade, 25th Infantry Division	Hawaii	col ocated	light/SBCT
3d Brigade, 25th Infantry Division	Hawaii	col ocated	light
1st Brigade, 82d Airborne Division	Fort Bragg, North Carolina	col ocated	airborne
2d Brigade, 82d Airborne Division	Fort Bragg, North Carolina	col ocated	airborne
3d Brigade, 82d Airborne Division	Fort Bragg, North Carolina	col ocated	airborne
1st Brigade, 101st Airborne Division	Fort Campbell, Kentucky	col ocated	air assault
2d Brigade, 101st Airborne Division	Fort Campbell, Kentucky	col ocated	air assault
3d Brigade, 101st Airborne Division	Fort Campbell, Kentucky	col ocated	air assault
172d Infantry Brigade	**Alaska**	**separate**	**light/SBCT**
173d Airborne Brigade	**Italy**	**separate**	**airborne**

Table 17. Brigades in the War with Iraq, 2003

Aviation Brigade, 3d Infantry Division (Mech)
1st Brigade, 3d Infantry Division (Mech)
2d Brigade, 3d Infantry Division (Mech)
3d Brigade, 3d Infantry Division (Mech)
1st Brigade, 101st Airborne Division (Air Assault)
2d Brigade, 101st Airborne Division (Air Assault)
3d Brigade, 101st Airborne Division (Air Assault)
101st Aviation Brigade, 101st Airborne Division (Air Assault)
159th Aviation Brigade, 101st Airborne Division (Air Assault)
2d Brigade, 82d Airborne Division
3d Brigade, 1st Armored Division (not employed as a unit during IRAQI FREEDOM)
173d Airborne Brigade

The 3d Mechanized Division's Brigade in the Iraqi 2003 Campaign

The V Corps' 3d Infantry Division (Mechanized) executed the main attack of the coalition ground assault to depose Saddam Hussein's Iraqi regime. The division's operation concept was to advance as fast and expeditiously to Baghdad as possible, acting as a dagger thrust to the heart of that regime. The daring thrust would deliberately bypass cities and, except for securing bridges for follow-on forces, remain on the Euphrates River's west bank until after defeating the Republic Guard forces defending the area around Karbala, 50 miles southwest of the capital. It was hoped the immediate presence of US forces near Baghdad would cause the collapse of the regime. Central Command (CENTCOM) deliberately designed its strategy to contrast with that used in 1991. The Iraqi command, advised by two former Russian generals, was expecting just such a replay.[17] The 1991 campaign had consisted of a long air campaign, followed by a large-scale ground campaign where most units moved with friendly units on their flanks and nothing was bypassed. The design of the new campaign capitalized on advances in precision munitions, digital communications, and intelligence gathering. Using these advantages, the goal was to move too swiftly and unpredictably for the Iraqi defenders to respond with an effective defense. This switch was euphemistically referred to as "the running start."[18]

For Operation IRAQI FREEDOM, the 3d Mechanized Division's BCTs were initially organized into one tank-heavy brigade force, one mechanized-heavy, and one balanced brigade force with two mechanized and two tank battalions. The task organization are shown in Table 18.

The division had additional attached assets including a PATRIOT antimissile battalion (5-52d ADA), and a logistical corps support group.

Table 18. Initial Brigade Organization, 3d Infantry Division (Mech), 2003

3d Infantry Division (Mech)
Major General G Buford C. Blount III, Commanding

1st Brigade Combat Team
COL William F. Grimsley, commanding

TF 2-7th Infantry (Mech)

TF 3-7th Infantry (Mech)

1 3-69th Armor

C-1st Cavalry (IR)

1-41st Field Artillery

Battery, 1-3 Air Defense Artillery

11th Engineer Battalion

3d Forward Support Battalion

2d Brigade Combat Team
COL David G. Perkins, Commanding

TF 3-15th Infantry (Mech)

TF 1-64th Armor

1 4-64th Armor

A-4th Cavalry (III-I)

1-9th Field Artillery

Battery, 1-3d Air Defense Artillery

10th Engineer Battalion

26th Forward Support Battalion

3d Brigade Combat Team
COL Daniel B. Allyn, Commanding

TF 1-15th Infantry (Mech)

TF 1-30th Infantry (Mech)

TF 2-69th Armor

2-70th Armor (from 2d Bde, 1st Armd Div)

C-10th Cavalry (BRT)

1-10th Field Artillery

Battery, 1-3 Air Defense Artillery

317th Engineer Battalion

203d Forward Support Battalion

Aviation Brigade
COL Curtis Potts, Commanding

3-7th Cavalry (Divisional
Reconnaissance)

1-3 Aviation

2-3 Aviation

The issuing of Force XXI Battle Command Brigade and Below (FBCB2) systems to all commanders, company and above, greatly enhanced the division's ability to command and control. This recently fielded digitalized system enabled commanders to have almost immediate situational awareness involving friendly forces, and to a lesser sense, enemy forces, by providing a display of force locations.[19]

The three brigades of the 3d Mechanized crossed the berm separating Kuwait from Iraq between dusk and dawn of 20-21 March 2003. The division was on the left of the coalition ground forces front. To the west (left) was open desert, a flank which intelligence sources indicated was devoid of Iraqi troops. To the east, 1st Marine Division elements of the I Marine Expeditionary Force (I MEF) crossed the frontier near Safwan, astride the main road (Highway 8) from Kuwait to Nasiriyah. The I MEF's initial mission was to secure the Rumaylah Oil Field, then to advance on Highway 8 to Nasiriyah, cross the Euphrates River, and move on

114

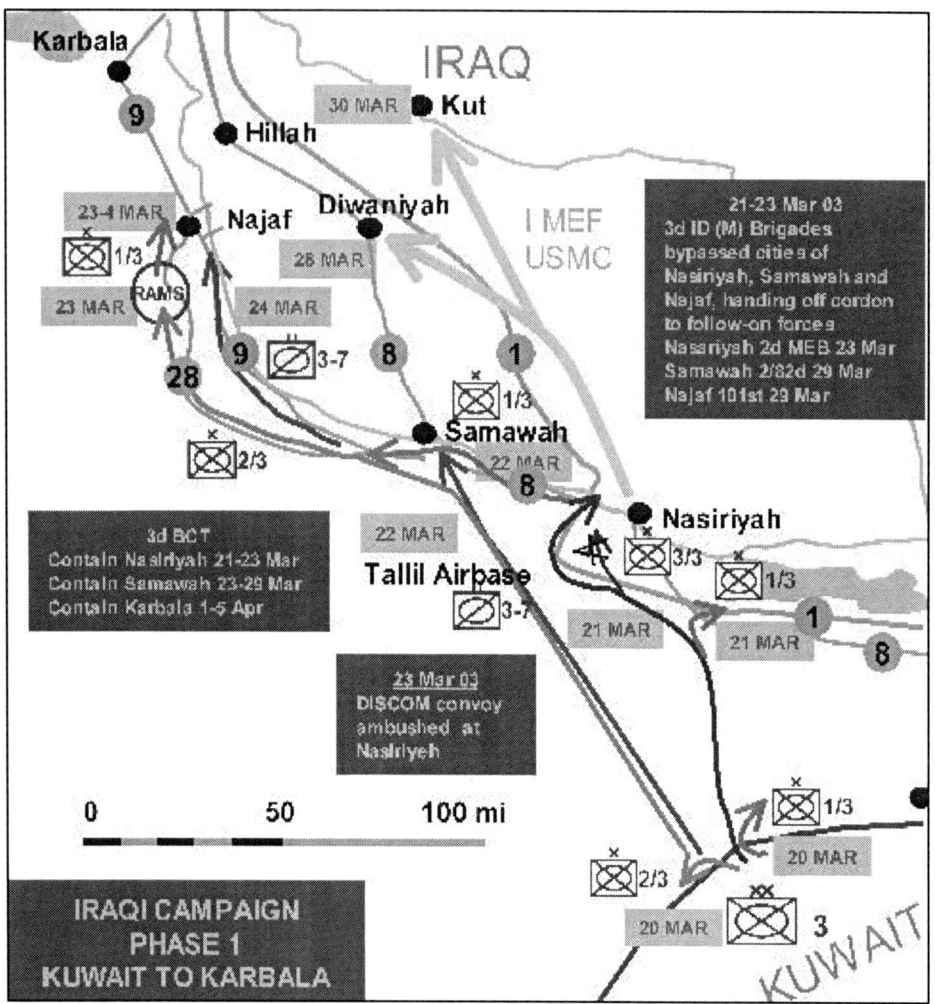

Figure 40. Drive on Karbala, 2003

Baghdad west of the river. To the right (east) of I MEF, was the UK 1st Armoured Division. Along with the UK 3d Commando Brigade, the division had the mission of securing the area around Basra.

The 3d ID was to advance cross-country in two columns from Kuwait to the Euphrates River Valley near Nasiriyah and Samawah. Each brigade had a specific mission as it crossed into Iraq. The 1st on the right and 2d Brigade on the left initially cleared the border defenses and established breaching lanes, allowing the divisional cavalry squadron, 3-7th Cavalry, and the bulk of the 1st and 3d Brigades to pass through and commence the two pronged advance to the Euphrates River. Each brigade then followed the forward elements.[20]

The cavalry squadron advanced rapidly on the left through open desert to the vicinity of Samawah, where its mission was to isolate the city from the south and east by securing two bridges over a canal southwest of the city, which also would secure Route 28, the main axis of advance the division intended to follow past Samawah. The tank heavy 2d Brigade was right behind the cavalry troopers, with the job of advancing north up Route 28, past the 3-7th Cavalry to the vicinity of Najaf to the northwest, and securing the projected site of the divisional and corps logistical base southwest of the city.[21]

The axis of advance on the right consisted of the 1st and 3d Brigades. The pincer had the mission of securing the line of advance near Nasariyah, including the large Tallil Airbase complex south of the city along with Routes 1 and 8, and the Highway 1 expressway bridge over the Euphrates River west of Nasariyah. This bridge was important because the Marines would use it later in their advance to the Tigris River. After securing these objectives, the brigades would then hand off to elements of the 2d Marine Expeditionary Brigade (MEB), which was responsible for rear area security in the Nasiriyah area, and continue the advance along the Euphrates River Valley to Samawah and Najaf. The initial advance was cross-country through empty desert with rear elements following on roads or trails.

The division advanced an average of 150 miles on the first day with an march rate of about 24 miles an hour. The brigades advanced differently. On the left, the 2d Brigade, following behind 3-7th Cavalry, divided into two elements. All the tracked vehicles moved rapidly cross-country through the rugged desert terrain, while the wheeled elements moved separately on a paved road at a slower pace. On the right, the 1st Brigade advanced cross-country, at first in a wedge formation with one battalion task force in the lead flanked by the other two, then later with all three abreast of each other.[22]

Except at the border, the Iraqis did not oppose the advance to the Nasariyah area. The 1st Brigade, tasked with covering the right (east) flank, moved and secured the Jalibah airfield east of Tallil Airbase and west of the Rumaylah oil fields then being secured by the Marines. After this, the 3d Brigade passing through the 1st to attack the Tallil area and defeat the defending Iraqi 11th Infantry Division.

The 3d BCT formed up southeast of Tallil at a desert location designated Assault Position Barrow, then attacked Tallil in a series of maneuvers utilizing its three forward task forces (one tank battalion was retained in reserve) to isolate the airfield then secure it. Advancing in the late afternoon of 21 March, TF 2-69th Armor, following behind the brigade reconnaissance troop, advanced on the left along the Route 1 expressway bypassing the airfield and up to the highway bridge over the Euphrates River, a location designated Objective Clay. Throughout the afternoon and evening, the task force fought and defeated dismounted Iraqi elements to secure the south side of the bridge, doing so by 2350 on 21 March and then crossing the river and securing the north bank by 0500 on 22 March.[23] While the bridge battle was raging, the brigade's other two committed task forces went into action. TF 1-15 Infantry's mission was to secure a barracks area northeast of the Tallil Airfield, designated Objective Liberty. Moving out in the evening of 21 March, the task force secured the objective in the early morning hours of the 22 March against minimal opposition that melted away (or surrendered including an Iraqi air defense general), completing the isolation of the airfield. TF 1-30th Infantry, with responsibility for clearing the airfield, then advanced directly on it from the southeast,

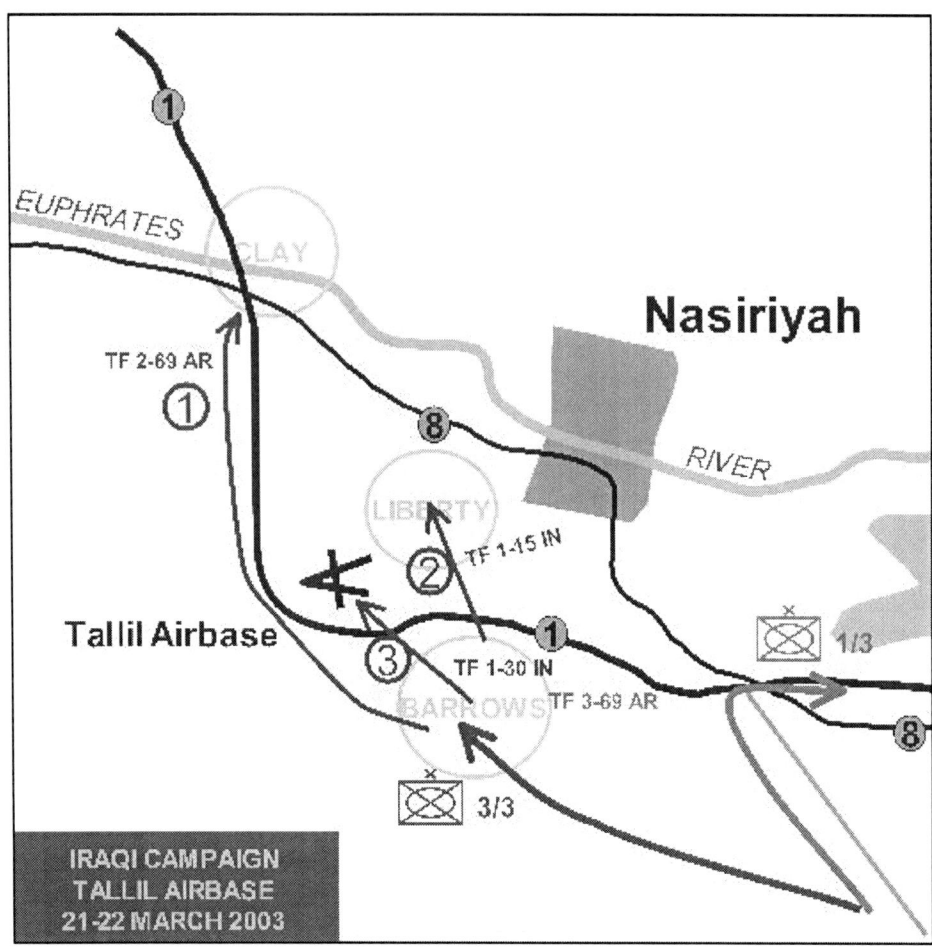

Figure 41. Tallil Airbase, 21-22 March 2003

breaching the berm surrounding the airfield and assaulting across it supported by artillery, attack helicopter, and air fires, seizing Tallil against light resistance.[24]

In a maneuver that would be repeated throughout the campaign, the 3d Brigade consolidated its gains and provided security forces to contain Nasariyah, while the 1st Brigade passed through it and advanced along Route 8 to Samawah to the west. The 3d Brigade remained in the Nasariyah area until relieved by the 2d MEB moving up from the east on Routes 8 and 1 on 23 March. The brigade then moved off to the northwest to secure the road to Samawah.

At Samawah, the 3-7th Cavalry's ground elements arrived after dawn on 22 March. The following 2d Brigade's tracked vehicle elements caught up with the cavalry troop and, after resting, bypassed the Samawah area, heading to Najaf. The cavalry squadron advanced to secure its objectives—two canal bridges—on the south side of the city, designated as Objective

Chatham, linking up with Special Forces elements on the way. The cavalrymen then became involved in a fierce firefight with Iraqi paramilitary forces, but soon gained the upper hand. On the same day, the 1st Brigade advanced along Route 8 beside the Euphrates River from the Nasiriyah area toward Samawah, engaging the enemy briefly before handing the battle off to the cavalry squadron and following the 2d Brigade around Samawah westward along Route 28 to the vicinity of Najaf. The cav squadron remained around Samawah containing the city and was attached to the 3d Brigade on the 23d.

After relief by the Marines, the 3d Brigade came forward and completed the isolation of Samawah after being relieved by the Marines at Nasariyah. While containing the city, Iraqi paramilitary forces repeatedly abandoned the defensive advantages of the urban landscape to execute charge-style attacks against the 3d Brigade's armored forces, with predictable results. The brigade remained around the city until relieved by the 2d Brigade, 82d Airborne Division, on 29 March. Upon relief, it moved to an assembly area northwest of Najaf to prepare for future operations near Karbala.[25]

Najaf, the sacred Shiite city, was next on the horizon for the 3d Mechanized's brigades, This large city was also to be isolated. As a Shiite city, resistance was expected to be less than fanatical. This was to prove not to be the case. Objective Rams, a patch of desert southwest of Najaf along Route 28, had been designated to be the division's main logistical base for the final drive on Baghdad. The battle to secure Objective Rams and isolate Najaf involved the 1st and 2d Brigades and the 3-7th Cavalry Squadron. The 2d Brigade, in the lead, was to secure Objective Rams, completing a 230-mile advance in less than 40 hours. 1st Brigade would then pass through Objective Rams and isolate Najaf from the north (the direction of Baghdad). The 3-7th Cavalry would come up Route 8 along the Euphrates River and isolate Najaf on the east.

As at Samawah, the Iraqi enemy resisted mostly with paramilitary forces operating out of, but not remaining within, the city. While Objective Rams was expected to be deserted, it was not. A mix of Iraqi irregulars and regulars occupied the site defending a radio tower communications facility. The defenders were not aware of the swift American advance, expecting instead an airborne insertion.[26] The 2d Brigade's lead elements, a tank-heavy battalion task force, arrived at Objective Rams in the last hours of 22 March, about a day earlier than originally projected, and then fought and defeated the fanatical, but suicidal Iraqi militia, securing the objective by 1000 on the 23d, assisted by close air support and field artillery fires. Subsequently, in a second phase of action, Iraqi raiders from Najaf repeatedly attacked brigade elements on Objective Rams. The brigade remained at Objective Rams in a defensive posture for the next two days.[27]

The 1st Brigade, after being relieved at Nasiriyah, had bypassed Samawah and followed the 2d Brigade to Objective Rams, then passing through to advance farther to the northwest along Route 28 to an intermediate objective, Raiders, late on the morning of the 23d. The advance on Objective Raiders cut Najaf off from the northeast and would be followed immediately by an advance to the east to secure a bridge over the Euphrates River at Kifal, designated Objective Jenkins. This latter move isolated Najaf from the northeast. Highway 28 from Objective Rams to Raiders cut across the high escarpment upon which Najaf sat. The road there, a cut through the escarpment, was a natural choke point with restrictive terrain on both sides and no place to maneuver. Iraqi forces were dug in astride Route 28 and along both sides of the escarpment with infantry and well-placed artillery. As the 1st Brigade began its advance from Objective Rams, direct and indirect fires started racking the lead elements. In response, the brigade called upon its supporting fire elements to clear the way. After firing smoke to obscure the column from enemy view, the direct support field artillery battalion, the 1-10th Field Artillery, unleashed 58 separate fire missions that suppressed the Iraqi resistance. 1st Brigade secured Raiders in the early morning hours of the 24th and prepared to move on Jenkins. Later in the day, the brigade established blocking positions along Route 9 running north out of Najaf between Raiders and Jenkins.

At dawn on the 25th, the advance on Jenkins commenced in the height of a sandstorm. A task force organized around an air defense artillery (ADA) battery and tank company secured the western approaches to the bridge on Jenkins several hours prior to the advance of the bulk of the brigade. The Iraqis defended the near side of the bridge from prepared positions with now typical fanaticism. The ADA team engaged the defenders for 9 hours with artillery fire until infantry from 1st Brigade's TF 3-69th Armor, including Company B, 3-7th Infantry, arrived and cleared that portion of Kifal west of the river. Immediately thereafter, a platoon of tanks forced its way across the bridge to the east bank while the Iraqis tried to blow it up. The detonation, while failing to topple the structure, damaged it to the point that tanks had to be led across one at a time. This the TF did, until it had moved its entire complement of tanks to the far bank. The forces now across the river then repulsed repeated Iraqi dismounted suicidal attacks, while establishing a strong defensive position. With the bridgehead achieved, the 1st Brigade had completed the isolation of Najaf from the north.[28]

Meanwhile near Nasiriyah on the 23d, while the forward elements of the division were at Najaf, the wheeled elements of the division support command continued their slower movement to Objective Rams. As the line of communications extended great distances, initially bypassing urban areas, the danger for rear area convoys was accordingly increased. One of the division support command convoys was ambushed after misrouting into unsecured portions of Nasiriyah resulting in prisoners of war and casualties, primarily from the maintenance company of the PATRIOT battalion attached to the division.

Back forward at Najaf, the divisional cavalry squadron now joined the 1st and 2d Brigades in the fight. To complete the isolation of the city, the 3-7th Cavalry Squadron, upon relief of its containment mission at Samawah, was to advance on 24 March up Route 9, 45 miles along the Euphrates River to Objective Floyd, centered on a two-part bridge across the Euphrates River near the town of Abu Sukhayr, south and east of Najaf. The cavalry's route paralleled to the east that of the 2d and 1st Brigades moving to Objective Rams. The advance along Highway 9, was, however, constricted by terrain to the one road and the movement quickly became a running fight. The cavalrymen had to break up a series of large ambushes established by Iraqi paramilitary and militia forces, who were equipped with rocket propelled grenades (RPGs) and antitank missiles. Additionally, the beginning of a three-day sandstorm, which restricted visibility, resulted in some combat taking place at close range. Fighting at Faysaliyah was the fiercest, particularly when a canal bridge collapsed, blocking a road, damaging an M1 tank, and requiring a detour and bypass, while temporarily stranding a tank—Bradley, hunter-killer team on the far bank. With the squadron still fighting all along the route, at dawn on 25 March, advance elements reached the southern edge of Floyd after a 9-hour, 45-mile movement down a road, now forever known to the troops as "Ambush Alley."[29]

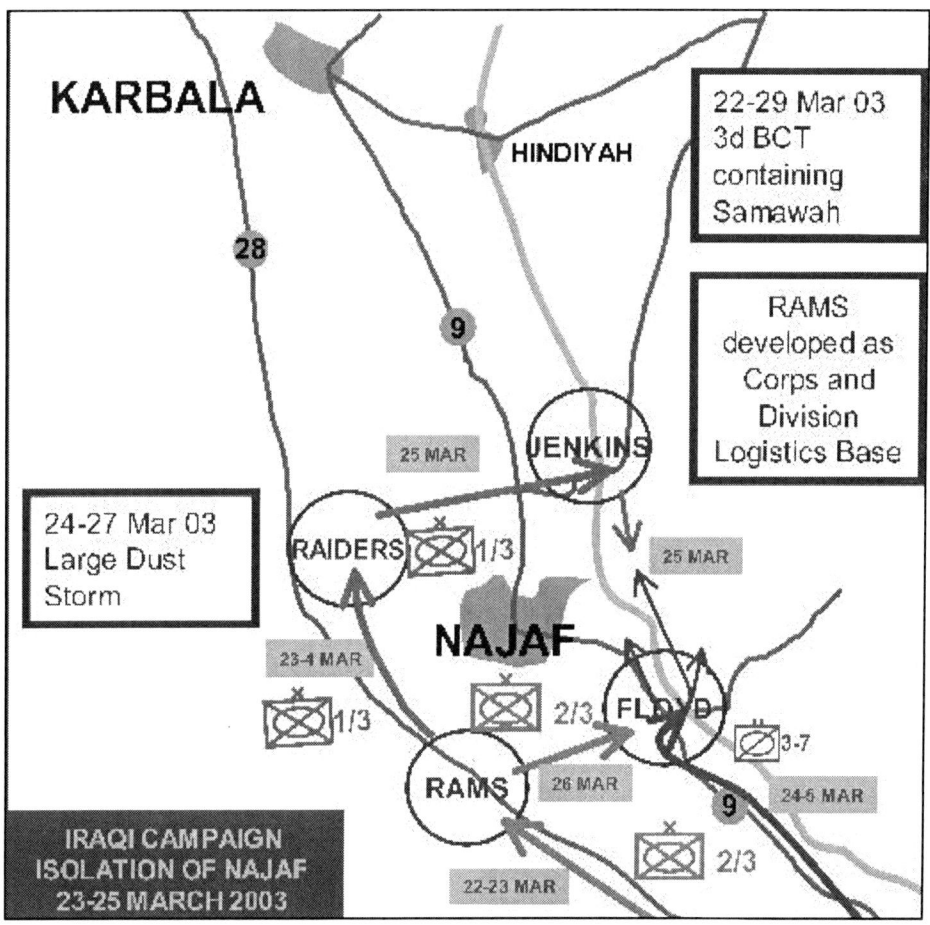

KARBALA

HINDIYAH

22-29 Mar 03
3d BCT
containing
Samawah

RAMS
developed as
Corps and
Division
Logistics Base

28

9

25 MAR

JENKINS

24-27 Mar 03
Large Dust
Storm

RAIDERS 1/3

25 MAR

23-4 MAR

NAJAF

1/3

2/3 FLOYD

3-7

RAMS

26 MAR

9

24-5 MAR

IRAQI CAMPAIGN
ISOLATION OF NAJAF
23-25 MARCH 2003

22-23 MAR

2/3

Figure 42. Isolation of Najaf, 23-25 March 2003

Upon finally reaching the vicinity of Objective Floyd, 3-7th Cavalry immediately attacked to secure the bridge. This attack, in the midst of the dust storm, relied on thermal and night vision sights. Iraqi paramilitary personnel fiercely defended the bridge. Nevertheless, by late morning it was secure and part of the squadron was able to move north along the east bank of the river through Abu Sukhayr to secure a dam and another bridge to the north. Again resistance was tooth and nail against the advance, with fighting at close range because of the poor visibility induced by the sandstorm.[30]

As Iraqi pressure increased, 3-7th Cavalry was soon fighting simultaneously on three separate fronts on both sides of the Euphrates River. Ammunition supply was soon running low. Division responded quickly by placing the 1st and 2d Brigades on alert to assemble forces to reinforce or link up with the cavalry squadron. At dusk on the 25th, the 1st Brigade dispatched elements from a tank task force, 2-69th Armor, out of its bridgehead at Kifal, down the east

120

bank of the Euphrates to the cavalry, bringing limited resupply. The two units linked up within 3 hours of the start of the 3d Brigade's movement. Meanwhile to the southwest, 2d Brigade, charged with securing Objective Rams and relieving the cavalry squadron in place, did so on the 26th, completely blocking Najaf off from the south. For this mission the brigade received two additional tank battalion task forces that had been guarding the division rear elements as they occupied Objective Rams.

Operations around Najaf were hindered by the massive sandstorm, which blanketed all of southern Iraq and Kuwait for three days (25-27 March) and reduce visibility to zero. The storm, however, did not prevent the brigades of the 3d Infantry Division (Mechanized) from completing the isolation of Najaf and the establishment of a large logistical base at Objective Rams, in preparation for expected subsequent operations against the Iraqi Republican Guard near Karbala and on to Baghdad.[31]

While the command was earmarked to take an operational pause before advancing against the Republican Guard units expected to be near Karbala, by the end of 26 March 2003, all three brigades of the 3d Mechanized Division had all been diverted from this primary mission, to conducting security missions along the route of that advance. From 25 to 29 March virtually all movement north ceased. To the south, the 3d Brigade was cordoning Samawah. Fifty miles to the northwest, the 2d Brigade from the south and the 1st Brigade from the north were containing Najaf.

In order to allow the brigades to begin preparations for the Karbala-Baghdad operation, V Corps dispatched the 101st Airborne Division (Air Assault) and the 2d Brigade, 82d Airborne Division, to relieve them of their security missions. Elements of the 82d relieved the 3d Brigade around Samawah on the 29th, while the same day, the 101st relieved the other two brigades around Najaf. Both the 101st and 82d would spend the next few days reducing these enemy resistance centers, located on the 3d Mechanized Division's lines of communication.[32]

Upon relief, the 3d Division's brigades moved to the vicinity of Objective Rams to continue refitting and reorganizing for the next operation, a process that had been ongoing even while the units were arrayed around Samawah and Najaf. During the Najaf operation, the division reorganized its task organization under its three maneuver brigade headquarters. With the 3d Brigade, first at Nasiriyah, then at Samawah, containing pockets of resistance, TF 2-69th Armor was detached to the 1st Brigade on 22 March for its advance on Objective Raiders. The tank battalion attached to the 3d Brigade from the 1st Brigade, 1st Armored Division, the 2-70th Armor, along with the 2d Brigade's 1-64th Armor, were detached to provide security for the Division Support Command at Objective Rams on 24 March. Both battalions were then attached to the 2d Brigade on the 26th for the relief operation at Objective Floyd. When the division began preparing for the Karbala operation on 29 March, the 2-70th Armor was permanently detached to the 101st Airborne Division (Air Assault) and TF 1-15th Infantry was detached from 3d Brigade to 2d Brigade for the duration of the Karbala-Baghdad operation. This gave the division a configuration of 1st Brigade with two mechanized infantry task forces and a tank task force, 3d Brigade with a mechanized and a tank task force and 2d Brigade with two mechanized and two tank task forces. 2d Brigade would, in turn, detach one of its mechanized TFs, TF 3-15 Infantry, to provide security for the division's Euphrates River crossing site for several days. The task organization would then revert to that of the start of the campaign once Baghdad was reached, with the 3d Brigade receiving back its original habitually attached battalions.[33]

The final operation of the campaign consisted of an advance to bypass Karbala, a crossing of the Euphrates River, and a movement directly on and then isolating Baghdad. With Baghdad isolated, the brigades would subsequently execute forays into the city, the intensity of which would depend on resistance and the status of the Iraqi regime. 3d ID had responsibility for isolating Baghdad west of the Tigris River, which bisected the city from the north to the south. I MEF advancing up from the southeast, had responsibility for the portion east of the Tigris River. For this operation all three divisional maneuver brigades would be employed in key roles, each with a final objective in the encirclement of Baghdad from the north (3rd Brigade), west (1st Brigade), and south (2d Brigade).[34]

Baghdad is east of the Euphrates River. With Army forces at Objective Rams west of the river, it had to be crossed before advancing on the Iraqi metropolis. The terrain west of the Euphrates River was restrictive to the movement of large armored forces, being cut with berms, canals, irrigation ditches, rock quarries, and the urban precincts of Karbala. The only passable terrain, both for forward movement and ultimately for the division's line of communications, was through the 2-mile wide gap between Karbala and the large lake referred to by the Iraqis as the Salt Sea, but commonly called Lake Karbala by the Americans. Intelligence analysis indicated that the enemy was shaping the Karbala Gap, west of the city, into an artillery and missile killing ground. Despite this, the terrain forced the US forces to advance through the gap. Accordingly, in the days before the renewal of offensive operations, V Corps made every effort to find and destroy all enemy weapons capable of ranging the gap.[35]

The nearest and best Euphrates crossing site to the Karbala Gap was northwest of Karbala where Route 9 crossed the river on two four lane highway bridges at Musayyib. Using this crossing site would be obvious to the defending Iraqis. In order to deceive them as to the true intentions of the US forces, V Corps devised various feints and misleading activities prior to the actual advance.

As part of this strategy, V Corps directed the 3d Mechanized Division to conduct a feint to deceive the Iraqis as to the division's planned Euphrates River crossing point. East of Karbala, a bridge crossed the Euphrates River at Hindiyah on a road that went on to Hillah, established next to the ruins of ancient Babylon. This bridge was designated Objective Murray. The real crossing site, a dual-span expressway bridge located northeast of Karbala on Route 9 in Musayyib, was designated Objective Peach. While elements of the 101st Airborne Division feinted from near Najaf toward Hillah from the southwest, as a prelude to the advance on the Karbala Gap, the 2d Brigade, 3d Infantry Division, would do the same from Objective Rams to Objective Murray. Additionally, the 2d Brigade would clear the area in front of the projected division advance of small enclaves of enemy soldiers.

On 30 March, the 2d Brigade moved out to clear the division front between Najaf and Karbala, using its two mechanized infantry task forces to clear enemy forces from rock quarries. Artillery and attack helicopters supported the task forces. The following day saw the whole V Corps in motion with various feints and air attacks designed to divert enemy attention from the Karbala Gap and allow for the destruction of Iraqi artillery and missile units. For the 3d Infantry Division, the main effort was the 2d Brigade's feint to the bridge at Hindiyah, Objective Murray. The 2d's mission was to drawn Iraqi units away from the main attack near Karbala and deceive the enemy into thinking the main crossing would occur at Hindiyah . Starting at 0600 on 31 March, with two mechanized task forces covering the flanks, TF 4-64th Armor moved down the main road through Hindiyah to the Euphrates bridge, clearing the town in the process, while being supported by field artillery and engineers. Resistance was intense, consisting of mortar and artillery fire and the ubiquitous RPGs fired from buildings and street corners. The defenders were a mix of irregular Fedayeen troops and elements of the Republican Guard Nebuchadnezzar Division's the 2d Battalion, 23d Infantry Brigade. This was the first encounter between the 3d Mechanized Division and elements of the Republican Guard. The tankers secured the west side of the Euphrates bridge in less than an hour and, after engineers removed demolitions from the structure, fought the enemy on the far bank for several additional hours. The defenders began using civilians as shields and hostages to cover their movements and firings. As the operation was a feint, TF 4-64 did not cross the river. Allowing the enemy to believe his defense had succeeded, 2d Brigade withdrew to blocking positions on Route 9 southeast of Hindiyah late in the afternoon. The blocking positions were designed to support the operations of the other two brigades the next day, as well as to deceive the Iraqis into expecting another attack at Hindiyah.[36]

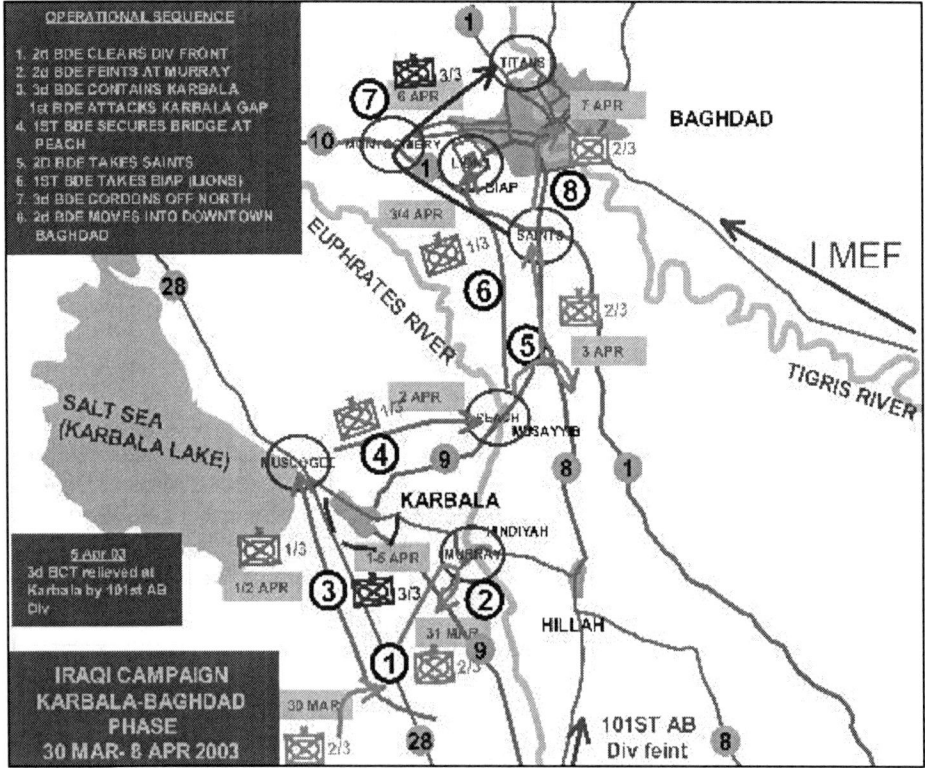

Figure 43. Drive on Baghdad, 2003

The real attack began during the night of 1-2 April. The 1st Brigade, led by TF 3-69th Armor on the right and TF 2-7th Infantry on the left, advanced through the Karbala Gap, securing the Gap by 0700 against surprisingly light opposition. The expected resistance from the Republican Guard's Medina Division did not materialize. Counterbattery fire, in coordination with 2d Brigade's feint, had shattered the Iraqi missile-artillery fire ambush before it could be executed . Objective Muscogee, a dam/bridge complex located in the northwest corner of the gap, received special attention from the tank task force, while the mechanized TF fended off the now routine attacks of irregulars from inside the western portion of Karbala. The bridges and dams were seized by 0600 on 2 April and the gap was cleared before full daylight. Artillery and attack helicopter fires supported the advance, particularly in suppressing Iraqi artillery. 1st Brigade elements contained Karbala to the west as the 3d Brigade moved up on the right, in its now familiar role, and set up positions to contain Karbala from the east.[37]

The division leadership, particularly the Assistant Division Commander (Maneuver), Brigadier General Lloyd Austin, wanted to maintain the momentum created by the quick seizure of the gap and advance straight to the Euphrates bridges (Objective Peach) and cross the river. Before 0700, the 3d Brigade assumed full responsibility for containing Karbala and securing the gap, while the 1st Brigade prepared to advance to Objective Peach. An attached engineer brigade headquarters, the 937th, was also brought forward to coordinate traffic flow through the gap.[38]

The 1st Brigade then advanced on Objective Peach at midday on 2 April. The lead element, TF 3-69th Armor, reached the area of the bridge very quickly and by 1500 had secured the west bank of the twin span Highway 9 expressway bridges which were located north of Musayyib. Artillery, close air, and attack helicopters mechanized infantrymen from the 3-7th Infantry battalion, along with engineer troops assigned to the brigade combat team's engineer battalion, crossed the river on rubber rafts to the far bank to secure the bridges before the Iraqis could blown them up. This attempt was only partially successful. The enemy fired the demolitions on the northern span before the engineers could stop them. Despite the explosion, the bridge still stood, though it had a big hole in its center and structural damage that caused its center to sag toward the river below. The southern span, however, was captured intact and soon TF 3-69th Armor was across. The rest of the day and night involved securing the bridgehead, defending it against the inevitable counterattacks on the east bank, and preparing to pass the 2d Brigade through the brigadehead to continue the advance.[39]

The 2d Brigade, fresh from its feint at Hindiyah, had the mission of following 1st Brigade and passing through it at Objective Peach and advancing to secure Objective Saints, on the south side of Baghdad. Objective Saints controlled the important intersection of Routes 1 and 8, blocking Baghdad west of the Tigris River from the southern part of the country. Urged to come forward rapidly, the 2d Brigade initially tried to move to the west of Karbala rather than through the gap itself. While geographically shorter, this route was on soft or rugged terrain unfavorable to armored and wheeled vehicles. The road network was poor, muddy, and laced with irrigation ditches and canals. As a result, part of the brigade had to ultimately turn back and go through the gap after all. Delayed so, the 2d Brigade was unable to reach Objective Peach until early on 3 April.[40]

While awaiting the 2d Brigade's arrival, the 1st Brigade, in its bridgehead positions, repulsed a major, well-coordinated Iraqi armored attack. The Medina Division's 10th Armored

Brigade executed perhaps the best counterattack conducted by the Iraqis in the whole campaign on the 2d Brigade at dawn. Despite its quality, the American defenders repulsed the attack and the Iraqi commander was killed.[41]

After the counterattack, 2d Brigade crossed to the east bank and passed through the 1st Brigade, leaving a mechanized TF (3-15th Infantry) behind to provide security at the bridges and advancing one mechanized TF (TF 1-15th Infantry) in an axis north along on the southern edge of Baghdad. The advance met light resistance, mostly of the paramilitary variety and some elements of the Nebuchadnezzar Republican Guard Division, and reached Objective Saints in roughly 3 hours. The mechanized infantrymen fought in the early afternoon of 3 April to secure that objective, supported by close air and artillery fires against dug-in Iraqi mechanized and dismounted forces. While the fight for Objective Saints was taking place, 2d Brigade dispatched an armored task force (TF 4-64th Armor) to secure Highway 8 south of its junction with Highway 9. The remnants of the Medina Division were supposed to be in that area. The TF defeated and destroyed small Iraqi armored forces whose defenses were facing the opposite direction, apparently attributed to the success of the feints at Hindiyah. The 2d Brigade's last crossing task force, TF 1-64th Armor, followed TF 1-15 Infantry to Objective Saints. All brigade units consolidated at Saints for the evening. Baghdad was effectively isolated from the south.[42]

After securing Objective Peach, 1st Brigade prepared to execute its on order mission of occupying the Saddam International Airport, codenamed Objective Lions, on the west side of Baghdad. The brigade began moving almost as soon as the last elements of 2d Brigade passed through on their way to Objective Saints. But many things were happening at once to slow up the 1st Brigade: 3-7th Cavalry, the division reconnaissance element, had to first pass through as it was to advance before the 1st Brigade to secure its left (west) flank; the brigade had to hand off crossing site security responsibilities first to the battalion left behind by the 2d Brigade, then to the divisional engineer brigade; all the brigade's units had to assemble to cross; and additional engineer units were arriving to add more bridges. While the advance started on time, 1st Brigade units were, however, strung out from the beginning of the movement and would arrive at the objective piecemeal rather than *en masse*.[43]

The 1st Brigade's advance would initially be via restrictive country roads directly north from the Objective Peach area to Highway 1, a major expressway running northwest to southeast below Baghdad. Once astride this road, brigade elements would travel down the highway to within a mile and a half of the Baghdad airport complex, then conduct a coordinated assault on the airfield. Traveling in advance of the brigade, the 3-7th Cavalry would continue down Route 1 to its intersection with another major highway, Route 10, northwest of the airport. There the squadron would guard the flank of the brigade as it attacked the airport.[44]

Late in the afternoon of 3 April, the advance began. During the first part, the movement through the countryside, 1st Brigade soldiers encountered their first positive reaction from Iraqi civilians who cheered the passing vehicles not very far south of Baghdad. The restrictive terrain and a small ambush delayed the movement. Nevertheless, Highway 1 was soon met and the BCT initiated planned supporting fires against Objective Lions. The lead element, TF 3-69th Armor, arrived in the environs of the airport at a little after 2200. With the rest of the brigade strung out to the rear, TF 3-69 commenced the attack on its own, advancing and assaulting the southern end of the large airfield complex, attacking throughout the night of 3-4 April. The task force secured a perimeter and repulsed counterattacks. Brigade follow-on elements began arriving at dawn, with TF 2-7th Infantry entering from the south and establishing blocking positions facing Baghdad on the eastern side of the complex. Engineers and other elements arrived to assist in clearing debris from the airfield. The 1st BCT cleared barracks, compounds, and bunkers methodically, while outside the airport, paramilitary forces and occasionally T-72 tanks fired at the Americans. One company-sized dismounted attack was repulsed mainly through the heroism of an engineer platoon sergeant who took over the .50 caliber machine gun mounted on a destroyed M113 APC and fired suppressive fires until he was mortally wounded. 1st Brigade had established a major base of operations blocking Baghdad from the west.[45]

While the 1st and 2d Brigades maneuvered against Baghdad, the 3d Brigade remained outside Karbala, screening the city, deflecting desultory charges from paramilitary forces and waiting for relief from the 101st Airborne Division. After this relief took place on 5 April, the brigade moved through the Objective Peach crossing site and up to 2d Brigade's operating base at Objective Saints, where the brigade had all its habitually attached elements rejoined it for the first time since the Battle of Tallil. From Saints, the 3d BCT began executing its mission of isolating Baghdad from the north by advancing down Highway 1 to its junction with Highway 10 (Objective Montgomery), where 3-7th Cavalry had been holding off Iraqi attacks since late on the 3d. From Objective Montgomery, the 3d Brigade advance to the northeast, along the way to establish blocking positions at major roads, intersections, and then securing the Highway 1 bridge over the Tigris River. These positions, collectively known as Objective Titans, were held by the brigade until Baghdad fell. Brigade elements fought the Iraqis sporadically and later sent a task force to support the defenders at Objective Lions. On 9 April Brigade elements advanced into Baghdad itself.[46]

Once Baghdad was isolated, the original plan was to probe the defenses of the large city gingerly. However, intelligence indicators, including the reactions of a captured Republican Guard colonel who was stunned to see American forces so close to Baghdad, showed that aggressiveness could possibly secure the city without a block by block fight.[47] The colonel was captured on 5 April when the 2d Brigade sent its TF 1-64th Armor on a raid north up Route 8 from Objective Saints into Baghdad then over to the west to Objective Lions, the now renamed Baghdad International Airport, and returned through the countryside to Objective Saints. The raid, while resisted fiercely, was also resisted erratically. No organized urban-style defense materialized, though one M1 tank was disabled when antitank fire hit its rear deck. With enemy fire not allowing the tank to be safely recovered, it was destroyed in place and abandoned, becoming an instant landmark. The success of the raid made a large-scale movement into downtown Baghdad seem very plausible.[48]

Accordingly, the 2d Brigade still south of the city at Objective Saints, received the mission to advance into the downtown districts of the city on 7 April on a brigade-sized raid. If successful, the raid would be transformed into a physical occupation of the center city. The brigade advanced in force to the center city early on the 7th, with its two tank battalion task forces racing into the downtown area to secure key installations, while the mechanized battalion task force followed to secure the supply line and key intersections. The Iraqi irregulars defending the city let the tank battalions pass after short firefights, having finally learned the futility of using RPGs and truck mounted machine guns against the formidable Abrams tank. These enemy fanatics, however, reappeared when the mechanized task force, TF 3-15th Infantry, moved to secure the key highway intersections between the airport and the Tigris River, which snaked its way through the heart of Baghdad. After a running daylight battle at three intersections, designated Objectives Moe, Larry, and Curly, the infantrymen totally routed the disorganized defenders, while the rest of the brigade completed its 12-mile advance into the heart of the city in 2 hours and secured key bridges, palaces, and government buildings in the former stronghold of Saddam's regime.

While the 2d Brigade advanced into downtown Baghdad, an Iraqi surface-to-surface missile made a direct hit on the brigade's tactical operations center (TOC) at Saints, killing or wounding a number of soldiers and putting that key communications node out of action for 2 hours. However, the flexibility of the brigade organization and its redundant command and control facilities allowed this hit to only have a minor impact on combat operations.[49]

The success of the mechanized infantrymen at securing the line of communications, allowing resupply into the forward elements deep in the city, transformed the 2d Brigade's raid into a permanent move into downtown Baghdad. The 2d Brigade and the US Army was in Baghdad to stay, securing the west bank of the Tigris River. The 2d Brigade remained and had two more days of steadily decreasing fighting. The arrival of elements of the I MEF on the opposite side of the Tigris River on 9 April marked the effective end of the Saddam regime's organized resistance. As Marine forces secured the east bank of the river, statues began toppling because the Iraqi people realized their moment of liberation had arrived.[50]

The 3d Mechanized Division's masterful use of the brigade in the Iraqi war was the climax of over 50 years of force design at the organizational level just below division. The brigades, formed up with supporting and attached elements as BCTs, provided the necessary flexibility and fightability to execute complicated combat maneuvers, fight several different battles at the same time, and shift missions almost on the head of a dime. At one point the three divisional maneuver brigades were each fighting outside a different key Iraqi city, Nasiriyah, Samawah, or Najaf, which were separated by between 60 and 75 miles, on a total frontage of over 150 miles. The ability of the brigade to disperse, then mass for operations like the Karbala-Baghdad drive, and its ability to fight alone or as part of the larger mix, bodes well on its future as a US Army organizational element.

NOTES

1. Memorandum, AFOP-TR, dated 20 Nov 2001, Subject: Active Component/Reserve Component (AC/RC) Integration Item 96-10, Active Component/Army National Guard (AC/ARNG) Integrated Divisions.

2. Despite its designation, the 116th Cavalry Brigade is by organization a standard separate armored brigade with two tank battalions (designated cavalry battalions) and a mechanized infantry battalion. The brigade designation comes from an old Idaho Army National Guard unit.

3. Jim Caldwell, "Army Leaders Announce New Design Framework for Army XXI Heavy Division," *Army Communicator* 23 (Summer 1998), 14.

4. The 4th Infantry division, as of April 2003, contained five tank battalions and four mechanized battalions.

5. "Army Announces Final Drawdown Plan," *Army News Service* (15 January 1999), <http://www.dtic.mil/armylink/news/Dec1998/a19981223downsize.html>.

6. Ibid. LCD XXI also reduced tank and mechanized battalions to three (rather than four companies) and had other small changes throughout divisional structure.

7. Discussion of the BRTs is primarily based on Captain Ross F. Lightsey, "Establishing and Using the Brigade Reconnaissance Troop," *Infantry*, (Jan-Apr 2000), 10-14.

8. Brochure produced by the GM-BDLS Defense Group, entitled "Stryker Family of Vehicle," in November, 2001; Major Gregory A. Pickell, "The New Interim Brigade Combat Team: Old Wine in New Bottles?" *Military Review* 82 (May-June 2002), 71-72; Brian J. Dunn, "Equipping the Objective Force," *Military Review* 82 (May-June 2002), 29-31; Richard J. Dunn III, "Transformation: Let's Get It Right This Time," *Parameters* 31 (Spring 2001), 22-28.

9. Ibid.

10. Scott R. Gourley, "Significant Events in Transformation: Stryker Battalions Enter Evaluation Phase," *Army* 53 (February 2003), 65-66. General Dynamics later bought out GMC's portion of the venture in March 2003. The MOH winners were PFC Stuart S. Stryker, World War II, and SP4 Robert F. Stryker, Vietnam.

11. Ibid. Headquarters, Department of the Army. Field Manual (FM) 3-21.31, *The Stryker Brigade Combat Team*. (Washington, DC: US Army, 2003), 1-14.

12. FM 3-21.31, 1-15.

13. Ibid., 1-20.

14. 3d Infantry Division, *Operation Iraqi Freedom After Action Report*, Final Draft, 12 May 2003, 6-3.

15. US Army Operation Iraqi Freedom Study Group. *On Point: The US Army in Operation Iraqi Freedom*. Draft Manuscript. (Fort Leavenworth, KS: US Army Combat Studies Institute, 15 August 2003), 4-87.

16. 3d Infantry Division, *Operation Iraqi Freedom After Action Report*, 5-5.

17. David A. Fulghum, "The Pentagon's Force-Transformation Director Takes an Early Swipe at What Worked and What Didn't in Iraq." *Aviation Week & Space Technology* 158 (28 April 2003).

18. *On Point*, 3-11

19. 3d Infantry Division, *Operation Iraqi Freedom After Action Report*, 8-2.

20. *On Point*, 3-35, 3-39-43, 3-45, 3-48.

21. Ibid., 3-48, 3-70, 4-16-7.

22. Ibid., 3-48, 3-85.

23. Ibid., 3-59, 3-62.

24. Ibid., 3-61-2.

25. Ibid., 3-80-1.

26. Ibid., 4-17.

27. Ibid., 4-17-9.

28. Ibid., 4-59-62.

29. Ibid., 4-23-5; Sean Naylor, Sean, "'Like Apocalypse Now' 7th Cavalry Squadron Runs Gauntlet of Iraqi Fire During Its Longest Day," *Army Times*, 7 April 2003, 14-16.

30. *On Point*, 4-63-4.

31. Ibid., 4-10-11.

32. Ibid., 4-69-70, 5-12. V Corps was holding the 101st back for use in isolating Baghdad; the 82d's brigade was the theater reserve.

33. 3d Infantry Division, *Operation Iraqi Freedom After Action Report*, xi-xix.

34. *On Point*, 5-6.

35. Ibid., 5-4-6.
36. Ibid., 5-19-20, 5-19-24-26.
37. Ibid., 5-52.
38. Ibid., 5-53.
39. Engineers would quickly rig the northern bridge so it could be used and install as float bridge next to it, minimizing the effects of the demolition. *On Point*, 5-55.
40. Ibid., 5-60.
41. Ibid., 5-61.
42. Ibid., 5-61-63.
43. Ibid., 5-65-66.
44. Ibid., 5-66. The Highway 10/Highway 1 intersection was codenamed Objective Montgomery.
45. Ibid., 5-66-68, 5-72-73.
46. Ibid., 5-82, 5-87.
47. John Diamond and Dave Moniz. "Iraqi Colonel's Capture Sped Up Taking of City." *USA TODAY*, 9 April 2003.
48. *On Point*, 6-17-18.
49. Ibid., 6-31-33.
50. Ibid., 6-51, 6-8-9. 6-22, 6-34-6

CONCLUSION AND THE FUTURE OF THE BRIGADE

Conclusion

The maneuver brigade is as viable a fighting formation in 2004 as it was in 1775. The combined arms brigade of the Revolutionary War soon gave way to a pure formation throughout the 19th and early 20th centuries. But combined arms returned with the adoption of the combat command task force concept for the new ROAD brigade in 1963 and its evolutionary ancestors, the AOE brigade, the 2003 BCT, and the 2004 UA Brigade, making the brigade, operating as part of a division or apart from a division, the true fulcrum for maneuver and firepower.

Before World War I, the brigade was the basic unit through which US commanders fought their armies. The reason for this was a historically poor replacement system. The replacement system allowed regiments to wane in strength. Brigades had to remain of a size suitable for command by a general officer and were maintained not by a state government, but by the Army. Therefore, they did not wane. Instead brigades were simply reorganized with more, but smaller regiments. Throughout the 19th century, a commander could expect that the brigades he would maneuver would be roughly 2,000 soldiers, no matter the state of his replacement system or the size of his regiments.

World War I saw the organization of the first permanent fixed brigades. The large size of the World War I square division, its organic brigades, and its design for use in trench warfare, saw the flexibility and maneuverability of the brigade wane. When the division was redesigned to fight in World War II, the brigade echelon was deleted completely, with the regiment taking over its former role.

However, modern armored warfare with its fluid movements and mission-oriented tactics, saw the adoption of the combat command in lieu of the regiment or brigade as the tactical headquarters between battalion and division levels in the armored division. The combat command concept—a flexible headquarters without any troops of its own except those temporarily assigned to execute specific missions—proved a highly successful way to execute armored operations.

In 1963, the Army adopted the combat command concept across the board, enlarged it and renamed the unit with the more traditional title of brigade. This brigade, controlling attached maneuver battalions and supported by combat support and service support units from the division, has remained ever since.

During the recent war in Iraq, the brigade played a prominent role as the basic maneuver unit. At one time, the 3d Infantry Division (Mechanized) was fighting three separate battles on three fronts, spread over a large geographical expanse. Each battle was directed by a reinforced brigade. The division maneuvered by employing its brigades as separate entities working in coordination. For example, when the 3d maneuvered to simultaneously bypass both Samawah and Najaf, cities about 50 miles apart, one brigade contained Samawah, while the other two maneuvered to surround Najaf. Once relieved at Samawah, the brigade there in turn moved around the other two brigades to advance an additional 50 miles beyond Najaf toward Karbala. Upon their own relief, the other two brigades moved up to Karbala from outside Najaf to participate in the operations to seize Baghdad. In the subsequent direct advance on

Baghdad, one brigade contained Karbala, one secured the Euphrates River crossing site, and the third passed through to advance onto Baghdad. After being relieved at the crossing site, the brigade there then passed through the advance brigade and secured the Baghdad airport. The commander of the 3d Mechanized Division continually rotated or flip-flopped his brigades to maintain initiative with fresh troops, while at the same time providing security and protection along a narrow axis of advance and long supply line, while simultaneously containing several major urban areas until follow-on troops could take over that mission.

The jury is still out on the effectiveness or reality of the combat aviation brigade as a maneuver brigade. While the Army considers it so, there are no real historical examples of the brigade being used in actual combat as a maneuver force, except to lay down fires, a task that division artillery and field artillery brigades also do quite well, with no claim of being a maneuver element.[1] During the 2003 Iraqi War, the 3d Infantry Division's Aviation Brigade retained this role, while also performing some limited reconnaissance and security missions for the division.

The Future of the Brigade: Stryker Brigades and Units of Action

In the last few years several military theorists, most notably Colonels Douglas MacGregor and John Brinkerhoff, have urged the Army to reorganize itself with the brigade as its basic tactical unit, rather than the division. MacGregor compares the division to the unwieldy, though highly successful, phalanxes of ancient Greece and favors a more flexible design based on the brigade. One of the oft-cited points is that European armies, particularly the German *Bundeswehr*, are organized on a brigade basis, with the division as primarily a command and control headquarters. However, this ignores the small size of the German army and its focus on fighting in central Europe.[2] MacGregor and Brinkerhoff would both place the brigade directly under a corps headquarters, deleting the division echelon of command completely from the force structure.[3] As will be seen below, the division has remained, at least for the foreseeable future, even as brigades assume more independent roles and missions.

The future of the brigade and division and which will be the Army's organizational building block, may well depend upon the size and future missions of the force. And even before the advent of the UA/UEx (unit of action/unit of employment) concept in 2003, explained below, while the division was still the primary unit, the brigade had, in any event, assumed many independent roles formerly associated primarily with the division. Size considerations after the drawdown had basically already converted the Army National Guard into a brigade-based force. Stationing considerations for the active force resulted in almost a third of the brigades, 8 out of 31, being either separate by design or detached from their parent division. The SBCT program virtually ignored the division in its organizational development, and the almost universal application of the BCT concept means, in many respects, that the US Army was already a brigade-based force.

The brigade's future as a key Army organizational element seems assured by its key role as the UA in the Army's Future Force program, originally called the Objective Force. This program, initially an extension of the Stryker Brigade, or "interim," program, is a long-term force development initiative aimed at the development and fielding of a Future Force, or final developmental force, capable of employing technological advances to accomplish military objectives in a joint environment in the 21st century. As part of this force development initiative, the Army focused on two levels of unit deployment packages, a force called the Unit of Employment , typically of division size, but capable of being army or corps in size, and a brigade-sized element, the Unit of Action.

While the UEx concept shows many innovative shifts from current divisional doctrine and organization, including an emphasis on tailorability, being able to command forces from other services, jointness, and a capability to command a theater operation or a portion of a theater operation, the UA falls in well with previous brigade force design concepts.

The brigade-sized UA is considered modular in design, with subunits and capabilities being added or subtracted based on mission, environment, and other factors.[4] In this respect, the UA meshes exactly with all brigade organizational schemes employed by the Army since the adoption of the ROAD brigade in 1963 and is, in fact, an extension of the current informal, but virtually universal use of BCTs. The first designed UA was an outgrowth of the Stryker Brigade Program. The Stryker Brigade UA was organized as a high-technological unit employing advances in digital communications and armored combat vehicles, not yet developed, with a quick deployment capability. Though modular in design concept, the Army's Objective Force Task Force developed a basic organizational structural design for the UA brigade, illustrated in Figure 44.

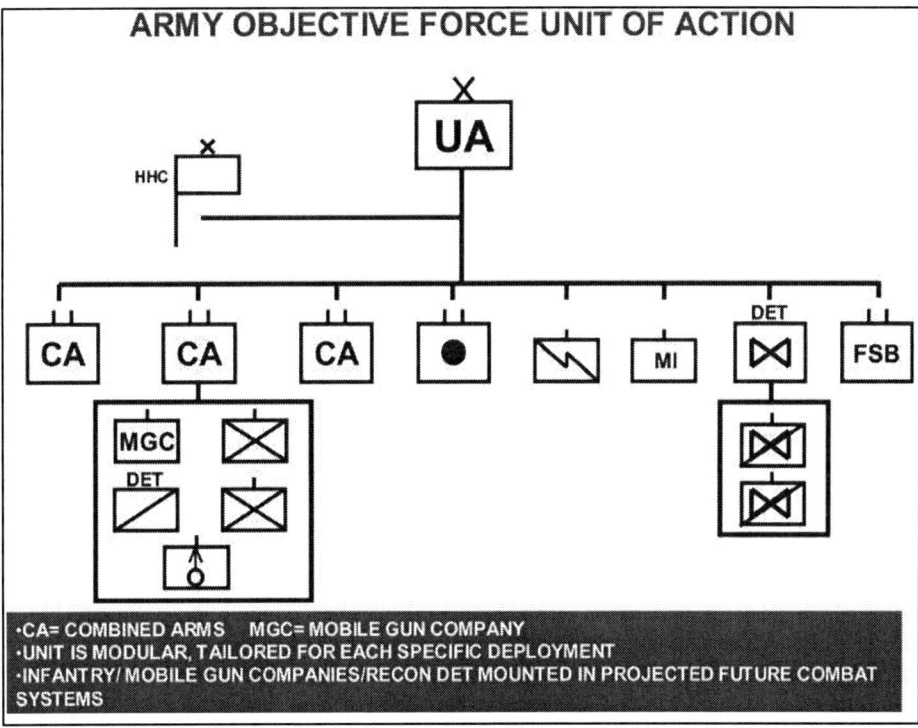

Figure 44. UA Brigade Design[5]

The brigade, as configured doctrinally, contained three combined arms battalions, composed of two infantry companies mounted in a Stryker wheeled, armored or a follow-on vehicle, a similarly mounted company-sized reconnaissance detachment, mortar battery, and a mobile gun company equipped with a armored gun Stryker wheeled or follow-on vehicle system.[6] In a departure from previous organizations, the logistical element of the brigade, a forward support battalion, would contain its own organic security element and the reconnaissance element would contain two air cavalry troops.[7]

The desired missions for the Stryker UA Brigade are outlined below:

Table 19. Projected Stryker Unit of Action Missions[8]

- Orchestrates engagements

- Smallest combined arms unit that can be committed independently (brigade and below)

- Enables massing of effects without massing of forces

- Deployable anywhere in 96 hours—fights immediately upon arrival

- Shift toward tactical standoff engagement with continuous operations at a higher tempo

- Complements precision strike with precision maneuver

- Gains and maintains positional advantage

- Interfaces with coalition forces and nongovernmental organizations on the ground

As mentioned in the previous chapter, the new revised Stryker Brigade UA was organized with an additional maneuver battalion called the Reconnaissance, Surveillance and Target Acquisition Squadron or RSTA. Under the UA implementation plan established in 2004 (discussed below), one maneuver battalion will be deleted from all UA maneuver brigades, except the Stryker UA, which would retain three combined arms battalions along with the RSTA squadron.

The development of the UA, first with the Stryker Brigades, then across the board to all Army brigades, light and heavy, and its establishment as the smallest combined arms unit that can be committed independently, is a direct evolutionary advance in the history of the maneuver brigade from its predecessors, the AOE brigade, the ROAD brigade, and the combat command. Its use as the new basic maneuver unit of the Army, with the UEx division becoming more a controlling headquarters and facilitating force, harkens back to the earliest days of the US Army, when Washington used his brigades as the basic maneuver unit of the Army.

In early 2004 the Army announced plans to adopt the UA concept Armywide. The concept extended the idea of modularity to mean that the brigades needed to be self-contained and as identical in structure as possible, so that they could be shifted between controlling divisions and missions as necessary. While divisions will continual as operational headquarters, usually controlling four maneuver brigades, in essence the Army redesign concepts for the 21st century, replace the division as the basic tactical unit with a "brigade-based modular Army."[9] The current mix of light brigades (infantry, light infantry, airborne, air assault) and heavy brigades (armored and mechanized infantry) will be transformed into three basic types by the end of the conversion process: heavy (from the former armored and mechanized infantry brigades), medium (the new Stryker brigade combat teams created from former light infantry divisional brigades), and light (from the remaining light, airborne and air assault brigades). The modular concept of interchangeability shuns specialized units. The formerly specialized air assault and airborne brigades will remain specialized, while at the same time being reorganized identical with the other light UA brigades.[10] The projected goal, as this work goes to press, is the creation of four brigades with the equivalent combat power, out of the division's previous three maneuver brigades, and to standardize all divisional aviation brigades.[11] To do this, the new brigades have been reduced from three maneuver battalions to two, but a cavalry squadron, RSTA, will replace the former brigade recon troop. Army leadership contended that the new, smaller brigades would have greater, up to one and a half times, the combat power than the previous, larger brigades. The creation of more, though smaller brigades, would increase the flexibility at the operational level by allowing brigade rotations and deployments based on personnel replacement cycles done by unit rather than by individual.[12] The new brigades most resemble in organization the combat commands in the light armored division in World War II, which, in typical organization, included a single tank battalion, a single armored infantry battalion, and a single armored field artillery battalion. This smaller structure had been maintained in the armored division up until the adoption of the ROAD brigades in 1963.[13] To make the brigades modular, each heavy brigade (armored and mechanized infantry) and each light brigade (infantry, light infantry, airborne, air assault) is to be organized similarly. The brigades would be capable of working under any division headquarters.[14] In a new concept, long debated within the Army, the two maneuver battalions in the heavy UA brigade are to be organized as a combined arms organizations, with two tank, two mechanized infantry, and one engineer companies. This made each maneuver battalion similar in organization. The eight maneuver companies organized in two battalions reflected well with the typical predecessor AOE brigade, which had nine maneuver companies organized in three battalions. The addition of three reconnaissance troops in the RSTA actually gives the new brigade (if the AOE recon troop is included) a net gain of one maneuver company in the heavy UA brigade over its immediate predecessor. This organization is depicted in Figure 45.[15]

The divisional aviation brigade would also be standardized. Each brigade would consist of two attack helicopter battalions with 24 Apache attack helicopters each, an assault aviation battalion with 30 UH-60 Blackhawk light utility helicopters, a medium company of eight CH-47 medium cargo helicopters, a command and control helicopter company with eight Blackhawks, organic aviation maintenance, and a unit, probably designated as a company, of unmanned aerial vehicles.[16] Division would come to resemble the integrated divisions. Previous practice saw different sized AH-64 and UH-60 battalions in aviation brigades in different divisions.

This reorganization of the aviation brigade into the modular configuration, however, still retains the dichotomy found in previous such organizations—on the one hand it controls maneuver fighting elements such as the attack helicopter battalions, and on the other administrative/support elements, such as the assault and medium aviation battalions and companies. The desire to consolidate all aviation assets into one organization creates this duality and continues the debate into the future as to whether the aviation brigade is a true maneuver element or an administrative one like the division artillery headquarters.

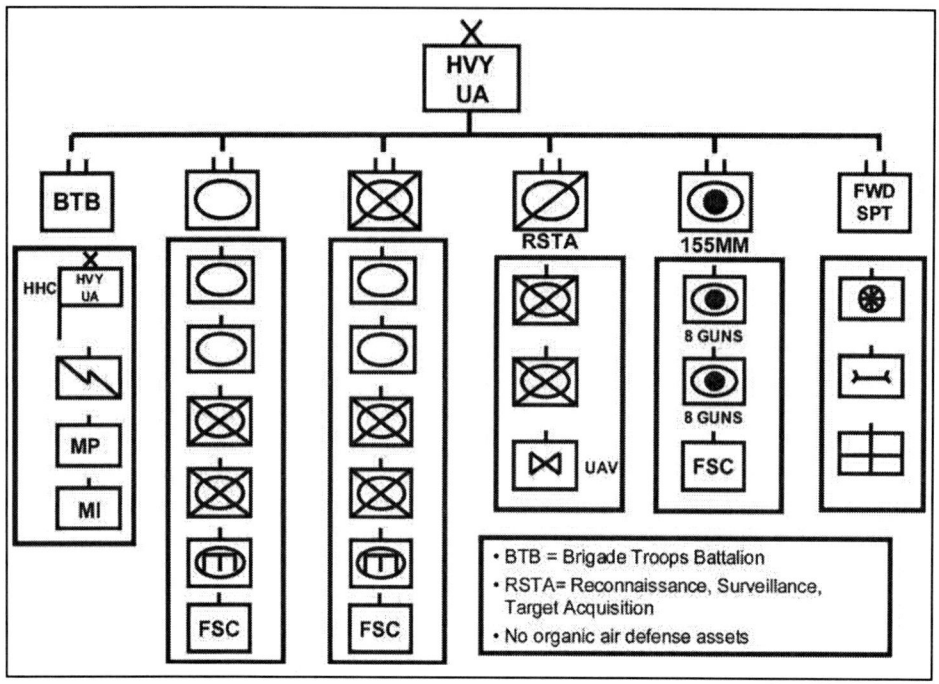

Figure 45. Heavy UA Brigade, 2004

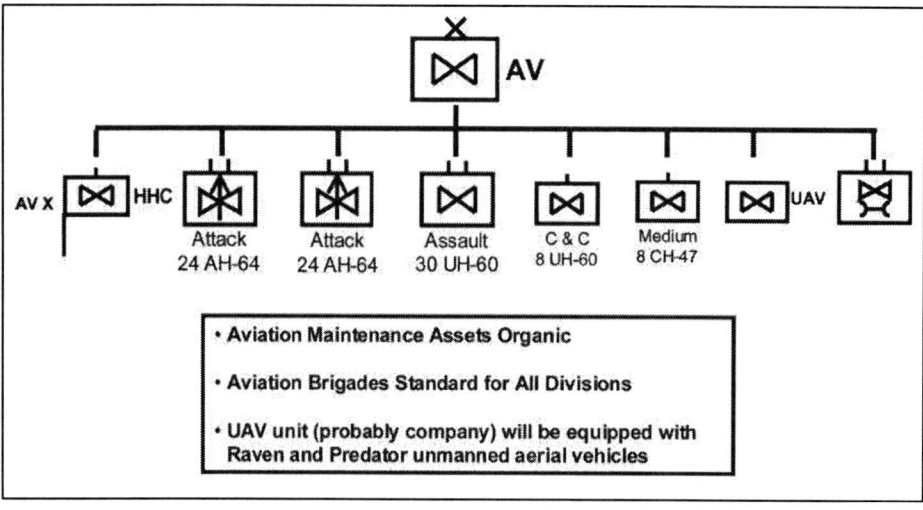

Figure 46. Modular Divisional Aviation Brigade, 2004

136

The reorganization of the divisional aviation brigade also reflects the concept Army force developers called modularity. As with the maneuver brigades, a divisional aviation brigade could fight under any division headquarters.[17]

When the modular brigade redesign is completed in 2007, the reshuffling of maneuver assets into the UA brigades will result in the creation of 15 new brigades in the active Army and the transformation of the 15 enhanced Army National Guard brigades into 22 UA BCTs. While the brigade has been a very flexible organization in its own structure since the creation of the first ROAD brigades in the early 1960s, the UA brigade, with its interchangeable, modular structure, will add a level of flexibility at the operational and strategic levels as well. For the first time since George Washington's reorganization in 1778, the brigade will be the Army's basic tactical combined arms unit. With the transformation of the division into essentially a controlling headquarters, the Army's future, as has been much of its past, clearly belongs to the brigade.

As this study concludes, it should be noted that there have been no recent historical examples to support the need for or desirability change the structure of the brigade. The latest military operations, particularly the 2003 Iraqi campaign, tend to validate the flexibly

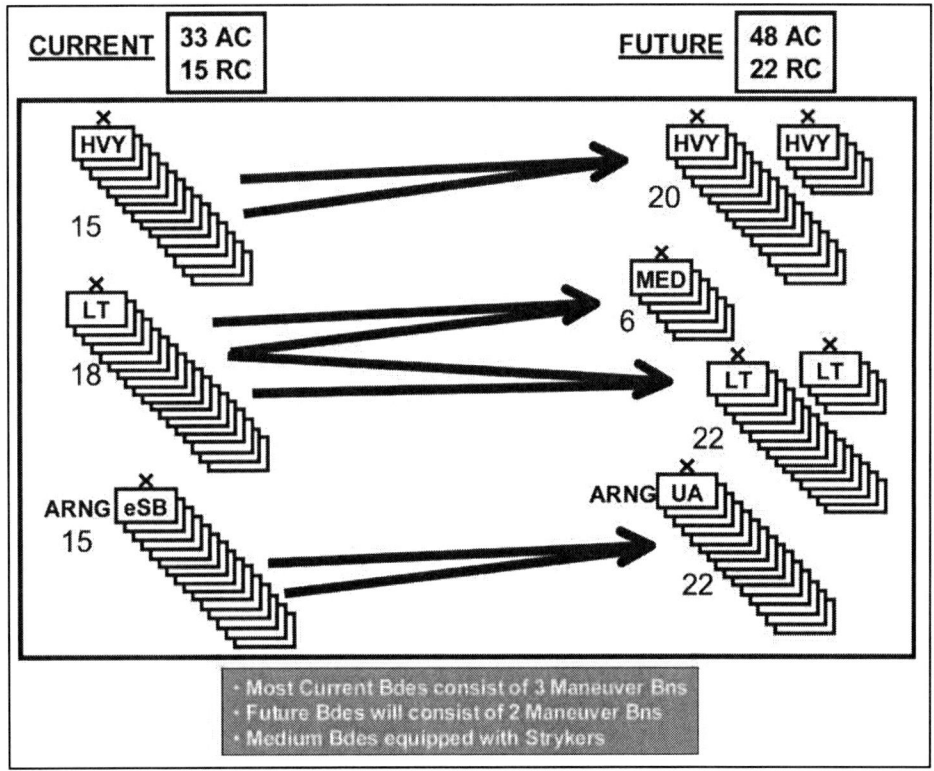

Figure 47. Army Brigade Restructuring, 2004

organized ROAD/AOE style BCT. At no time were brigades broken up into smaller units to add flexibility to maneuver. Under the AOE concept, the modular elements are the combat and combat support battalions and companies, not brigades. In the 2003 campaign, the 3d Infantry Division (Mechanized) commander had the capability to organize his brigades by their particular missions, a capability he used often. It remains to be seen whether the UA brigades will provide similar flexibility while adding flexibility at levels above brigade. For a historical example of the Army's use of a similarly sized unit at the brigade level, the armored division combat command which lasted from 1943 to 1963, was similarly organized to the new UA brigade, with a battalion each of infantry, tanks, and field artillery. The adoption of the combined arms maneuver battalion in the UA brigade, permanently organized as it fights, is the most revolutionary change in the brigade since the adoption of ROAD in 1963.The UA brigades may, due to their additional numbers, provide a flexibility to Army operations at a level higher than that of the AOE brigades, enhancing the rotation of brigade-level units and allowing for a unit replacement personnel system keyed into the brigade level rather than the individual. Level as was done previously With additional brigades, some units can be allowed to be unready as they take in an influx of new soldiers. The lessons for this will be those of the future rather than those of past history of the brigade.

NOTES

1. The 10th Mountain Division's Aviation Brigade was used as a command and control headquarters in the Mogidishu peacekeeping operation from August 1993 to February 1994. The brigade, which was heavily augmented, controlled two infantry battalions, an assault aviation battalion, and a forward support battalion, the 46th, apparently activated in anticipation of the division activating a third brigade, which it never did, and the forward support battalion was inactivated in 1993, and armored and mechanized elements from the 24th ID (M). See Colonel Lawrence E. Casper, "The Aviation Brigade as a Maneuver Headquarters," *Army* 45 (March 1995), 20-23.

2. Jonathan M. House, *Combined Arms Warfare in the Twentieth Century* (Lawrence, KS: University Press of Kansas, 2001), 261-63.

3. Douglas A. Macgregor, *Breaking the Phalanx: A New Design for Landpower in the 21st Century*, (Westport, CT: Praeger, 1997), 68-69, 227; John R. Brinkerhoff, "The Brigade-Based New Army," *Parameters* (Autumn 1997), 62.

4. US Army Training and Doctrine Command (TRADOC) Pamphlet 525-3-90, *O&O, The United States Army Objective Force Operational and Organizational Plan for Maneuver Unit of Action*, TRADOC, dated 22 July 2002, 25.

5. Ibid., 26-47.

6. Ibid., 33-40.

7. Ibid., 41, 47. Recent plans to modularize the Army brigade would indicate that this Stryker brigade model will lose one of its combined arms battalions.

8. Lieutenant General John M. Riggs, "Building an Army... FCS [Future Combat Systems] as Part of the Objective Force," briefing dated 9 November 2001, US Army Objective Force Task Force, slide 6R.

9. Ann Roosevelt, "Army Chief Approves Major Aviation Restructuring," *Defense Daily* (January 30, 2004), 4. The redesign into four smaller maneuver brigades and an aviation brigade does bare more than a passing resemblance to the Pentomic redesign of the 1950s, with its five small subordinate elements.

10. Jim Garamore, "Army to Restructure, Will Grow by 30,000," *American Forces Information Service News Articles* (January 29, 2004); Roosevelt, 5.

11. The fourth maneuver brigade headquarters would come from conversion of the divisional engineer brigade headquarters.

12. SFC Marcia Triggs, "New CSA Vision: More Brigades—Smaller But Lethal, " *Army News Service* (October 8, 2003); Jon R. Anderson, Army Studies Forming Careerlong Brigades," *Stars and Stripes* (February 17, 1004)

13. Of course, the original concept for the combat command was to only have two of them in the armored division, making each somewhat larger. However, in practice, the Reserve Command became a third combat command. This structure was formalized after the war as mentioned in the section of the text dealing with the combat command.

14. Donald H. Rumsfeld, "New Model Army," *Wall Street Journal* (February 3, 2004); Rowan Scarborough, "Major Overhaul Eyed for Army: Schoomaker Crafts Retooling," *Washington Times* (February 3, 2004), 1; Garamore.

15. Elaine M. Grossman, "Army Eyes 'Joint Fire Control Teams to 'Enable' Lighter Troops," *Inside the Pentagon*, (January 29, 2004), 1; Schoomaker, 1.

16. Ann Roosevelt, 4.

17. Ibid.

Bibliography

1st Battalion, 506th Airborne Infantry. *Combat Operations After Action Report, Operation Apache Snow,* dated 18 June 1969.

101st Airborne Division (Airmobile). *Description of Operation vic Dong Ap Bia.* Fact Sheet. May 1969.

101st Airborne Division (Airmobile). *Operational Report- Lessons Learned, 101st Airborne Division (Airmobile) for Period 31 July 1969.* RCS CSFOR-65 (R1) (U), dated 9 December 1969.

22d Military History Detachment. *Narrative Operation "Apache Snow" 101st Airborne Division,* 1969.

3d Battalion, 187th Airborne Infantry. *Combat Operations After Action Report, Operation Apache Snow,* dated 20 June 1969.

3d Brigade, 101st Airborne Division (Airmobile). *Combat Operations After Action Report- Summary APACHE SNOW,* dated 25 June 1969.

3d Infantry Division (Mechanized). *Operation Iraqi Freedom After Action Report.* Final Draft, dated 12 May 2003.

ABC News. *Airport Seized. Baghdad Airport Seized by U.S. Forces.* Posted on ABC News website <http://www.ABCNews.com> accessed on 3 April 2003.

Aldridge, Frederick S. *Organization and Administration of the Militia System of Colonial Virginia.* Ph.D. diss. American University, 1964.

American Armies and Battlefields in Europe. Washington, DC: US Army Center of Military History (CMH), 1992. Reprint of 1938 edition.

Anderson, Jon R. "Army Studies Forming Careerlong Brigades," *Stars and Stripes* (February 17, 1004).

"Army Announces Divisions to Remain in the 10-Division Force." DOD New Release Reference Number 067-95, February 10, 1995.

"Army Announces Final Drawdown Plan." *Army News Service* (15 January 1999) <http://www.dtic.mil/armylink/news/Dec1998/a19981223downsize.html> accessed on 1 May 2003.

Associated Press. "Three-Pronged Assault Paved Way to Baghdad." Posted on Fox News <http://www.foxnews.com> accessed on 8 April 2003.

Atkinson, Rick. "Army Enters Holy City. Troops Move Within Half-Mile of Revered Tomb." *Washington Post,* 2 April 2003, A1.

Balck, William. *Taktik (Tactics),* vol. 3, *Kriegsgliederung, Nachrichten, Befehle. Marschdienst (Military Organization, Communication, Orders, Marches).* 4th ed. Berlin: R. Eisenschmidt, 1907.

Barnett, Correlli. *Britain and Her Army 1509-1970*. Warmondsworth, England; Allen Lane, Penguin Press, 1974.

Barto III, Major Joseph C. *Task Force 2-4 Cav-"First In, Last Out": The History of the 2d Squadron, 4th Cavalry Regiment, During Operation Desert Storm*. Fort Leavenworth, KS: Combat Studies Institute (CSI), 1993.

"Battalions Declared Inactive." *Infantry Journal* 30 (June 1927), 660.

Beall, John A. "Revisions of ROCAD." *Armor* 68 (March-April 1959), 48-51.

Bigelman, Paul A. "Force Designs for the Future." *Army* 31 (June 1981), 22-23.

Bodge, George M. *Brief History of King Philip"s War*. Boston: Printed Privately, 1891.

Boatner, Mark M., III. *The Civil War Dictionary*. New York: Vintage Books, 1991.

Bowman, Lieutenant Colonel Stephen. ""The Old Reliables" One of a Kind." *Army* 38 (February 1988), 26-34.

Branigin, William. "3 Key Battles Turned Tide of Invasion: Infantry Soldiers Broke Last Significant Lines of Iraqi Resistance in Close-Quarters Combat." *Washington Post*, 20 April 2003, A20.

_____. "A Gruesome Scene on Highway 9: 10 Dead After Vehicle Shelled at Checkpoint." *Washington Post*, 1 April 2003, A1.

Brownlee, Romie L., and William J. Mullen III, *Changing an Army: An Oral History of General William E. DePuy, USA Retired.* Washington, DC: CMH, 1985.

Cable News Network (CNN). *Pentagon: 2 Republican Guard Divisions Destroyed.* Posted on CNN website <http://www.CNN.com> accessed at 4:55 PM EST, 2 April 2003.

Caldwell, Jim. "Army Leaders Announce New Design Framework for Army XXI Heavy Division," *Army Communicator* 23 (Summer 1998), 13-16.

Candy, Colonel Charles E. "From ACCB to the 6th Cavalry Brigade (Air Combat)." *US Army Aviation Digest* 21 (May 1975), 1-4.

Casper, Colonel Lawrence E. "The Aviation Brigade as a Maneuver Headquarters," *Army* 45 (March 1995), 20-23.

Chaffee, Adna R. "The Maneuvers of the First Cavalry Division, September-October 1923." *Cavalry Journal* 33 (April 1924), 133-62.

Chandrasekaran, Rajiv and Peter Baker. "Baghdad-Bound Forces Pass Outer Defenses: Marines, Army Approach City On Two Fronts." *Washington Post*, 3 April 2003, A1.

Cheng, Christopher C.S. *Air Mobility: The Development of a Doctrine*. Westport, CT: Praeger, 1994.

Coakley, Robert W. *The Role of Federal Military Forces in Domestic Disorders 1789-1878*. Washington, DC; US Army, 1988.

Combat Studies Institute. *Sixty Years of Reorganizing for Combat: A Historical Trend Analysis.* Fort Leavenworth: CSI, 1999.

Conmy, Joseph B. Jr., "Crouching Beast Cornered." *Vietnam* (December 1990), 31-36.

Cooper, SFC (no first name cited). *Army (V Corps) Tactical Lessons Learned from Iraq.* E-mail to author, dated 1 April 2003.

Cordesman, Anthony. *The Instant Lessons of the Iraq War Main Report.* Third Working Draft, April 14, 2003. Washington, DC: Center for Strategic and International Studies. 2003.

Cosmas, Graham A. *An Army for Empire. The United States in the Spanish-American War.* Columbia: University of Missouri Press, 1971.

Cronin, Francis D. *Under the Southern Cross, the Saga of the Americal Division.* Washington, DC: Combat Forces Press, 1971.

Crossland, Richard B., and James T. Currie. *Twice the Citizen: A History of the US Army Reserve, 1908-1983.* Washington, DC: Office of the Chief, Army Reserve, 1984.

Diamond, John and Dave Moniz. "No Answer for U.S. Firepower." *USA TODAY,* 6 April 2003.

_____. "Iraqi Colonel"s Capture Sped Up Taking of City." *USA TODAY,* 9 April 2003.

Dickinson, John. *The Building of an Army.* New York: Century Co., 1922.

Division Organization in WWI. CMH unpublished Word document 2002.

Duane, William. *A Hand Book for Infantry.* Philadelphia. William Duane, 1814.

Dunn, Brian J. "Equipping the Objective Force." *Military Review* 82 (May-June 2002), 28-33.

Dunn Richard J., III. "Transformation: Let"s Get It Right This Time." *Parameters* 31 (Spring 2001), 22-28.

Dwyer, Jim. "A Gulf Commander Sees a Longer Road. V Corps Commander." *New York Times,* 28 March 2003.

Edwards, Major John E. *Combat Service Support Guide.* Second Edition. Harrisburg, PA: Stackpole Books, 1993.

Epstein, Robert M. "The Creation of the Army Corps in the American Civil War." *Journal of Military History* 55 (January 1991), 41-46.

Frazier, Donald S., ed. *The United States and Mexico at War: Nineteenth-Century Expansionism and Conflict.* New York: Simon & Schuster Macmillan, 1998.

Ford, Worthington Chauncy., ed. *Journals of the Continental Congress, 1774-1789,* 34 vols. Washington, DC: Government Printing Office (GPO), 1904-1937.

_____. *The Writings of George Washington.* New York: Putnam, 1890.

Fortesque, J.W. *A History of the British Army*. London: MacMillan, 1910.

Foss, John W., Donal S. Pihl, and Thomas E. Fitzgerald. "The Division Restructuring Study: The Heavy Division." *Military Review* 57 (March 1977), 11-21.

Fulghum, David A. "The Pentagon"s Force-Transformation Director Takes an Early Swipe at What Worked and What Didn"t in Iraq." *Aviation Week & Space Technology* 158 (28 April 2003).

Fuller, J.F.C. *British Light Infantry in the Eighteenth Century.* London: Hutchinson, 1925.

Fulton, Major General William B. *Riverine Operations 1966-1969*. Vietnam Studies Series. Washington, DC: Department of the Army, 1985.

Garamore, Jim. "Army to Restructure, Will Grow by 30,000," *American Forces Information Service News Articles* (January 29, 2004).

The General Board, United States Forces, European Theater. *Organization, Equipment and Tactical Employment of the Armored Division*, Study Number 48.

Genesis of the American First Army. Washington, DC: GPO, 1987.

Gilmore, Gerry J. "Army to Develop Future Force, says Shinseki." Army Link News, 13 October 1999.

Gourley, Scott R. "Significant Events in Transformation: Stryker Battalions Enter Evaluation Phase." *Army* 53 (February 2003), 62-66.

Grant, Greg. "An Up-Close View of the Capture of Baghdad." *Salt Lake City Tribune,* 20 April 2003.

Gray, Andrew. *U.S Forces Edge Toward Baghdad After Fierce Fight*. Reuters News Story posted at <http://www.washingtonpost.com> accessed on 31 March 2003.

Grossman, Elaine M. "Army Eyes 'Joint Fire Control Teams' to 'Enable' Lighter Troops," *Inside the Pentagon*, (January 29, 2004), 1.

"The Guard Goes ROAD." *National Guardsman* 17 (February 1963), 2-4.

Hay, John H., Jr. *Tactical and Materiel Innovations*. Washington, DC: GPO, 1974.

Hawkins, Glen R and James Jay Carafano. *Prelude to Army XXI: US Army Division Design Initiatives and Experiments 1917-1995.* Washington, DC: CMH, 1997.

Headquarters, Department of the Army. Field Manual 3-21.31, *The Stryker Brigade Combat Team*. Washington, DC: US Army, 2003.

Headquarters, Department of the Army. Field Manual 71-123, *Tactics And Techniques For Combined Arms Heavy Forces: Armored Brigade, Battalion Task Force, And Company Team*. Washington, DC: US Army, 1992.

Hechler, Ken. *The Bridge at Remagen.* New York: Ballantine, 1957.

Historical Resources Branch, CMH. *The American Division in World War I*. Undated document.

144

Hodierne, Robert. "Into the Fight: Rapid Ground Assault First, Then "Shock and Awe." *Army Times*, 31 March 2003, 4-7.

Hodierne, Robert, and Alex Neill. "Regime Comes Tumbling Down: Fall of Baghdad Came Quicker than Most Anyone Expected." *Army Times*, 21 April 2003, 8, 11.

House, Jonathan M. *Combined Arms Warfare in the Twentieth Century*. Lawrence, KS: University Press of Kansas, 2001.

_____. *Toward Combined Arms Warfare: A Survey of 20th-Century Tactics, Doctrine, and Organization*. Combat Studies Institute Research Survey Number 2. Fort Leavenworth, KS: US Army Command and General Staff College (CGSC), 1984.

Hunt, Roger D., and Jack R. Brown. *Brevet Brigadier Generals in Blue*. Old Soldier Books, 1998.

Ingles, Harry C. "The New Division." *Infantry* 49 (November-December 1939), 521-29.

Jamieson, Perry D. *Crossing the Deadly Ground: US Army Tactics, 1865-1899*. Tuscaloosa: University of Alabama Press, 1994.

Johnson, Thomas M. and Fletcher Pratt. *The Lost Battalion*. New York: Bobbs-Merrill, 1938.

Kelly, Michael. "Across The Euphrates." *Washington Post*, 3 April 2003, A23.

King, James I., and Melvin A. Goers. "Modern Armored Cavalry Organization." *Armored Cavalry Journal* 57 (July-August 1948), 47-50.

Landry, Colonel John R. and Lieutenant Colonel Bloomer D. Sullivan. "CSS: Resourcing and Sustaining the AirLand Battle: Forward Support Battalion," *Military Review* 67 (January 1987), 24-30.

Leach, Douglas. *Arms for Empire: A Military History of the British Colonies in North America, 1607-1763*. New York: Macmilllan, 1973.

Lee, David D. *Sergeant York: An American Hero*. Lexington, KY: University Press of Kentucky, 1985.

Lelinek, Pauline. *U.S. Force 20 Miles Outside of Baghdad*. Associated Press Wire News Story, 2 April 2003.

Lider, Julian. *Origins and Development of West German Military Thought*. 2 vols. Aldershot, England, 1986-88.

Liewer, Steve. "Apache Copter Crews Second Al Hillah Mission a Success." *Stars and Stripes, European Edition*, 15 April 2003.

Lightsey, Captain Ross F. "Establishing and Using The Brigade Reconnaissance Troop," *Infantry* 90 (Jan-Apr 2000), 10-14.

Lippman, Thomas W. "Hussein"s Baghdad Falls as U.S. Establishes Control.

Jubilant Iraqis Take to Streets, Topple Baghdad Statue of Dictator." *Washington Post* 10 April 2003, A1.

Lupfer, Timothy T. *The Dynamics of Doctrine: The Changes in German Tactical Doctrine During the First World War*. Leavenworth Paper Number 4. Fort Leavenworth, KS: CGSC, 1981.

MacGarrigle, George L. *Taking The Offensive: October 1966 to October 1967*. The US Army in Vietnam. Washington, DC: CMH, 1998.

MacGregor, Douglas A. *Breaking the Phalanx: A New Design for Landpower in the 21st Century*. Westport, CT: Praeger, 1997.

Mahon, John K. and Romana Danysh. *Infantry Part I: Regular Army*. Army Lineage Series. Washington, DC: GPO, 1972.

Maltz, R., *Update from the Front*. E-mail to author, dated 9 April 2003.

Marshall, Steve. "Accuracy of Battlefield News Often Hazy" *USA TODAY*, April 8, 2003, 7A.

Martin, Lieutenant Colonel Donald R. "First Cavalry Division Reorganization." *Armor* 83 (July-August 1974), 51-52.

Maurer, Kevin. "82nd Learns To Spot Threats." *Fayetteville (NC) Observer*, April 1, 2003.

May, Commander (RN) W.E., W.Y. Carman and John Tanner. *Badges and Insignia of the British Armed Services*. New York: St. Martin"s Press, 1974.

McClure, N.F. "The Infantry Division and Its Composition." *Journal of Military Service Institute* 50 (January-February 1912), 5-9.

McGrath, John J. *Arab Allied Armies in the Gulf War*. Unpublished Word document, 2002.

_____. *Creation of the Airmobile Division 1965*. Unpublished PowerPoint document, 2002.

_____. *Gulf War Build Up*. Unpublished PowerPoint document, 2001.

_____. *Gulf War Organization*. Unpublished PowerPoint document, 2001.

_____. *History of the 187th Support Battalion*. Brochure created for the inactivation of the battalion. Brockton, Massachusetts, 1994.

_____. *Iraqi Army Order of Battle*. Unpublished Word document, 2001.

_____. "A New Concept for Combined Arms." *Armor* 43 (January-February 1984), 46-47.

_____. *Spanish American War US Army Order of Battle*. Unpublished Word document, 2001.

_____. *US Army Corps Flags and Commanders Down to Brigade Level*. Unpublished Word document, 2000.

McKenney, Janice E. *Air Defense Artillery*. Army Lineage Series. Washington, DC: GPO, 1985.

Morrissey, Brendan. *Boston 1775: The Shot Heard Around the World*. Osprey Campaign Series Number 37. Osprey: London, 1993.

Murphy, Caryle "Baghdad Air Campaign Intensifies on 12th Day of War U.S., Iraqi Forces Battle for Control of Hindiyah." *Washington Post*, 31 March 2003.

Myers, James P., Jr. "General Forbes Roads to War." *Military History* 18 (December 2001), 30-36.

Myers, Steven Lee. "U.S. Columns Roll Forward Near Baghdad." *New York Times*, 2 April 2003, A1.

Naisawald, L. van Loan. *The US Infantry Division: Changing Concepts in Organization, 1900-39*. Project Shop, Organized Reserve O-S 23. Baltimore: Johns Hopkins University, 1952.

Naylor, Sean. "Allies Destroy Iraqi Republican Guard Force." *USATODAY*, 26 April 2003.

_____. "'Like Apocalypse Now.' 7th Cavalry Squadron Runs Gauntlet of Iraqi Fire During Its Longest Day." *Army Times*, 7 April 2003, 14-16.

_____. "Sights Set on Baghdad: Soldiers Overcome Unexpected Resistance, Stand Poised at City"s Outskirts." *Army Times*, 14 April 2003, 14-16.

Ney, Virgil. *Evolution of the US Army Infantry Battalion: 1939-1968*. Fort Belvoir, VA: US Army Combat Developments Command, 1968.

_____. *Evolution of the Armored Infantry Rifle Squad*. Fort Belvoir, VA: US Army Combat Developments Command, 1965.

Norton, John. "TRICAP." *Army* 21 (June 1971),14-19.

Oleson, Ivan H. "TriCap: A New Logistics Challenge," *Army Logistician* 3 (September-October 1971), 5-7, 33.

O"Meara, Walter. *Guns at the Forks*, Englewood Cliffs, NJ: Prentice-Hall 1965.

"Operation Iraqi Freedom: A Chronology." *Army* 53 (May 2003).

Order of Battle, US Army, World War II, European Theater of Operations: Divisions Paris: Office of the Theater Historian, European Theater, 1945.

Order of Battle of the United States Land Forces in the World War (1917-19): American Expeditionary Forces: General Headquarters, Armies, Army Corps, Services of Supply, Separate Forces; Directory of Troops; Divisions; Zone of the Interior. 5 vols. Washington, DC: GPO, 1931-49, reprinted Washington, DC: GPO, 1988.

"Our Floundering Army Reserve Program." *Reserve Officer* 25 (July 1948), 4-6ff.

Perret-Gential, J. "Divisions—Three or Five elements?" *Military Review* 41 (February 1961), 16-25.

Pew, Frank W. *The US Army Forces Command and the Development of the Brigade 75/76 Concept for the Support of Europe*. Fort McPherson, GA: US Army Forces Command, 1980.

Pfanz, Henry. *Gettysburg- The Second Day.* Chapel Hill, NC: University of North Carolina Press, 1987.

Phillips, Noelle. "3rd Infantry Travels by Night to Seize Crucial City." *Savannah Morning News,* 3 April 2003.

Pickell, Major Gregory A. "The New Interim Brigade Combat Team: Old Wine in New Bottles?" *Military Review* 82 (May-June 2002), 71-72.

Pittman, J. M. "Reorganization of the Armored Division." *Military Review* 24 (April 1944), 44-47.

Quimby, Robert S. *The Background of Napoleonic Warfare.* New York: AMS Press, Inc., 1957.

Radabaugh, Jack S. "The Militia of Colonial Massachusetts." *Military Affairs* 18 (Spring 1954), 1-18.

Report of the Assistant Inspector General. First Army, Subject: 77th Division, cutting off of seven companies and one machine gun company, October 3, 1918, dated 8 October 1918. Found in the papers of Major H.A. Drum. *Papers Relating to Lost Battalion, 77th Division,* Document 12. Military History Institute, 25 March 2003, <http://carlisle-www.army.mil/cgi-bin/usamhi/DL/showdoc.pl?docnum=12>.

Riggs, Lieutenant General John M. "Building an Army... FCS as Part of the Objective Force." Briefing dated 9 November 2001, US Army Objective Force Task Force.

Romjue, John S. *A History of Army 86. Division 86: The Development of the Heavy Division.* Fort Monroe, VA: US Army Training and Doctrine Command (TRADOC), 1982.

_____. *A History of Army 86. Division 86: The Development of the Light Division, the Corps and Echelons Above Corps.* Fort Monroe, VA: TRADOC, 1982.

_____. *The Army of Excellence: The Development of the 1980s Army.* Fort Monroe, VA: TRADOC, 1993.

_____. *From Active Defense to Airland Battle: The Development of Army Doctrine, 1973-1982.* Fort Monroe, VA: TRADOC, 1984.

Roosevelt, Ann. "Army Chief Approves Major Aviation Restructuring," *Defense Daily* (January 30, 2004), 4.

_____. "Army Reorganization Aims for 2007 Completion," *Defense Daily* (February 19, 2004), 5.

Rumsfeld, Donald H. "New Model Army," *Wall Street Journal* (February 3, 2004).

Saoud, Dalal. *Baghdad: A Battle That Did Not Happen.* United Press International. Posted on UPI website <http://www.UPI.com> accessed on 9 April 2003.

Sawicki, James. *Cavalry Regiments of the US Army.* Dumfries, VA: Wyvern Publications, 1985.

_____. *Infantry Regiments of the US Army* Dumfries, VA: Wyvern, 1981.

_____. *Tank Battalions of the US Army.* Dumfries, VA; Wyvern, 1983.

Scarborough, Rowan. "Major Overhaul Eyed for Army: Schoomaker Crafts Retooling," *Washington Times*, (February 3, 2004), 1.

Sepp, Kalev I. "The Pentomic Puzzle: The Influence of Personality and Nuclear Weapons on US Army Organization 1952-1958." *Army History* 51 (Winter 2001), 1-13.

Stanton, Shelby. *Anatomy of a Division: The First Cav in Vietnam.* Novato, CA: Presidio, 1987.

_____. *Order of Battle: US Army, World War II.* Novato, CA: Presidio, 1984.

_____. *Vietnam Order of Battle.* Washington, DC: US News Books, 1981.

Stubbs, Mary Lee, and Stanley R. Connor. *Armor-Cavalry.* Army Lineage Series. Washington, DC: GPO, 1969.

Symonds, Craig L. *A Battlefield Atlas of the American Revolution.* Baltimore, MD: Nautical and Aviation Publishing, 1986.

Tolson, John J. *Airmobility, 1961-1971.* Washington, DC: GPO, 1973.

Tomlinson, Chris. *For One Infantry Officer, War is a Test Of Courage, Endurance and Simple Decency.* Associated Press. Posted on Mercury News website <http://www.MercuryNews.com> accessed on 17 April 2003.

Triggs, SFC Marcia "New CSA Vision: More Brigades—Smaller But Lethal, " *Army News Service* (October 8, 2003).

US Army Combined Arms Combat Development Agency. *The Light Infantry Division: The Army of Excellence: Final Report,* 1 October 1984.

US Army Corps of Engineers History Office. *Engineer Memoirs: General William M. Hoge.* EP 870-1-25, Fort Belvoir, VA: US Army Corps of Engineers, 1993.

US Army Training and Doctrine Command, TRADOC Pamphlet 525-3-90, *O&O, The US Army Objective Force Operational and Organizational Plan for Maneuver Unit of Action.* Fort Monroe, VA: TRADOC, 2002.

US Army Logistics Management College. *Support Operations Course (Phase I).* Lesson Book. Fort Lee, VA: US Army Logistics Management College, 1992.

US Army Operation Iraqi Freedom Study Group. *On Point: The US Army in Operation Iraqi Freedom.* Draft Manuscript, Fort Leavenworth, KS: CSI, 15 August 2003.

Warner, Ezra. *Generals in Blue: Lives of the Union Commanders.* Baton Rouge, LA: Louisiana State University Press, 1984.

The War of the Rebellion: A Compilation of the Official Records of the Union and Confederate Armies. Ser. 1, 53 vols. Washington, DC: GPO, 1881-1898.

Wike, John W. "The Wearing of Army Corps and Division Insignia in the Union Army." *Military Collector and Historian* 4 (June 1952), 353-58.

Wilson, Dale E. *Treat "Em Rough: The Birth of American Armor 1917-20*. Novato, CA: Presidio, 1989.

Wilson, John B. *Armies, Corps, Divisions, Separate Brigades*. Army Lineage Series. Washington, DC: GPO, 1987.

_____. *Maneuver and Firepower: The Evolution of Divisions and Separate Brigades*. Army Lineage Series. Washington, DC: GPO, 1998.

_____. "Mobility Versus Firepower: The Post-World War I Infantry Division." *Parameters* 13 (September 1983), 47-52.

Wolf, Duquesne A. *The Infantry Brigade in Combat: First Brigade, 25th Infantry Division ("Tropic Lightning") in the Third Viet Cong/North Vietnamese Army Offensive, August 1968*. Manhattan, KS: Sunflower University Press, 1984.

Wright, Robert K, Jr. *The Continental Army*. Army Lineage Series. Washington, DC: GPO, 1989.

Zoroya, Gregg. "At Last, Smiles Greet U.S. Troops As They Enter Holy City In Iraq." *USA Today*, 3 April 2003, A1.

GLOSSARY

AAA	antiaircraft artillery
AAsslt	air assault
AC	active component
ACCB	air cavalry combat brigade
ACR	armoed cavalry regiment
AD	armored division
ADA	air defense artillery; branch of Army responsible for tactical and operational defense against air attack
AEF	American Expeditionary Force
AGS	assault gun system
air assault	units moved into battle via helicopter
airborne	units moved into battle via aircraft, usually synonymous with paratroopers
airmobile	units moved into battle via helicopter (term used between 1965 and 1974)
ANGB	Air National Guard Base
AOE	Army of Excellence
AO	area of operation
APC	armored personnel carrier
armored	units composed of elements mounted in armored tracked vehicles; tank units
ARNG	Army National Guard
Arty	artillery (term used between 1957 and 1972 when field artillery and air defense artillery were one branch)
ARVN	Army of the Republic of Vietnam
assault	aviation units equipped with light utility helicopters, designed to land combat troops under fire
assault support	aviation units equipped with medium utility helicopters, designed to land combat troops and equipment, usually not under fire
AT	antitank
ATP	ammunition transfer point
battalion	a unit of roughly 500 soldiers composed of companies and commanded by a lieutenant colonel; in regimental organizations with only one battalion (before 1898), virtually synonymous with term regiment
battery	lettered company-sized unit in the artillery
BCT	brigade combat team
Bde	brigade
BG	battle group (1957-1963)
BMMC	brigade materiel management center
Bn	battalion

brevet	system of honorary promotions used in US Army before1914
brigade	unit of either regiments or battalions of roughly 3,000 soldiers, commanded by either a brigadier general or colonel
BRT	brigade reconnaissance troop
BSA	brigade support area
BSB	brigade support battalion
Bundeswehr	Army of the Federal Republic of Germany
CAB (H)	combined arms battalion (heavy)
CAB (L)	combined arms battalion (light)
CARS	Combat Arms Regimental System
Cav cavalry	reconnaissance troops; troops mounted on horses (before1943)
CCA	Combat Command A
CCB	Combat Command B
CCC	Combat Command C
CCR	Combat Command Reserve
CD	cavalry division
CENTCOM	Central Command
CFV	cavalry fighting vehicle, M3Bradley
CMH	US Army Center of Military History
Co	company
COHORT	Cohesion, Operational Readiness, Training; US Army program of the1980s-1990s which trained company-sized units of soldiers together and retained them as a unit throughout their Army term of enlistment
COLT	Combat Observation Laser Team
Combat Command	task organized command found in US Army armored divisions from 942 to 1963
company	lettered unit composed of platoon, of roughly 100 soldiers, commanded by a captain
component	major subdivisions of the Army-active component (Regular Army and nonregular soldiers on active duty) and the reserve components-Army Reserve and Army National Guard
CONARC	US Army's Continental Army Command
corps	large units consisting of divisions and designated by Roman numeral identifiers (since 1917)
COSVN	Central Office for South Vietnam
CS	combat support; units whose function is to directly support combat units, such as engineers, signal troops, military police, and military intelligence
CSC	combat support company
CSG	corps support group
CSI	Combat Studies Institute
CSS	combat service support; logistics support units such as supply, maintenance, transportation

152

direct support	support unit placed in exclusive support of a specific unit, while not being technically assigned to it
DISCOM	Division Support Command
DIVARTY	division artillery
Division	unit consisting of brigades or regiments, with a strength of between 10,000 and 20,000 soldiers, typically commanded by a major general
dragoon	mounted infantry (term replaced in US Army in 1861 when dragoons became part of the cavalry)
DRB	division ready brigade
DRS	Division Restructuring Study
DSC	Distinguished Service Cross
DZ	drop zone; designated point for paratroopers to be airdropped
eHSB	enhanced heavy separate brigade
EOY	end of year
eSB	enhanced separate brigade
EXFOR	experimental force
FA	field artillery; branch of Army responsible for providing fire support (cannons, rockets, missiles) to support the Army in the field
FASCO	forward area support coordination officer
FAST	forward area support team
FAV	fast attack vehicle
FBCB2	Force XXI Battle Command Brigade and Below
FCS	Future Combat Systems
Field Force	corps-sized headquarters used in Vietnam
FM	field manual
force structure	the design and structural organization of the Army
FROG	free rocket over ground
FSB	fire support base; forward support battalion
FSSE	forward service support element
functional	a combat service support unit with only one type of function (a transportation company, a supply company, etc.)
GHQ	general headquarters
GMG	grenade machine gun
Group	Army organization, commanded by a colonel, consisting of non-organic subordinate battalions,
HHC	headquarters and headquarters company
HMMWV	high mobility multipurpose wheeled vehicle; replaced jeep and other vehicles in Army in 1980s
HQ/HQs	headquarters
HTLD	High Technology Light Division

HTMD	High Technology Motorized Division
HTTB	High Technology Test Bed
IA	Operations officer
IAP	International Airport
IBCT	Interim Brigade Combat Team renamed Stryker Brigade Combat Team (SBCT)
ID, ID (M)	infantry division; infantry division (mechanized)
I MEF	I Marine Expeditionary Force
Joint	a military operation or organization in which the forces come from more than one armed service, such as the Army and the Air Force
KTO	Kuwaiti Theater of Operations
LAB	light attack battalion
LAV	land assault vehicle
LCD XXI	Limited Conversion Division XXI
legion	brigade-sized unit consisting of infantry, artillery and cavalry, used by the Army briefly in the 1790s
LOGPAC	logistics package (consolidated convoy of logistics resupply)
LST	landing ship, tank
LW	*Landwehr*- in World War I (a category of German reservist troops)
LZ	landing zone (for helicopter-borne troops)
maneuver	combat troops capable of maneuvering against enemy forces on the battlefield-usually refers to infantry, cavalry, and tank units and sometimes attack helicopter units
MARCENT	US Marine Corps Central Command
MEB	Marine Expeditionary Brigade; US Marine Corps organization consisting of an infantry regiment reinforced with support elements including tactical air (fixed wing)
Mech	Mechanized (infantry); mechanical; shorthand term used to indicate a mechanized infantry unit
mechanized	troops mounted on tracked vehicles
MEF	Marine Expeditionary Force; US Marine command roughly equivalent to a corps, consisting of a division (sometimes two) reinforced with various assets including tactical air
MG	machine gun
MGS	mobile gun system
MI	military intelligence
MMC	also DMMC, BMMC; Materiel Management Center; Division Materiel Management Center; Brigade Materiel Management Center

MOS	Military Occupational Specialty
Mot	motorized; on wheels; not mech
MRF	Mobile Riverine Force
multifunctional	combat service support units organized to do various CSS functions
NA	National Army
NBC	nuclear, biological, chemical
NCO	noncommissioned officer
NVA	North Vietnamese army
Obj	objective
OPCON	operational control
OPFOR	opposing force
ORC	Organized Reserve Corps
ord	ordnance; branch of the Army responsible for ammunition and maintenance
PATRIOT	Phased Array Tracking Radar Intercept On Target
PDF	Panamanian Defense Force
pentomic	Army organizational structure used from 1957 to 1963 which had five battle groups subordinate to infantry divisions in lieu of regiments or brigades
PL	phaseline
Platoon, plt	Army unit of about 30 soldiers led by a lieutenant
POW	prisoner of war
RC	Reserve Components (the Army National Guard and Army Reserve)
RCT	regimental combat team
RDJTF	Rapid Deployment Joint Task Force
REFORGER	Return of Forces to Germany; annual exercise where Army units from the continental United States practiced deploying to Central Europe, begun in ate 1960s when 24th Infantry Division (Mechanized) redeployed to United States, leaving one brigade in Germany
Regiment	Army unit commanded by colonel traditionally consisting of subordinate companies or battalions (partially after 1861 and totally after 1898); after 1957 purely an administrative entity (with several exceptions such as the ACR); regiments are usually referred to by branch without the regimental designation: 3d Infantry instead of 3d Infantry Regiment
Reserve	in World War I (a category of unit in the German army initially made up of reservist personnel)
rgt, regt	regiment
RIF	reconnaissance-in-force (operation conducted in Vietnam when the enemy's location was not known)

ROAD	Reorganization Objective Army Division; Army organization adopted in 1963 which restored the brigade as the major subordinate unit of the division
ROCID	Reorganization of the Current Infantry Division; official name of the Pentomic division concept
roundout	program where RC units filled out AC force structure
RPG	Rocket-propelled grenade launcher; a very common Soviet-made short-range shoulder fired antitank rocket launcher; unlike the US LAW, the RPG was reloadable; the latest version was the RPG-7
RSTA	reconnaissance, surveillance, and target acquisition
Salv	salvage
SBCT	Stryker Brigade Combat Team
separate	a unit not an organic component of any higher unit
signal	communications branch of the Army
Spt	support
squadron	battalion-sized unit in the cavalry
SROTC	Senior Reserve Officer's Training Course
SWA	Southwest Asia (i.e., the Persian Gulf region)
TAOR	tactical area of responsibility
team	company-sized combined arms force formed on a temporary basis
TF	task force; battalion-sized combined arms force formed on a temporary basis; in World War II also sometimes used for larger-sized such forces
TOC	Tactical Operations Center
TOE	table of organization and equipment
TOW	highly effective antitank guided missile (ATGM) used in US Army in 1970s to present
TRADOC	US Army Training and Doctrine Command
trains	company and battalion CSS assets pooled together for self-defense and operations
TRICAP	triple capability; experimental US Army division 1971-1975
troop	company-sized unit in the cavalry
UA	Unit of Action
UAV	unmanned aerial vehicle
UE, UEx, UEy	Unit of Employment Doctrinally, the acronyms UEx and UEy have supplanted UE. UEx indicates a deployable unit of employment at the division or corps level, while UEy indicates a deployable unit of empoyment at levels higher than corps

UK	United Kingdom
USAC	United States Army Corps
USAR	United States Army Reserve
USAREUR	United States Army, Europe
USARF	United States Army Reserve Forces; designation used for Army reserve school units
USARS	United States Army Regimental System
VC	Viet Cong
VHF	very high frequency; type of radios used by aviation and higher headquarters organizations
Volksgrenadier	honorific designation given some low grade German divisions near end of World War II
Volunteers	component of the Army before 1917, in which individuals and units were formed to fight specific wars or campaigns, with most units formed on a state basis

APPENDIXES

Appendix 1

DIVISIONAL VERSUS SEPARATE BRIGADES

The major differences between separate brigades and divisional brigades since the introduction of ROAD in 1963, and continued under AOE are as follows:

	Divisional Brigade	**Separate Brigade**
Commander	Colonel	Brigadier General
Maneuver Forces	Two to five attached battalions	Two to five organic battalions
Reconnaissance Troops	Organic brigade recon troop (in heavy brigades)	Organic armored cavalry troop
Combat Support	Attached MI company, signal company; direct support engineer battalion/company, field artillery battalion, ADA battery	Organic engineer company, MI company, signal company, field artillery battalion, ADA battery
Combat Service Support	Forward support battalion in direct support	Organic support battalion

The difference between the support battalions are as follows:

	Divisional Forward Support Battalion	**Separate Brigade Support Battalion**
Materiel Management Center	None at division-level	BMMC in headquarters company
Support Operations Section	In headquarters company	None
Admin Company	None	Organic; later attached as a separate personnel service company
Supply and Transportation Company	Yes	Yes
Medical Company	Yes	Yes
Maintenance Company	Yes	Yes

Appendix 2

BRIGADE COLORS

Civil War

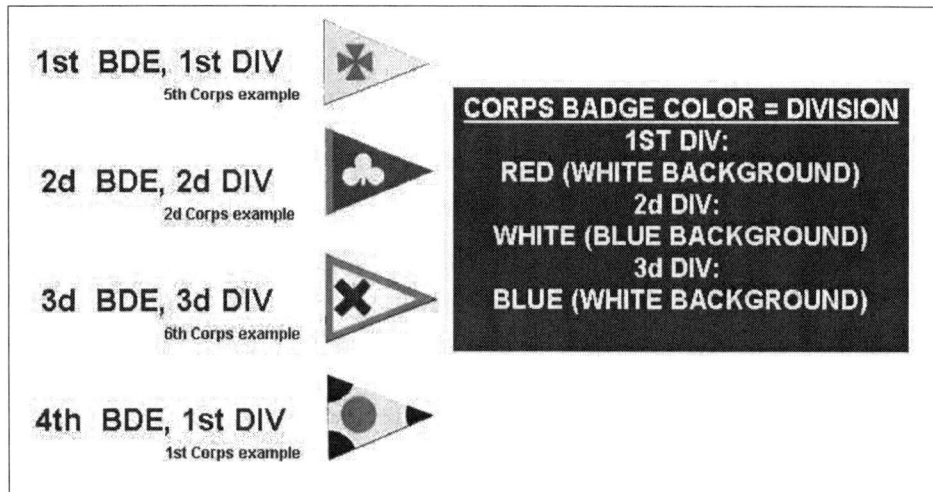

Spanish-American War

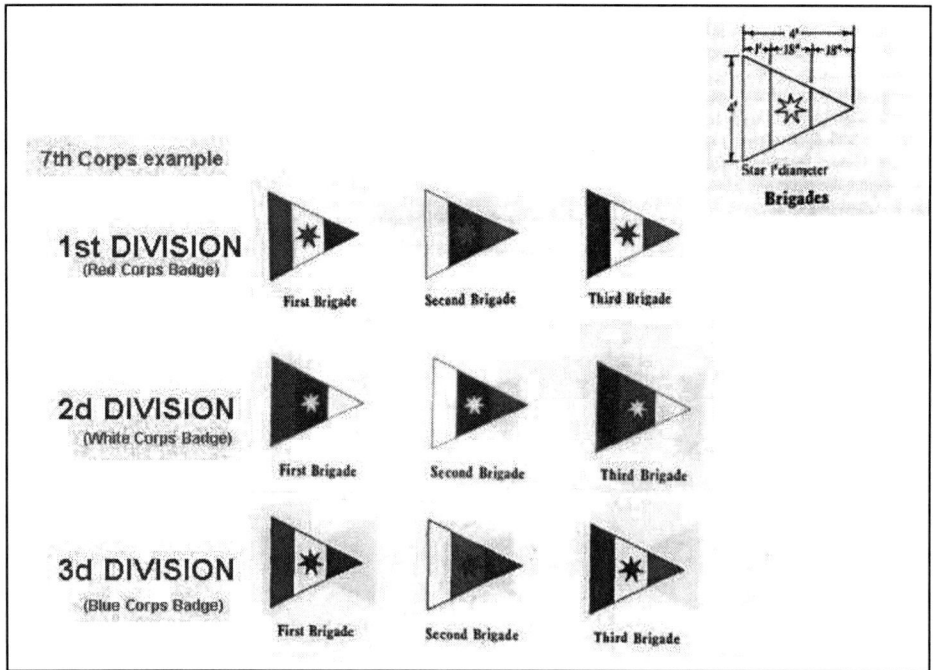

World War I/Interwar (Square Division)

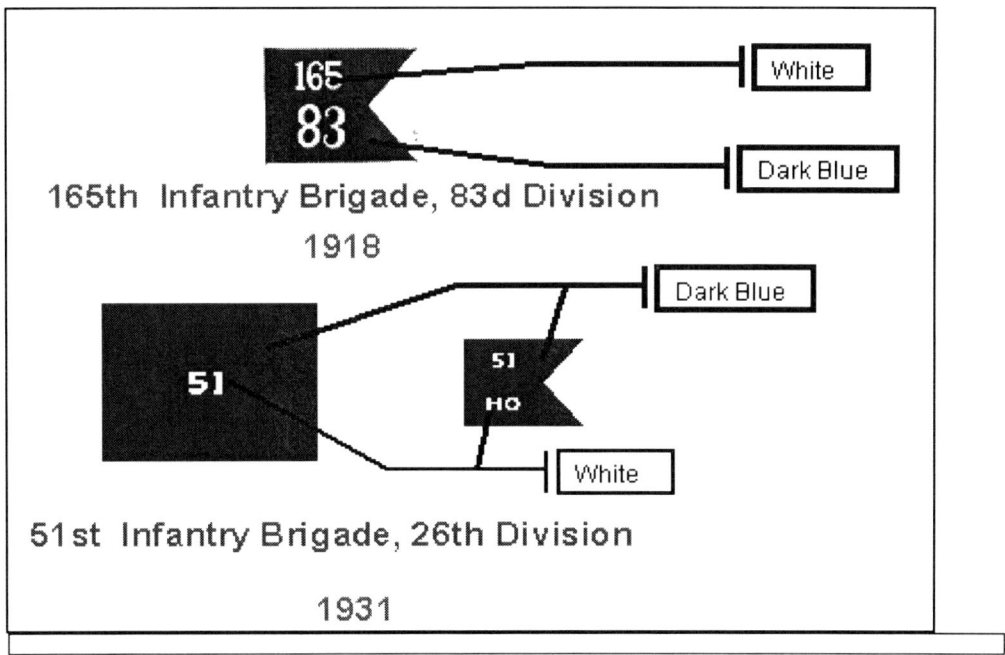

165th Infantry Brigade, 83d Division
1918

51st Infantry Brigade, 26th Division
1931

World War II (Armored Division Combat Command)

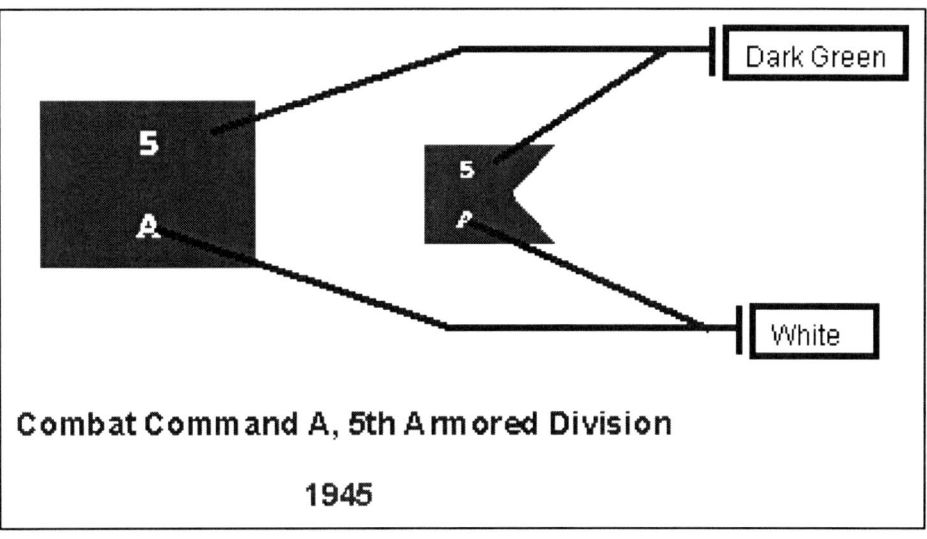

Combat Command A, 5th Armored Division
1945

Current (Since 1963)

Infantry, Airborne, Mechanized

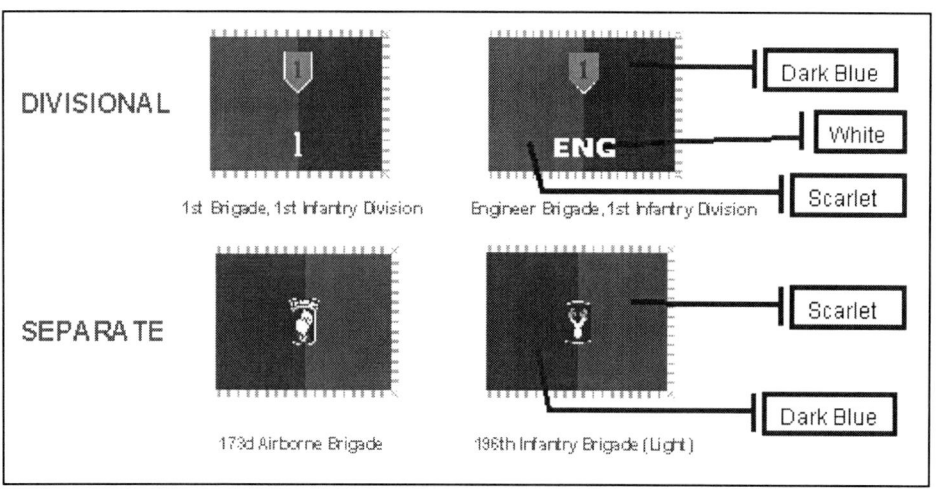

Armored & Cavalry

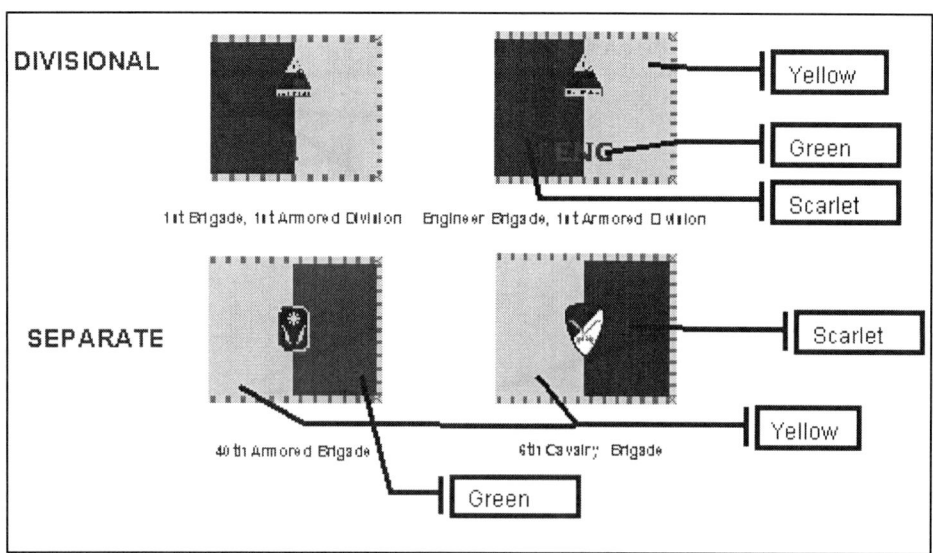

Cavalry & Aviation

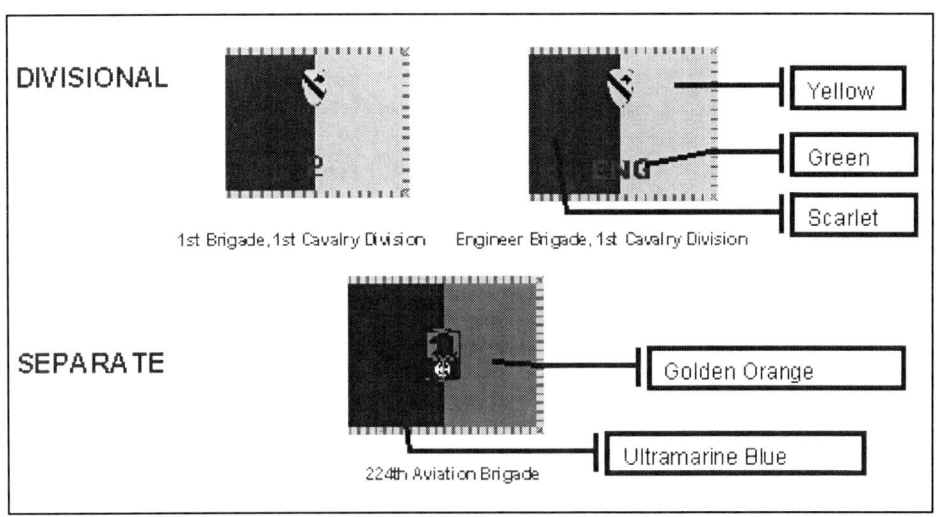

DIVISIONAL

1st Brigade, 1st Cavalry Division   Engineer Brigade, 1st Cavalry Division

Yellow

Green

Scarlet

SEPARATE

Golden Orange

Ultramarine Blue

224th Aviation Brigade

Appendix 3

WORLD WAR I AND INTERWAR INFANTRY BRIGADES

Designation	Regiments		Division	Service Dates	Remarks
1st Infantry Brigade	16th	18th	1st	Jun 1917-1939	Lineage to current 1st Brigade, 1st Infantry Division
2d Infantry Brigade	26th	28th	1st	Jun 1917-1939	Lineage to current 2d Brigade, 1st Infantry Division
3d Infantry Brigade	9th	23d	2d	Oct 1917-1939	Lineage to current 3d Brigade, 2d Infantry Division
4th Infantry Brigade	1st	20th	2d	Oct 1920-1939	4th Brigade in WW1 consisted of two USMC Regiments; Lineage to current 2d Brigade, 2d Infantry Division
5th Infantry Brigade	4th	7th	3d	Jan 1918-Oct 1939	Lineage to current 2d Brigade, 3d Infantry Division
6th Infantry Brigade	30th	38th	3d	Jan 1918-Oct 1939	Lineage to current 3d Brigade, 3d Infantry Division
7th Infantry Brigade	39th	47th	4th	Dec 1917-1921	Inactivated 1921
				1927-1939	7th Division 1927-1933; 47th replaced by 29th after 1927; Lineage to current 2d Brigade, 4th Infantry Division
8th Infantry Brigade	58th 8th	59th 22d	4th	Dec 1917-Oct 1939 1922-1940	Lineage to current 3d Brigade, 4th Infantry Division
9th Infantry Brigade	60th	61st	5th	Dec 1917-1921	Inactivated 1921
				1922-1939	8th Division 1927-1933; Lineage to current 1st Brigade, 5th Infantry Division
10th Infantry Brigade	6th 10th	11th	5th	Dec 1917-Oct 1939 1922-1939	Lineage to current 2d Brigade, 5th Infantry Division
11th Infantry Brigade	51st	52d	6th	Dec 1917-1921	Inactivated 1921
				1922-1939	9th Division 1927-1933 designation later used by Vietnam era brigade and current 1st Brigade, 6th Infantry Division

Designation	Regiments		Division	Service Dates	Remarks
12th Infantry Brigade	53d	54th	6th	Nov 1917-Oct 1939	Lineage to current 2d Brigade,
	2d	6th		1922-1939	6th Infantry Division
13th Infantry Brigade	55th	56th	7th	Dec 1917-1921	Inactivated 1921
	53d	54th		1922-1939	47th replaced 53d after 1927; Lineage to current 2d Brigade, 7th Infantry Division
14th Infantry Brigade	34th	64th	7th	Dec 1917-1940	Lineage to current 3d Brigade, 7th Infantry Division
	3d	17th		1922-1940	6th Division 1927-1933
15th Infantry Brigade	12th	62d	8th	Jan 1918-Feb 1919	Inactivated 1921; Lineage to current 2d Brigade, 8th Infantry Division
16th Infantry Brigade	8th	13th	8th	Dec 1917-Nov 1918	
	12th	34th		1923-1927 1933-1940	4th Infantry Division 1927-1933; Lineage to current 3d Brigade, 8th Infantry Division
17th Infantry Brigade	45th	67th	9th	Dec 1917-Feb 1919	
	36th	37th			Inactivated 1921; Lineage to current 2d Brigade, 9th Infantry Division
18th Infantry Brigade	46th	68th	9th	Jun 1918-Feb 1919	
	5th	13th		1923-1927 1933-1940	5th Infantry Division 1927-1933; Lineage to current 3d Brigade, 9th Infantry Division
19th Infantry Brigade	41st	69th	10th	Aug 1918-Feb 1919	
	14th	65th	Panama Canal	1919-1927	65th in Puerto Rico
20th Infantry Brigade	20th	70th	10th	Aug 1918-Feb 1919	
	33d	42d	Panama Canal	1919-1927	
21st Infantry Brigade	17th	71st	11th	Aug 1918-Feb 1919	
	19th	21st	Hawaiian	1921-1941	24th Infantry Division

Designation	Regiments		Division	Service Dates	Remarks
22d Infantry Brigade	63d	72d	11th	Sep 1918-Feb 1919	
	27th	35th	Hawaiian	1921-1941	25th Infantry Division
23d Infantry Brigade	36th	73d	12th	Aug 1918-Jan 1919	
	44th	57th	Philippine	1921-1941 (44th 1931-1942)	44th not manned and Division triangularized 1941; Brigade inactivated Apr 1941
24th Infantry Brigade	42d	74th	12th	Aug 1918-Jan 1919	
	45th	31st	Philippine	1921-1930	44th not manned
25th Infantry Brigade	1st	75th	13th	Aug 1918-Mar 1919	
26th Infantry Brigade	44th	76th	13th	Aug 1918-Mar 1919	
27th Infantry Brigade	10th	77th	14th	Jul 1918-Feb 1919	
28th Infantry Brigade	40th	78th	14th	Jul 1918-Feb 1919	
29th Infantry Brigade	43d	79th	15th	Sep 1918-Feb 1919	Currently designation used by HI ARNG brigade
30th Infantry Brigade	57th	80th	15th	Sep 1918-Feb 1919	
31st Infantry Brigade	21st	81st	16th	Sep 1918-Feb 1919	
32d Infantry Brigade	32d	82d	16th	Sep 1918-Feb 1919	
33d Infantry Brigade	5th	83d	17th	Sep 1918-Feb 1919	
34th Infantry Brigade	29th	84th	17th	Jan 1919-Feb 1919	
35th Infantry Brigade	19th	85th	18th	Aug 1918-Feb 1919	
36th Infantry Brigade	35th	86th	18th	Aug 1918-Feb 1919	
37th Infantry Brigade	14th	87th	19th	Oct 1918-Jan 1919	
38th Infantry Brigade	2d	88th	19th	Oct 1918-Jan 1919	
39th Infantry Brigade	48th	89th	20th	Oct 1918-Feb 1919	
40th Infantry Brigade	50th	90th	20th	Oct 1918-Feb 1919	

Designation	Regiments		Division	Service Dates	Remarks
51st Infantry Brigade	101st	102d	26th	Aug 1917-Apr 1919	MA, CT, RI, NH, VT, ME Army National Guard
	101st	182d		1921-1941	MA Army National Guard
	164th	182d		1941-1942 (Americal Division May 1942)	Officially became HHC, Americal Division, 1 May 1943; 132d Infantry arrived May 1942
52d Infantry Brigade	103d	104th	26th	Aug 1917-Apr 1919	MA, CT, RI, NH, VT, ME Army National Guard
	181st	104th		1923-1941	MA Army National Guard
53d Infantry Brigade	105th	106th	27th	Oct 1917-Apr 1919 1921-1940	NY Army National Guard
54th Infantry Brigade	107th	108th	27th	Oct 1917-Apr 1919 1921-1940	NY Army National Guard
55th Infantry Brigade	109th	110th	28th	Sep 1917-May 1919 1921-1941	PA Army National Guard; Designation used by current 55th Brigade, 28th Infantry Division
56th Infantry Brigade	111th	112th	28th	Sep 1917-May 1919 1921-1941	PA Army National Guard; Designation used by current 56th Brigade, 28th Infantry Division
57th Infantry Brigade	113th	114th	29th	Sep 1917-May 1919	NJ Army National Guard
	113th	114th	44th	1921-1941	NJ Army National Guard
58th Infantry Brigade	115th	116th	29th	Sep 1917-May 1919	MD, DE, VA Army National Guard
	115th	175th	29th	1923-1941	MD Army National Guard; Lineage linked to current 3d Brigade, 28th Infantry Division
59th Infantry Brigade	117th	118th	30th	Sep 1917-Apr 1919	NC, SC Army National Guard
	118th	121st		1921-1942	SC, GA Army National Guard
60th Infantry Brigade	119th 117th	120th 120th	30th	Sep 1917-Apr 1919 1921-1942	NC Army National Guard

Designation	Regiments		Division	Service Dates	Remarks
61st Infantry Brigade	121st	122d	31st	Aug 1917-Nov 1918	GA Army National Guard
	155th	156th		1921-1942	MS, LA Army National Guard
62d Infantry Brigade	123d	124th	31st	Aug 1917-Nov 1918	FL, AL Army National Guard
	124th	167th		1921-1942	
63d Infantry Brigade	125th	126th	32d	Sep 1917-May 1919	MI Army National Guard
				1921-1942	
64th Infantry Brigade	127th	128th	32d	Sep 1917-May 1919	WI Army National Guard
				1921-1942	
65th Infantry Brigade	129th	130th	33d	Aug 1917-May 1919	IL Army National Guard
				1921-1942	
66th Infantry Brigade	131st	132d	33d	Sep 1917-Jun 1919	IL Army National Guard; Designation linked to current 66th Brigade, 35th Infantry Division
				1921-1942	
67th Infantry Brigade	133d	134th	34th	Aug 1917-Feb 1919	IA, NE Army National Guard
		168th		1921-1942	IA Army National Guard; Designation linked to current 67th Brigade, 35th Infantry Division
68th Infantry Brigade	135th	136th	34th	Aug 1917-Feb 1919	MN Army National Guard
				1921-1942	
69th Infantry Brigade	137th	138th	35th	Aug 1917-May 1919	KS, MO Army National Guard
		134th		1921-1942	KS, NE Army National Guard; Designation used by KS Army National Guard Brigade 1963-1984
70th Infantry Brigade	139th	140th	35th	Sep 1917-May 1919	MO Army National Guard
	138th			1921-1942	
71st Infantry Brigade	141st	142d	36th	Sep 1917-Jun 1919	TX Army National Guard; Designation later used by TX Army National Guard sep airborne brigade
				1921-1942	

Designation	Regiments		Division	Service Dates	Remarks
72d Infantry Brigade	143d	144th	36th	Sep 1917-Jun 1919 1921-1942	TX Army National Guard; Lineage carried by 49th AD; Designation later used by TX Army National Guard sep Infantry brigade
73d Infantry Brigade	145th	146th 148th	37th	Sep 1917-Apr 1919 1921-1942	OH Army National Guard
74th Infantry Brigade	147th	148th 166th	37th	Sep 1917-Apr 1919 1921-1942 1921-1942	OH Army National Guard
75th Infantry Brigade	149th	150th	38th	Sep 1917-Nov 1918 1921-1942	KY Army National Guard
76th Infantry Brigade	151st	152d	38th	Sep 1917-Nov 1918 1921-1942	IN Army National Guard; Currently designation used by IN Army National Guard Brigade
77th Infantry Brigade	153d	154th	39th	Aug 1917-Jan 1919	Army National Guard
78th Infantry Brigade	155th	156th	39th	Aug 1917-Jan 1919	Army National Guard
79th Infantry Brigade	157th	158th	40th	Aug 1917-Apr 1919	CO, AZ Army National Guard
	159th	184th		1921-1942	CA Army National Guard
80th Infantry Brigade	159th 185th	160th	40th	Aug 1917-Apr 1919 1921-1942	CA Army National Guard
81st Infantry Brigade	161st	162d 163d	41st	Sep 1917-Mar 1919 1921-1942	 WA Army National Guard; Currently designation used by WA Army National Guard Brigade
82d Infantry Brigade	163d 162d	164th 186th	41st	Sep 1917-Feb 1919 1921-1942	 Organized Reserve Army National Guard
83d Infantry Brigade	165th	166th	42d	Aug 1917-Feb 1919	Army National Guard
84th Infantry Brigade	167th	168th	42d	Sep 1917-May 1919	Army National Guard
85th Infantry Brigade	102d	169th	43d	1921-1941	CT Army National Guard

Designation	Regiments		Division	Service Dates	Remarks
86th Infantry Brigade	103d	172d	43d	1922-1941	ME, VT Army National Guard; current designation used by 86th Brigade, 42d Division
87th Infantry Brigade	71st	174th	44th	1921-1941	NY Army National Guard
88th Infantry Brigade	116th	176th	29th	1921-1941	VA Army National Guard
89th Infantry Brigade	157th	158th	45th	1921-1941	CO, AZ Army National Guard
90th Infantry Brigade	179th	180th	45th	1921-1941	OK Army National Guard
92d Infantry Brigade	205th	206th	Sep	1924-1940	MN Army National Guard; brigade converted to 101st Coast Artillery Brigade, 1940 and 205th and 206th converted to 215th and 216th Cost Artillery Regiments
92d Infantry Brigade			Sep	1940-1942	PR Army National Guard; Currently designation used by PR Army National Guard Brigade
93d Infantry Brigade	10th (NY)	14th (NY)	Sep	1924-1940	NY Army National Guard; 10th later became new 106th in 27th Infantry Division; brigade headquarters converted to 71st FA Brigade 1940
151st Infantry Brigade	301st	302d	76th	Aug 1917-Feb 1919	National Army
	304th	385th		1921-1940	CT/RI Organized Reserve
152d Infantry Brigade	303d	304th	76th	Aug 1917-Feb 1919	National Army
	417th	418th		1921-1940	CT Organized Reserve
153d Infantry Brigade	305th	306th	77th	Aug 1917-May 1919	National Army; Lineage perpetuated by 2d Brigade, 77th Infantry Division
154th Infantry Brigade	307th	308th	77th	Aug 1917-May 1919	National Army; Lineage perpetuated by 3d Brigade, 77th Infantry Division
155th Infantry Brigade	309th	310th	78th	Aug 1917-Jun 1919	National Army; Lineage linked to current 2d Brigade, 82d Airborne Division

Designation	Regiments		Division	Service Dates	Remarks
156th Infantry Brigade	311th	312th	78th	Aug 1917-May 1919	National Army; Lineage linked to current 3d Brigade, 82d Airborne Division
157th Infantry Brigade	313th	314th	79th	Aug 1917-Jun 1919 1921-1942	National Army; PA Organized Reserve; Designation later used by USAR brigade and briefly in 1998-1999 by the current 5th Brigade, 87th Division
158th Infantry Brigade	315th	316th	79th	Aug 1917-Jun 1919	National Army; Lineage linked to current 2d Brigade, 81st Infantry Division; Designation briefly used in 1998 by current 2d Brigade, 87th Infantry Division
159th Infantry Brigade	317th	318th	80th	Aug 1917-Jun 1919	National Army; Lineage to current 2d Brigade, 101st Airborne Division
160th Infantry Brigade	319th	320th	80th	Aug 1917-May 1919	National Army; Lineage to current 3d Brigade, 101st Airborne Division
161st Infantry Brigade	321st	322d	81st	Aug 1917-Jun 1919	National Army; Linked to current 2d Brigade, 81st Infantry Division
162d Infantry Brigade	323d	324th	81st	Aug 1917-Jun 1919	National Army; Lineage linked to current 2d Brigade, 81st Infantry Division
163d Infantry Brigade	325th	326th	82d	Sep 1917-May 1919	National Army
164th Infantry Brigade	327th	328th	82d	Aug 1917-May 1919	National Army
165th Infantry Brigade	329th	330th	83d	Aug 1917-Feb 1919	National Army; Lineage linked to current 2d Brigade, 83d Infantry Division
166th Infantry Brigade	331st	332d	83d	Aug 1917-Feb 1919	National Army; Lineage linked to current 3d Brigade, 83d Infantry Division
167th Infantry Brigade	333d	334th	84th	Aug 1917-Feb 1919	National Army; Lineage to current 1st Brigade, 25th Infantry Division

Designation	Regiments		Division	Service Dates	Remarks
168th Infantry Brigade	335th	336th	84th	Aug 1917-Feb 1919	National Army; Lineage to current 2d Brigade, 25th Infantry Division
169th Infantry Brigade	337th	338th	85th	Aug 1917-Apr 1919	National Army; Lineage to current 1st Brigade, 24th Infantry Division
170th Infantry Brigade	339th	340th	85th	Aug 1917-Apr 1919	National Army; Lineage to current 2d Brigade, 24th Infantry Division
171th Infantry Brigade	341st	342d	86th	Sep 1917-Nov 1918	National Army; Designation used by AC Infantry Brigade 1963-1973
172th Infantry Brigade	343d	344th	86th	Aug 1917-Nov 1918	National Army; Designation used by AC Infantry Brigade 1963-1986; 1998-present
173th Infantry Brigade	345th	346th	87th	Aug 1917-Feb 1919	National Army; Designation used by AC airborne Brigade 1963-1972; 2002-present
174th Infantry Brigade	347th	348th	87th	Aug 1917-Feb 1919	National Army; Designation briefly used by current 2d Brigade, 78th Division 1998
175th Infantry Brigade	349th	350th	88th	Sep 1917-Jun 1919	National Army
176th Infantry Brigade	351st	352d	88th	Aug 1917-Jun 1919	National Army
177th Infantry Brigade	353d	354th	89th	Aug 1917-Jun 1919	National Army; Designation used by AC armored Brigade 1991-1994, 1998
178th Infantry Brigade	355th	356th	89th	Aug 1917-Jun 1919	National Army
179th Infantry Brigade	357th	358th	90th	Aug 1917-Jun 1919	National Army; Lineage linked to current 1st Brigade, 90th Division
180th Infantry Brigade	359th	360th	90th	Aug 1917-Jun 1919	National Army; Lineage linked to current 2d Brigade, 90th Division
181st Infantry rigade	361st	362d	91st	Aug 1917-Jun 1919	National Army
182d Infantry Brigade	363d	364th	91st	Sep 1917-Apr 1919	National Army
183th Infantry Brigade	365th	366th	92d	Nov 1917-Mar 1919	National Army

Designation	Regiments		Division	Service Dates	Remarks
184th Infantry Brigade	367th	368th	92d	Nov 1917-Mar 1919	National Army
185th Infantry Brigade	369th	370th	93d	Dec 1917-May 1918	NY, IL Army National Guard
186th Infantry Brigade	371st	372d	93d	Dec 1917-May 1918	National Army from Army National Guard units from DC, OH, CT, MD, MA, TN
187th Infantry Brigade	301st	302d	94th	1921-1940	MA Organized Reserve; Designation later used by USAR brigade 1963-1994
188th Infantry Brigade	376th	419th	94th	1921-1940	MA Organized Reserve; Designation used briefly in 1999 by 4th Brigade, 87th Division
189th Infantry Brigade	377th	378th	95th	1921-1940	OK Organized Reserve; Designation briefly used by current 4th Brigade, 78th Division 1998
190th Infantry Brigade	379th	380th	95th	1921-1940	OK Organized Reserve; Lineage to current 3d Brigade, 24th Infantry Division
191st Infantry Brigade	381st	382d	96th	1921-1942	Organized Reserve Organized Reserve; Designation used later by USAR brigade 1963-1968
192d Infantry Brigade	383d	384th	96th	Sep 1918-Dec 1918 1921-1942	National Army; Organized Reserve Organized Reserve
193d Infantry Brigade	303d	386th	97th	1921-1940	RI/ME Organized Reserve; Designation later used by AC brigade in Panama 1962-1994
194th Infantry Brigade	387th	388th	97th	Oct 1918-Dec 1918	National Army
	387th	388th		1921-1940	NH/VT Organized Reserve; Designation used by AC armored Brigade 1962-1995
195th Infantry Brigade	389th	390th	98th	1921-1940	NY Organized Reserve; Lineage to current 3d Brigade, 25th Infantry Division
196th Infantry Brigade	391st	392d	98th	1921-1940	NY Organized Reserve; Designation used by AC Infantry Brigade 1965-1972

Designation	Regiments		Division	Service Dates	Remarks
197th Infantry Brigade	393d	394th	99th	1921-1940	PA Organized Reserve; Designation used by AC Infantry Brigade 1962-1991
198th Infantry Brigade	395th	396th	99th	1921-1940	PA Organized Reserve; Designation used by AC Infantry Brigade 1967-1971
199th Infantry Brigade	397th	398th	100th	1921-1940	WV Organized Reserve; Designation used by AC Infantry Brigade 1966-1970; 1991-1992
200th Infantry Brigade	399th	400th	100th	1921-1940	KY Organized Reserve
201th Infantry Brigade	401st	402d	101st	1921-1940	WI Organized Reserve
202d Infantry Brigade	403d	404th	101st	1921-1940	WI Organized Reserve
203d Infantry Brigade	405th	406th	102d	1921-1940	AR, MO Organized Reserve; Lineage to current 2d Brigade, 102d Infantry Division
204th Infantry Brigade	407th	408th	102d	1921-1940	MO Organized Reserve; Lineage to current 3d Brigade, 102d Infantry Division
205th Infantry Brigade	409th	410th	103d	1921-1942	AZ, NM Organized Reserve; Designation used later by USAR brigade 1963-1994; Designation used briefly in 1998-1999 by current 4th Brigade, 70th Division
206th Infantry Brigade	411th	412th	103d	1921-1942	CO Organized Reserve
207th Infantry Brigade	413th	414th	104th	1921-1942	Organized Reserve, 104th Infantry Division Organized Reserve
208th Infantry Brigade	415th	416th	104th	1921-1942	WA, MT Organized Reserve

Appendix 4

US ARMY BRIGADES SINCE 1958

Divisional Brigades

Designation	Dates Active	Remarks	Other Designations	Nickname
1st Brigade, 1st ID	1917-1939 1943-1944 1958-1962 1964-present	Organized 1917; Disbanded 1939; Reconstituted 1943; Disbanded 1944; Reconstituted 1958; Inactivated 1962; Redesignated and reactivated 1964; Fort Riley 1964-1965; Vietnam 1965-1970; Fort Riley 1970-present; Deployed to SWA 1990-1991	1st Bde (1 ID) (1917-1921) 1st Infantry Bde (1 ID) (1921-1925) 1st Bde (1 ID) (1925-1936) 1st Infantry Bde (1 ID) (1936-1939) 1st Airborne Infantry Bde (1943-1944) 1st Infantry Bde (1958-1962)	Devil Brigade
2d Brigade, 1st ID	1917-1939 1943-1945 1958-1962 1964-present	Organized 1917; Inactivated 1940; Reconstituted 1943; Disbanded 1945; Reconstituted 1958; Inactivated 1962; Redesignated and reactivated 1964; Fort Riley 1964-1965; Vietnam 1965-1970; Fort Riley 1970-1996; Deployed to SWA 1990-1991;replaced 3d ID (Mech) at Schweinfurt, Germant 1996; Bosnia 1996-1997; Kosovo 1999-2000; Operation IRAQI FREEDOM 2004	2d Bde (1 ID) (1917-1921) 2d Infantry Bde (1 ID) (1921-1925) 2d Bde (1 ID) (1925-1936) 2d Infantry Bde (1 ID) (1936-1939) 2d Infantry Bde (1939-1940) 2d Airborne Infantry Bde (1943-1945) 2d Infantry Bde (1958-1962)	Dagger

Designation	Dates Active	Remarks	Other Designations	Nickname
3d Brigade, 1st ID	1964-1991 1996-present	HQs Troop, 1st Div (1917-1921) HQS and MP Co, 1st Div (1921-1942) HQS Co, 1st ID (1942-1960); Disbanded 1960; Reconsitituted 1963 and activated 1964; Fort Riley 1964-1965; Vietnam 1965-1970; Germany 1970-1991; Deployed to SWA 1990-1991 and served as Port Support Activity at Dammam; Between 1991 and 1996, 218th Infantry Bde (Mech), SC ARNG, served as roundout brigade; Vilseck, Germany 1996-present; Bosnia 1996-1997; Operation IRAQI FREEDOM 2004	1st ID (Forward) (1975-1991)	Iron
1st Brigade, 1st AD	1962-present	Organized as CCA, 1942; Redesignated 1946; Inactivated 1947; Reactivated and redesignated 1951; Redesignated 1962 at Fort Hood; Flag moved to Germany, 1971 (to replace 4th AD); Germany 1971-present; Did not deploy to SWA in 1990 with rest of division (replaced by 3d Bde, 3d ID; Bosnia 1995-1996: Kosovo 1999-2000: Operation IRAQI FREEDOM 2004	CCA, 1st AD (1942-1946) 3d Constabulary Regt (1946-1947) CCA, 1st AD (1951-1962)	Forerunners
2d Brigade, 1st AD	1962-present	Organized as CCB, 1942; Inactivated 1946; Reactivated 1951; Inactivated 1957; Redesignated and reactivated 1962 at Fort Hood; Flag moved to Germany, 1971 (to replace 4th AD); Germany 1971-present: Deployed to SWA 1990-1991: Bosnia 1995-1996; Kosovo 2000-2001: Operation IRAQI FREEDOM 2004	CCB, 1st AD (1942-1946; 1951-1957)	Iron Brigade

178

Designation	Dates Active	Remarks	Other Designations	Nickname
3d Brigade, 1st AD	1962-1995 1996-present	Organized as Reserve Command, 1944; Inactivated 1946; Reactivated 1951; Redesignated CCC, 1954; Inactivated 1957; Redesignated and reactivated 1962 at Fort Hood; Flag moved to Germany, 1971 (to replace 4th AD); Deployed to SWA 1990-1991; Fort Lewis, 1994-1995 Inactivated 1995; Reactivated 1996 at Fort Riley; Operation IRAQI FREEDOM 2003-2004	Reserve Command, 1st AD (1944-1946) CCR, 1st AD (1951-1954) CCC, 1st AD (1954-1957)	Bulldogs
1st Brigade, 1st CD	1918-1949 1963-present	Organized 1917; Activated 1918; Demobilized 1919; Reconstituted 1921; Inactivated 1949; Redesignated 1949 and reactivated; Inactivated 1951 and disbanded; Reconstituted and redesignated and reactivated 1963; Korea 1963-1965; Flag moved from Korea to Fort Benning 1965, replaced by 2d ID; Airmobile bde 1965-1971; Vietnam 1965-1971; Replaced 1st AD elements at Fort Hood in 1971 (1st AD replaced 4th AD in Germany); Fort Hood, 1971-present: Armored bde in TriCap division 1971-1974; Deployed to SWA 1990-1991; Operation IRAQI FREEDOM 2004	1st Cavalry Bde (15 CD) (1918-19) 1st Cavalry Bde (1 CD) (1921-1949) 1st Constabulary Bde (1949-1951) 1st Bde, 1 CD (1963-present)	Iron Horse

Designation	Dates Active	Remarks	Other Designations	Nickname
2d Brigade, 1st CD 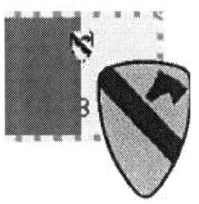	1918-1949 1963-present	Organized 1917; Activated 1918; Demobilized 1919; Reconstituted 1921; Inactivated 1949; Redesignated 1949 and reactivated; Inactivated 1951 and disbanded; Reconstituted and redesignated and reactivated 1963 in Korea; Flag shifted to Fort Benning 1965; Troops came from 2d Bde, 2d ID; Brigade airmobile-airborne 1965-1968; airmobile Bde 1968-1971:Vietnam 1965-1971; Replaced 1st AD elements at Fort Hood in 1971 (1st AD replaced 4th AD in Germany); Fort Hood, 1971-present; Air Cavalry Combat Bde 1971-1974; Assests used to form 6th ACCB 1974; deployed to SWA 1990-1991; Operation IRAQI FREEDOM 2004	2d Cavalry Bde (15 CD) (1918-19) 2d Cavalry Bde (1 CD) (1921-1949) 2d Constabulary Bde (1949-1951)	Black Jack
3d Brigade, 1st CD	1917-1919 1940-1942 1963-1980 1991-present	Organized 1917; Activated 1918; Demobilized 1919; Reconstituted 1921 but not activated until 1940; Redesignated 1942 and inactivated 1945; Converted and redesignated and reactivated 1963; Vietnam 1965-1972; served as separate brigade in RVN, 1971-1972; Fort Hood 1972-1990, 1991-present; airmobile bde 1972-1974; 155th Armd Bde (MS ARNG) roundout brigade 1984-1991; 1st Bde, 2d AD redes 3d Bde, 1st CD, 1991; [see next column]	3d Cavalry Bde (15 CD) (1917-1918) 3d Cavalry Bde (1918-19) 3d Cavalry Bde (2 CD) (1940-1942) HHC, 9th AD Trains (1942-1945) 3d Bde, 1 CD (1963-present) separate brigade in Vietnam (1971-1972) [from left] Operation IRAQI FREEDOM 2004	Grey Wolf

Designation	Dates Active	Remarks	Other Designations	Nickname
4th Brigade, 1st CD	1971-1972	Organized at Fort Hood to fill out the 1st Cavalry Div while the 3d Bde remained in Vietnam; Replaced 1st AD elements at Fort Hood in 1971 (1st AD replaced 4th AD in Germany); Airmobile bde inTriCap Division 1971-1972: Inactivated upon 3d Bde's return		
1st Brigade, 2d AD	1963-1991 1992-1996	Redesignation of CC A under ROAD reorganization in 1963; Fort Hood 1963-1991; Deployed to SAW with 1st Cavalry Div 1990; Fought with MARCENT 1991; Fort Polk, 1992-1996 (redesignation of 1st Bde, 5th ID (Mech); Replaced at Fort Polk by 2d ACR	CCA, 2d AD (1942-1963)	Tiger Brigade
2d Brigade, 2d AD	1963-1990 1992-1996	Redesignation of CC B under ROAD reorganization in 1963; Fort Hood 1963-1991; Inactivated Sep 90 while other two brigades were going to SWA; Reactivated at Fort Polk by redesignation of 2d Bde, 5th ID (Mech), 1992; Fork Polk 1992-1996	CCB, 2d AD (1942-1963)	St. Lo Brigade
3d Brigade, 2d AD	1963-1992	Garrisoned in Garlstedt, Germany 1979-1992; Deployed to SWA with the 1st ID (Mech) 1990-1991; Inactivated in Germany 1992; Replaced by 256th Infantry Bde (Mech), LA ARNG roundout brigade 1994-1997	HQs, 41st Armored Infantry (1942-1946) CCR, 2d AD (1946-1949) Bde 75 (1975) 2d AD Forward (1976-1991)	Blackheart

181

Designation	Dates Active	Remarks	Other Designations	Nickname
4th Brigade, 2d AD	1975-1979	Fort Hood; Replaced Bde 75; Inactivated upon PCS of 3d Bde to Germany	3d Armor Group 1944-1947; 1954-1955)	
1st Brigade, 2d ID	1963-present	Redesignated from former HQS Co, 2d ID under ROAD; Fort Benning 1963-1965; Korea, 1965-present; Replaced 1st Cavalry Division elements in Korea		Iron
2d Brigade, 2d ID	1963-present	Redesignated under ROAD from dormant square division brigade; Fort Benning 1963-1965; Bde attached to 11th Air Assault Division 1964-1965; Korea 1965-present; Replaced 1st Cavalry Division elements in Korea	4th Infantry Bde (1920-1939)	Strike Force
3d Brigade, 2d ID	1963-1992 1995-present	Redesignated under ROAD from dormant square division brigade; Korea 1965-1992; Replaced 1st Cavalry Division elements in Korea; 81st Infantry Bde (Mech), WA ARNG, served as roundout brigade, 1992-1995; Reactivated 1995 at Fort Lewis; Stryker Bde 1999-present	1st Provisional Bde (1917) 3d Infantry Bde (1917-1939)	Arrowhead Brigade

Designation	Dates Active	Remarks	Other Designations	Nickname
1st Brigade, 3d AD	1963-1991	Germany 1963-1990; Deployed to SWA 1990-1991; Germany 1991; remainder of division inactivated 1992	CCA, 3d AD (1942-1945; 47-1963)	
2d Brigade, 3d AD	1963-1992	Germany 1963-1990; Deployed to SWA 1990-1991; Germany 1991-1992	HQS, 36th Armored Infantry (1942-1945) Reserve Command, 3d AD (1947-1954) Combat Command C, 3d AD (1954-1963)	
3d Brigade, 3d AD	1963-1992	Germany 1963-1990; Deployed to SWA 1990-1991; Germany 1991-1992	CCA, 3d AD (1942-1945; 47-1963)	
1st Brigade, 3d ID	1963-present	Redesignated from former HQS Co, 3d ID under ROAD; Germany 1963-1996; Fort Stewart 1996-present; Replaced 24th ID (Mech) 1996; Operation IRAQI FREEDOM 2003		Raider

Designation	Dates Active	Remarks	Other Designations	Nickname
2d Brigade, 3d ID	1963-1994 1996-present	Redesignated under ROAD from dormant square division brigade; Germany 1963-1994; Fort Stewart, 1996-present: Replaced 24th ID (Mech) 1996; Operation IRAQI FREEDOM 2003	5th Infantry Bde (1917-1939)	Spartan
3d Brigade, 3d ID	1963-present	Redesignated under ROAD from dormant square division brigade; Germany 1963-1990, 1991-1996 deployed to SWA with 1st AD, 1990-1991; Fort Stewart 1996-present: Replaced 24th ID (Mech) 1996; Operation IRAQI FREEDOM 2003	6th Infantry Bde (1917-1939)	Hammer
1st Brigade, 4th AD	1963-1971	Germany; Replaced by 1st AD	CCA, 4th AD (1942-1946; 1954-1963) 2d Constabulary Bde (1946-1949)	
2d Brigade, 4th AD	1963-1971	Germany; Replaced by 1st AD	CCB, 4th AD (1942-1946; 1954-1963) 3d Constabulary Bde (1946-1947)	
3d Brigade, 4th AD	1963-1971	Germany; Replaced by 1st AD	Reserve Command, 4th AD (1943-1946) CC C, 4th AD 1954-1963)	

Designation	Dates Active	Remarks	Other Designations	Nickname
1st Brigade, 4th ID	1963-1995 1996-present	Created from former HQS Co, 4th ID; Fort Lewis 1963-1966; Vietnam, 1966-1970; Fort Carson (where replaced 5th ID (M); 1970-1995; Fort Hood 1996-present (replaced 2d AD); Operation IRAQI FREEDOM 2003-2004		
2d Brigade, 4th ID	1963-1989 1996-present	Fort Lewis 1963-1966; Vietnam, 1966-1970; Fort Carson (where replaced 5th ID (M); 1970-1989; Replaced by r oundout brigade 116th Cavalry Bde (ID ARNG); Fort Hood, 1996-present (replaced 2d AD); Operation IRAQI FREEDOM 2003-2004	7th Infantry Bde (1917-1940)	
3d Brigade, 4th ID	1963-1970 1970-present	Fort Lewis 1963-1966; Vietnam, 1966-1970: 1967 swapped designation with 3d Bde, 25th ID; 1970 redeployed to Fort Lewis where inactivated; Reactivated at Fort Carson 1970; Brigade remained at Fort Carson while rest of division shifted to Fort Hood in 1996: Operation IRAQI FREEDOM 2003-2004	8th Infantry Bde (1917-1940)	
4th Brigade, 4th ID	1975-1984 Jan-Mar 1996	Activated at Fort Carson in 1975 as the 4th ID's contribution to Bde 76, a temporary duty brigade for service in Germany; Deployed to Germany 1976 and made permanent in 1977-stationed at Wiesbaden AB and attached to 8th ID (M); Fort Carson 1996	Bde 76 (1975-1977)	

Designation	Dates Active	Remarks	Other Designations	Nickname
1st Brigade, 5th ID	1962-1972 1974-1997	Fort Carson 1962-1968; Vietnam 1968-1971; 69th Infantry Bde (Mech), KS ARNG, mobilized to replace brigade at Carson (1968-1969); Fort Carson 1971; Fort Polk 1974-1997; Replaced at Fort Polk by 2d AD	9th Infantry Bde (1917-1940)	
2d Brigade, 5th ID	1962-1970 1977-1992	Created by conversion of Pentomic 2d Infantry Bde at Fort Devens; Fort Devens 1962-1965; Replaced at Fort Devens by 196th Infantry Bde; Fort Carson 1965-1970; Replaced at Fort Polk by 2d AD	10th Infantry Bde (1917-1939)	
3d Brigade, 5th ID	1962-1970	Fort Carson 1962-1970; Replaced by roundout brigade 256th Infantry Bde (Mech), LA ARNG 1975-1992	HQS Co, 5th ID	
4th Brigade, 5th ID	1969-1970	Fort Carson 1969-1970; organized to replace 69th Infantry Bde (Mech), KS ARNG, which was filling in for 1st Bde which was in Vietnam and had demobilized	HQS Co, 5th ID	
1st Brigade, 6th ID	1985-1996	Alaska, 1985-1996; 11th Infantry Bde fought in Vietnam separately and as part of the American Div (see sep listing); Roundout to 10th Mountain Div 1994-1996; Redesignated 172d Infantry Bde 1996	11th Infantry Bde (1917-1939) 11th Infantry Bde (Light) (1966-1971)	

Designation	Dates Active	Remarks	Other Designations	Nickname
2d Brigade, 6th ID	1967-1968 1986-1994	Ft Campbell, 1967-1968; Alaska 1986-1994	12th Infantry Bde (1917-1939)	
3d Brigade, 6th ID	1967-1968 1986-1994	Ft Campbell, 1967-1968; Alaska 1986-1994	HQS Co, 6th ID	
4th Brigade, 6th ID	1967-1968	Hawaii, 1967-1968		
1st Brigade, 7th ID	1963-1971 1974-1995	Korea 1963-1971; Inactivated at Fort Lewis 1971; Fort Ord 1974-1994; Fort Lewis 1994-1995; Replaced at Fort Lewis by 1st Bde, 25th ID 1995	HQS Co, 7th ID	
2d Brigade, 7th ID	1963-1971 1974-1993	Korea 1963-1971; Inactivated at Fort Lewis 1971; Fort Ord 1974-1993	13th Infantry Bde (1917- 1940)	

Designation	Dates Active	Remarks	Other Designations	Nickname
3d Brigade, 7th ID	1984-1993	Korea 1963-1971; Inactivated at Fort Lewis 1971; Replaced by roundout brigade 41st Infantry Bde (OR ARNG) 1977-1985; Fort Ord 1984-1993	14th Infantry Bde (1917-1940)	
1st Brigade, 8th ID	1963-1992	Mannheim, Germany; Replaced by 1st AD	HQS Co, 8th ID	
2d Brigade, 8th ID	1963-1992	Baumholder, Germany; Replaced by 1st AD	15th Infantry Bde (1917-1940)	
3d Brigade, 8th ID	1963-1992	Mainz, Germany; Replaced by 1st AD; airborne-mechanized bde from 1963 to 1973 with two airborne mechanized battalions and an airborne qualified slice assigned from division	16th Infantry Bde (1917-1940)	
1st Brigade, 9th ID	1966-1969 1972-1990	Ft Riley 1966; Vietnam 1966-1969; Inactivated in Hawaii 1969; Fort Lewis 1972-1988; HTMD 1984; motorized 1986	HQS Co, 9th ID	

188

Designation	Dates Active	Remarks	Other Designations	Nickname
2d Brigade, 9th ID	1966-1969 1972-1988	Ft Riley 1966; Vietnam 1966-1969; Mobile Riverine Force 1966-1969: Inactivated in Hawaii 1969; Fort Lewis 1972-1988; HTMD 1984; Motorized 1986; Replaced by rondout brigade 81st Infantry Bde (Mech) WA ARNG 1989-1991	15th Infantry Bde (1917) 17th Infantry Bde (1917-1940)	
3d Brigade, 9th ID	1966-1970 1973-1991	Ft Riley 1966; Vietnam 1966-1970; Separate brigade in Vietnam, 1969-1970, under OPCON of 25th ID; Inactivated 1970, Fort Lewis; Fort Lewis 1973-1991; HTMD 1984; Motorized 1986	18th Infantry Bde (1918-1940)	
1st Brigade, 10th Mountain Div	1986-present	Ft Drum; Somalia 1992-1994; Haiti 1994-1995; Afghanistan 2001-2002, 2003-2004	HQS Co, 10th ID	
2d Brigade, 10th Mountain Div	1985-present	Fort Benning 1985-1988; Fort Drum 1988-present; Afghanistan 2001-2002, 2003: Operation IRAQI FREEDOM 2004-2005		

Designation	Dates Active	Remarks	Other Designations	Nickname
1st Brigade, 11th AAslt Div	1963-1965	Ft Benning; Converted to 1st Cavalry Div (Airmobile) elements		

Designation	Dates Active	Remarks	Other Designations	Nickname
2d Brigade, 11th AAslt Div	1963-1965	Ft Benning; Converted to 1st Cavalry Div (Airmobile) elements		

Designation	Dates Active	Remarks	Other Designations	Nickname
3d Brigade, 11th AAslt Div	1964-1965	Ft Benning; Converted to 1st Cavalry Div (Airmobile) elements		

Designation	Dates Active	Remarks	Other Designations	Nickname
1st Brigade, 24th ID	1963-1970 1974-1996	Germany 1963-1968; Fort Riley 1968-1970; Fort Stewart, 1974-1996; Deployed to SWA 1990-1991; Replaced by 3d ID (M), 1996	169th Infantry Bde (85 Div) (1921-1942)	

Designation	Dates Active	Remarks	Other Designations	Nickname
2d Brigade, 24th ID	1963-1970	Germany 1963-1968; Fort Riley 1968-1970; Fort Stewart, 1974-1996; Deployed to SWA 1990-1991; Replaced by 3d ID (M), 1996	170th Infantry Bde (85 Div) (1921-1942)	

190

Designation	Dates Active	Remarks	Other Designations	Nickname
3d Brigade, 24th ID	1963-1970 1991-1996	Germany 1963-1970; Replaced by roundout 48th Infantry Bde (Mech) GA ARNG 1975-1991; Fort Benning 1991-1996; Replaced 197th Infantry Bde, 1991; Replaced by 3d ID, 1996	190th Infantry Bde (95 Div) (1921-1942)	
1st Brigade, 25th ID	1963-present	Schofield Barracks 1963-1966; Vietnam 1966-1970; Schofield Barracks 1970-1971; Fort Lewis 1995-present; Replaced 1st Bde, 7th ID 1995; Stryker Bde 1999-present	167th Infantry Bde (84 Div) (1921-1942)	Lancers
2d Brigade, 25th ID	1963-present	Schofield Barracks 1963-1966; Vietnam 1966-1971; Separate brigade in Vietnam 1970-1972; Schofield Barracks 1971-present; Haiti 1995: announced as future Stryker Bde, 2003; Operation IRAQI FREEDOM 2004	168th Infantry Bde (84 Div) (1921-1942)	Warrior
3d Brigade, 25th ID	1963-1972 1985-present	Schofield Barracks 1963-1966; Vietnam 1966-1970; 1967-19 swapped designation with 3d Bde, 4th ID; Schofield Barracks 1970-1972; Roundout 29th Infantry Bde (HI ARNG) 1973-1985; Schofield barracks 1985-present: Haiti 1995; Afghanistan 2004	195th Infantry Bde (98 Div) (1921-1942)	Bronco
4th Brigade, 25th ID	1969-1970	Schofield Barracks 1969-1970; Replaced 2d Bde still in Vietnam		

Designation	Dates Active	Remarks	Other Designations	Nickname
1st Brigade, 26th ID	1963-1988	MA ARNG; Dorchester 1963-1967; Waltham 1967-1975; Lexington 1975-1988; Replaced by 86th Bde in 1988	HQS, 1st BG, 101st Inf	
43d Brigade, 26th ID	1967-1993	CT ARNG; former CT portion of 43d ID	HQs, 43d ID	
3d Brigade, 26th ID	1963-1993	MA ARNG; Springfield 1963-1974; Holyoke 1974-1976; Westover AFB 1976-1993; became 26th Bde, 29th ID, 1993	HQS, 1st BG, 104th Inf	
1st Brigade, 27th AD	1963-1968	NY ARNG; Division amalgamated into 27th Bde, 50th AD 1968	CCA, 27th AD (1955-1963)	
2d Brigade, 27th AD	1963-1968	NY ARNG; Division amalgamated into 27th Bde	CCB, 27th AD (1955-1963)	

Designation	Dates Active	Remarks	Other Designations	Nickname
3d Brigade, 27th AD	1963-1968	NY ARNG; Division amalgamated into 27th Bde	CCC, 27th AD (1955-1963)	
2d Brigade, 28th ID (Mech)	1963-1978 1975-present	PA ARNG; Washington, PA	HHC, 1st BG,110th Inf 689th MP Co (1968-199) 408th Gen SupportCo (1969-1975)	
55th Brigade, 28th ID (Mech)	1963-present	PA ARNG; Created from 109th Inf elements; New 3d Bde, 28th ID created from MD ARNG elements 1968-1971 and redesignated 58th Bde, 28th ID 1971-1975; Scranton, PA	3d Bde, 28th ID (1963-1968)	
56th Brigade, 28th ID (Mech)	1963-1968 1975-present	PA ARNG; Replaced in 28th ID by 116th Bde (VA ARNG) 1968-1975; designated as future Stryker Bde 2001; Philadelphia, PA; Kosovo 2003-2004	1st Bde, 28th ID (1963-1968) 56th Bde, 42d ID (1968-1975)	Independence
1st Brigade, 29th ID	1963-1968 1986-present	VA ARNG; Staunton, VA	116th Infantry Bde (1975-1986)	

Designation	Dates Active	Remarks	Other Designations	Nickname
2d Brigade, 29th ID	1963-1968 1985-1993	VA ARNG; Replaced by 26th Bde (MA ARNG) 1993	116th Bde, 28th ID (1968-1975)	
3d Brigade, 29th ID	1963-1968 1985-present	MD ARNG; Baltimore, MD 1963-1968; Pikeville, MD 1985-present	3d Bde, 28th ID (1968-1971) 58th Bde, 28th ID (1971-1975) 58th Infantry Bde (1975-1985)	
26th Brigade, 29th ID	1993-present	MA ARNG; Springfield, MA	Former 3d Bde, 26th ID and elements of HQs, 26th ID	Yankee
1st Brigade, 30th AD	1963-1973	MS ARNG; Converted to 155th Armored Bde; Tupelo	108th ACR	
2d Brigade, 30th AD	1963-1973	TN ARNG; Amalgamated into 30th Armored Bde 1973	CCB, 30th AD (1955-1963)	

Designation	Dates Active	Remarks	Other Designations	Nickname
3d Brigade, 30th AD 	1963-1973	TN ARNG; Amalgamated into 30th Armored Bde 1973	CCC, 30th AD (1955-1963)	
31st Brigade, 30th AD 	1968-1973	AL ARNG; Became 31st Armored Bde 1973; Tuscaloosa, AL	2d Bde, 31st ID (1963-1968)	
1st Brigade, 30th ID 	1963-1973	NC ARNG; 3d and 1st Bdes merged 1968 as new 1st Bde; Clinton, NC; Amalgamated into 30th Infantry Bde 1973	Co B, 1st BG, 119th Inf 3d Bde, 30th ID (1963-1968)	
2d Brigade, 30th ID 	1963-1973	AL ARNG; Tuscaloosa, AL		
3d Brigade, 30th ID 	1968-1973	GA ARNG; Macon; Converted to 48th Armored Bde 1973	1st Bde, 48th AD (1963-1968)	

Designation	Dates Active	Remarks	Other Designations	Nickname
1st Brigade, 31st ID	1963-1968	AL/MS ARNG		

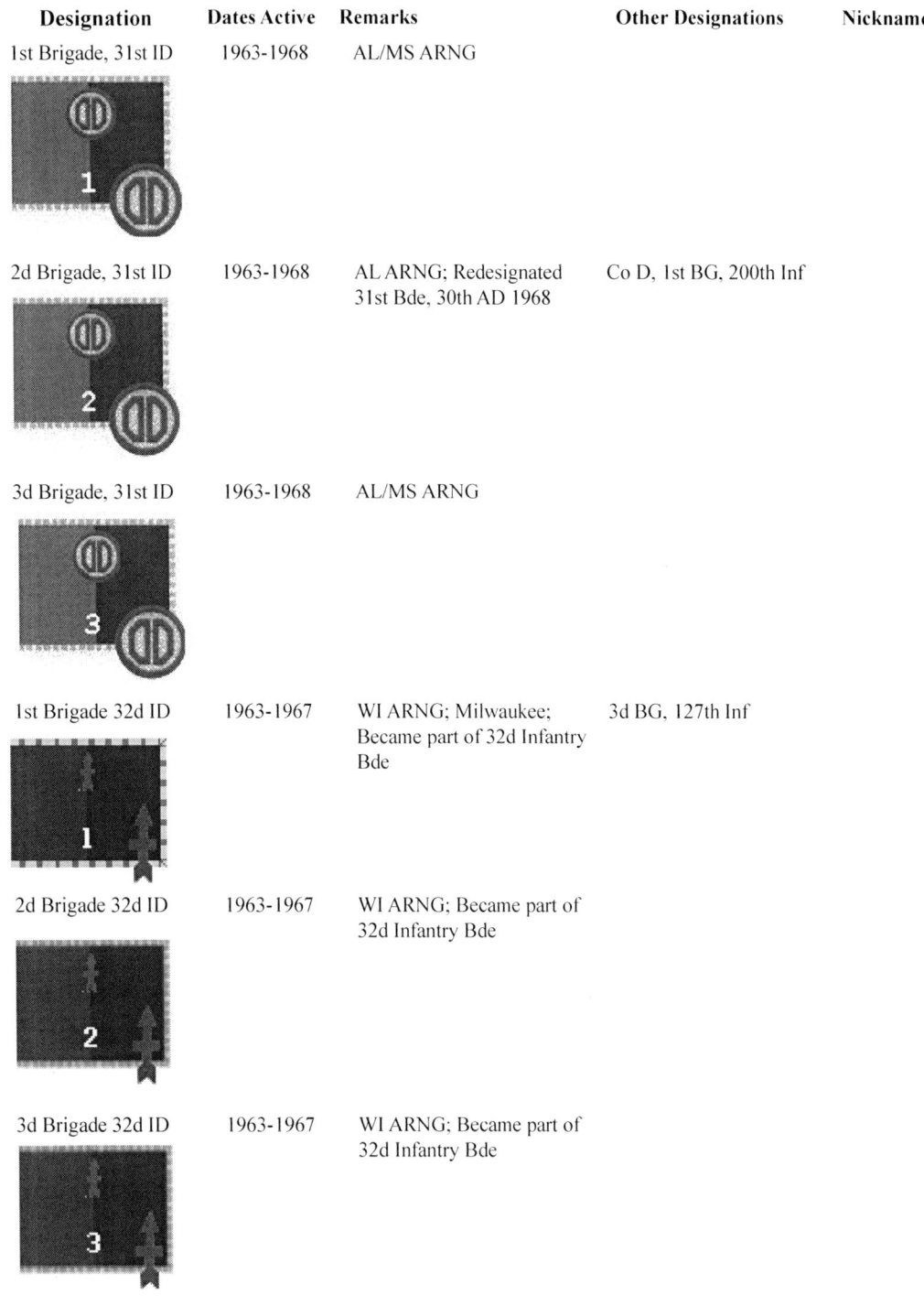

2d Brigade, 31st ID	1963-1968	AL ARNG; Redesignated 31st Bde, 30th AD 1968	Co D, 1st BG, 200th Inf	
3d Brigade, 31st ID	1963-1968	AL/MS ARNG		
1st Brigade 32d ID	1963-1967	WI ARNG; Milwaukee; Became part of 32d Infantry Bde	3d BG, 127th Inf	
2d Brigade 32d ID	1963-1967	WI ARNG; Became part of 32d Infantry Bde		
3d Brigade 32d ID	1963-1967	WI ARNG; Became part of 32d Infantry Bde		

Designation	Dates Active	Remarks	Other Designations	Nickname
1st Brigade 33d ID	1963-1968	IL ARNG; Became part of 33d Infantry Bde		
2d Brigade 33d ID	1963-1968	IL ARNG; Became part of 33d Infantry Bde		
3d Brigade 33d ID	1963-1968	IL ARNG; Became part of 33d Infantry Bde	1st BG, 131st Inf	
1st Brigade, 34th ID	1991-present	MN ARNG; Stillwater, MN; Replaced 47th ID: Kosovo 2004	1st Bde, 47th ID (1968-1991)	
2d Brigade, 34th ID	1991-present	IA ARNG	34th Bde, 47th ID (1963-1991)	

Designation	Dates Active	Remarks	Other Designations	Nickname
32d Brigade, 34th ID	1991-2001	WI ARNG; designation from former 32d ID; became seperate light inf bde 2001	HQs, 32d ID 32d Infantry Bde (1967-1997)	Red Arrow
66th Brigade, 35th ID	1997-present	IL ARNG; mobilized 2002 and deployed to Germany	66th Bde, 47th ID (1968-1991)	
67th Brigade, 35th ID	1985-2002	NE ARNG; converted to 67th Area Support Group, 2003	67th Infantry Bde (1964-1985)	Nebraska Brigade
149th Brigade, 35th ID	1985-present	KY/AL ARNG; Louisville, KY; AL portion added 2002 from former 31st Armored Bde; designation comes from old 149th Infantry	149th Armored Bde (1980-1985)	Louisville Legion
2d Brigade, 38th ID	1977-present	IN ARNG; Kokomo, IN	1st Bn, 150th FA	

Designation	Dates Active	Remarks	Other Designations	Nickname
37th Brigade, 38th ID	1968-1977 1994-present	OH ARNG; Columbus 1968-1977; North Canton 1994-present; designation from former 37th ID; projected Kosovo deployment 2005	HQS, 37th ID 73d Bde, 38th ID (1968-1977) 73d Infantry Bde (1977-1992) 37th Bde, 28th ID (1992-1994)	
46th Brigade, 38th ID	1968-present	MI ARNG; Wyoming, MI; designation from former 46th ID	2d Bde, 46th ID (1963-1968)	
1st Brigade, 39th ID	1963-1967	LA ARNG; Converted to 256th Infantry Bde 1967		
2d Brigade, 39th ID	1963-1967	LA/AR ARNG; Converted to 39th Infantry Bde		
3d Brigade, 39th ID	1963-1967	LA/AR ARNG; Converted to 39th Infantry Bde		

Designation	Dates Active	Remarks	Other Designations	Nickname
1st Brigade, 40th AD 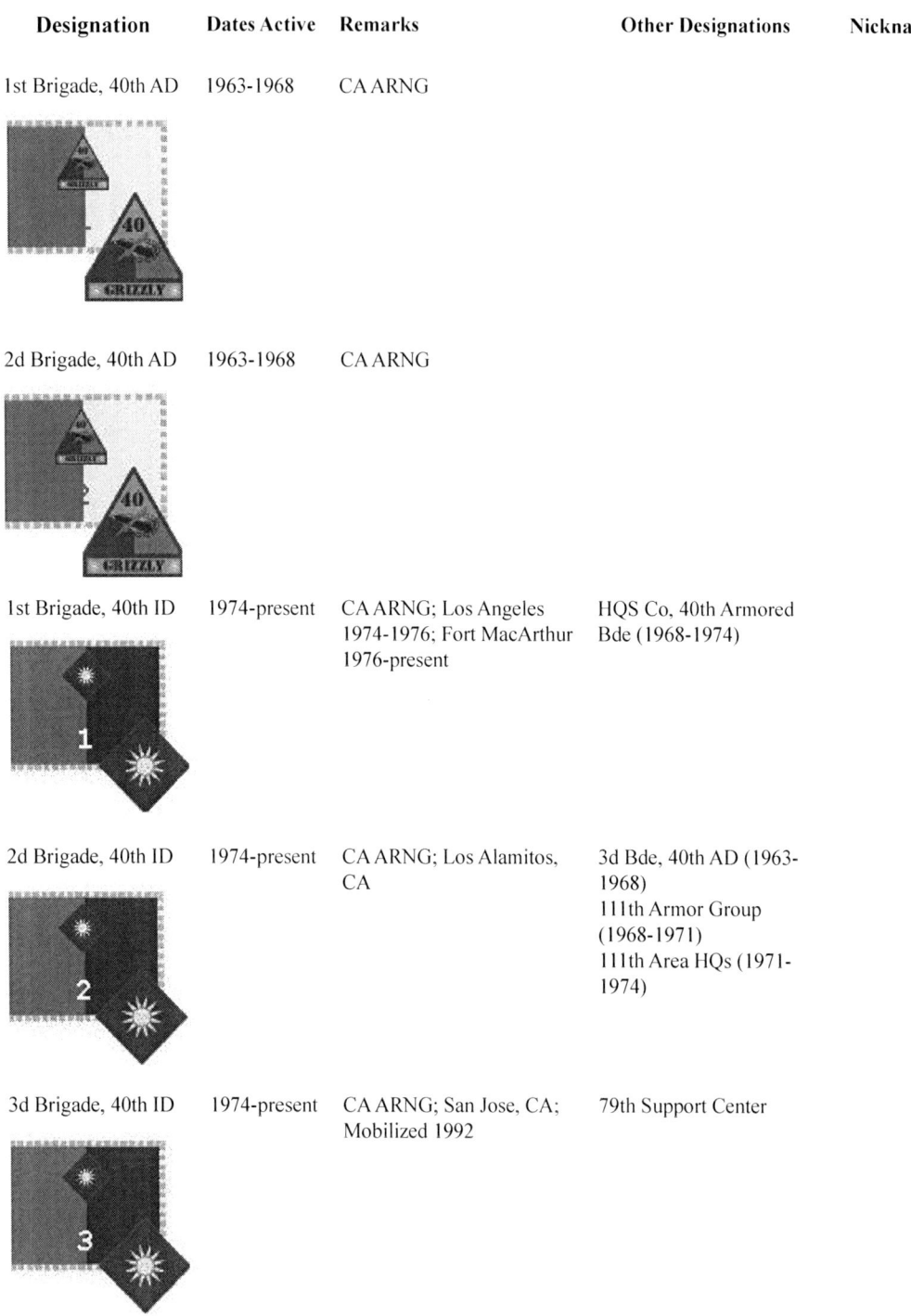	1963-1968	CA ARNG		
2d Brigade, 40th AD	1963-1968	CA ARNG		
1st Brigade, 40th ID	1974-present	CA ARNG; Los Angeles 1974-1976; Fort MacArthur 1976-present	HQS Co, 40th Armored Bde (1968-1974)	
2d Brigade, 40th ID	1974-present	CA ARNG; Los Alamitos, CA	3d Bde, 40th AD (1963-1968) 111th Armor Group (1968-1971) 111th Area HQs (1971-1974)	
3d Brigade, 40th ID	1974-present	CA ARNG; San Jose, CA; Mobilized 1992	79th Support Center	

Designation	Dates Active	Remarks	Other Designations	Nickname
1st Brigade, 41st ID	1963-1965	OR ARNG; Became 41st Infantry Bde		
2d Brigade, 41st ID	1963-1968	WA ARNG		
3d Brigade, 41st ID	1963-1968	WA ARNG		
3d Brigade, 42d ID	1986-present	NY ARNG; Buffalo, NY; Replaced 27th Bde which became roundout to 10th Mtn Div		
50th Brigade, 42d ID	1993-present	NJ ARNG; Fort Dix; designation from former 50th AD	HQS, 50th Armored DIv	Jersey Blues

Designation	Dates Active	Remarks	Other Designations	Nickname
86th Brigade, 42d ID	1993-present	VT ARNG; Berlin, VT; designation from former 86th Infantry Bde	86th Infantry Bde (1963-1964) 86th Armored Bde (1964-1968) 86th Bde, 50th AD (1968-1988) 86th Bde, 26th ID (1988-1993)	Vermont Brigade
1st Brigade, 45th ID	1963-1968	OK ARNG		
2d Brigade, 45th ID	1963-1968	OK ARNG		
3d Brigade, 45th ID	1963-1968	OK ARNG		
1st Brigade, 46th ID	1963-1968	MI ARNG		

Designation	Dates Active	Remarks	Other Designations	Nickname
2d Brigade, 46th ID	1963-1968	MI ARNG; Became 46th Bde, 38th ID; Grand Rapids 1963-1965; Wyoming 1965-1968		
3d Brigade, 46th ID	1963-1968	MI ARNG		
1st Brigade, 47th ID	1968-1991	MN ARNG	1st Bn, 135th Inf	
34th Brigade, 47th ID	1968-1991	IA ARNG		Red Bull
66th Brigade, 47th ID	1968-1991	IL ARNG	2d Bn, 130th Inf	

Designation	Dates Active	Remarks	Other Designations	Nickname
1st Brigade, 48th AD	1963-1968	GA ARNG; Became 3d Bde, 30th ID 1968	CCB, 48th AD (1955-1963)	
2d Brigade, 48th AD	1963-1968	GA ARNG		
3d Brigade, 48th AD	1963-1968	GA ARNG		
1st Brigade, 49th AD	1973-1992	TX ARNG; San Antonio	1st Bde, 36th ID (1963-1965) 36th Infantry Bde (1965-1973)	Texas Brigade
2d Brigade, 49th AD	1963-1968 1973-present	TX ARNG; Fort Worth	CCA, 49th AD (1955-1963) 49th Armor Group (1968-1971) 49th Armored Bde (1971-1973)	

204

Designation	Dates Active	Remarks	Other Designations	Nickname
3d Brigade, 49th AD	1963-1968 1973-present	TX ARNG; Dallas	HQS Infantry Bde (1968-1973)	
36th Brigade, 49th AD	1992-present	TX ARNG; Houston; designation from former 36th ID	71st Airborne Bde (1968-1973) 36th Airborne Bde (1973-1980) 36th Bde, 50th AD (1988-1992)	Arrowhead
1st Brigade, 50th AD	1968-1993	NJ ARNG; Woodbridge, NJ; Became 50th Bde, 42d ID		
2d Brigade, 50th AD	1975-1993	NJ ARNG; Cherry Hill, NJ; 86th Bde was division's 3d Bde 1968-1988; 36th Bde 1988-1992		
1st Brigade, 63d ID	1963-1965	USAR; Bell, CA	HQS Co, 63d ID	

Designation	Dates Active	Remarks	Other Designations	Nickname
2d Brigade, 63d ID	1963-1965	USAR; Pasadena, CA	181st Bde (1921-1942)	
3d Brigade, 63d ID	1963-1965	USAR; Los Angeles, CA	182d Bde (1921-1942)	
1st Brigade, 70th Div	1968-1995	USAR; Fraser, MI 1968-1980; Livonia, MI 1980-1990; Inkster, MI 1990-1995; Mobilized 1991	HQS Co, 70th ID	
2d Brigade, 70th Div	1968-1995	USAR; Flint, MI 1968-1996	883d FA Bn	
3d Brigade, 70th Div	1968-1995	USAR; Fort Wayne, IN; Mobilized 1991	270th Engineer Bn	

Designation	Dates Active	Remarks	Other Designations	Nickname
4th Brigade, 70th Div	1968-1995	USAR; Indianapolis , IN 1968-1969; Camp Atterbury, IN 1969-1995	770th Ordnance Bn (205th Infantry Bde)	
1st Brigade, 75th Div	1993-present	USAR; Houston, TX; Simulations training		
2d Brigade, 75th Div	1993-present	USAR; Fort Sam Houston, TX; Exercise training		
3d Brigade, 75th Div	1993-present	USAR; Fort Worth, TX 1993-1999; Fort Riley, KS 1999-present; Exercise training		
4th Bde, 75th Div	1993-present	USAR; Oklahoma City, OK 1993-1999; Fort Sill, OK 1999-present; Exercise training	(479th FA Bde)	

Designation	Dates Active	Remarks	Other Designations	Nickname
5th Brigade, 75th Div	1993-present	USAR; Kansas City, KS; Exercise training		
1st Brigade, 76th Div	1968-1995	Portsmouth, NH 1968-1993; Saco, ME 1993-1995	HQS, 76th ID	
2d Brigade, 76th Div	1968-1996	USAR; Warwick, RI 1968-1973; East Windsor, CT 1973-1993; Lodi, NJ 1993-1996	901st FA Bn	
3d Brigade, 76th Div	1968-1973 1993-1995	USAR; East Hartford, CT 1968-1971; East Windsor, Ct 1971-1973; Red Bank, NJ 1993-1995	301st Engineer Bn	
4th Brigade, 76th Div	1968-1996	USAR; Providence, RI; Replaced by 98th Division Bde	776th Ordnance Bn	

Designation	Dates Active	Remarks	Other Designations	Nickname
1st Brigade, 77th ID	1963-1965	USAR; New York, NY	HQS Co, 77th ID	
2d Brigade, 77th ID	1963-1965	USAR; Bronx, NY	153d Infantry Bde (1917-1942)	
3d Brigade, 77th ID	1963-1965	USAR; Hampstead, NY	154th Infantry Bde (1917-1942)	
1st Brigade, 78th Div	1968-present	USAR; Fort Hancock, NJ 1968-1983; Red Bank, NJ 1983-1993; Camp Kilmer, Edison, NJ 1993-present; Simulation training	HQS Co, 78th ID	
2d Brigade, 78th Div	1968-present	USAR/AC; Lodi, NJ 1968-1993; Mobilized 1991; Fort Dix, NJ 1993-1999; Fort Drum, NY 1999-present; Exercise training/training support	903d FA Bn (174th Infantry Bde)	

Designation	Dates Active	Remarks	Other Designations	Nickname
3d Brigade, 78th Div	1968-1973 1993-2002	USAR/AC; Kearny, NJ 1968-1973; Fort Devens, MA 1993-2002; Exercise training/training support	303d Engineer Bn (3d Support Bde)	
4th Brigade, 78th Div	1968-present	USAR/AC; Nixon, NJ 1968-1975; Edison, NJ 1975-1992; Richmond, VA 1992-1999; Fort Bragg, NC 1999-present; Exercise training/training support	778th Ordnance Bn (189th Infantry Bde)	
5th Brigade, 78th Div	1993-present	USAR/AC; Baltimore, MD, 1993-1999; Fort Meade, MD 1999-present; Exercise training/training support	78th Committee Group (1968-1978) 78th Training Command (1978-1984) (15th Support Bde)	
6th Brigade, 78th Div	1993-1999	USAR; Oakdale, PA 1993-1994; Uniontown, PA 1994-1999; Exercise training		
7th Brigade, 78th Div	1993-1999	USAR; North Syracuse, NY 1994-1999; Exercise training		
8th Brigade, 78th Div	1993-1995	USAR; Fort Dix, NJ; Exercise training		

210

Designation	Dates Active	Remarks	Other Designations	Nickname
9th Brigade, 78th Div	1993-1995	USAR; Fort Dix, NJ; Exercise training		
1st Brigade, 80th Div	1968-1995 1996-present	USAR; Alexandria, VA 1968-1995; Fort Meade, MD 1996-present; MP OSUT	HQS Co, 80th ID	
2d Brigade, 80th Div	1968-present	USAR; Salem, VA; IET	905th FA Bn	
3d Brigade, 80th Div	1968-1973 1988-1995 1996-present	USAR; Richmond, VA 1968-1973; Charleston, WV 1988-1990; Big Chimney, WV 1990-1995; Harrisburg, PA 1996-present; Combat support MOS training	305th Engineer Bn	
4th Brigade, 80th Div	1968-present	USAR: Norfolk, VA 1968-1977; Fort Story, VA 1977-1996; Charleston, WV 1996-present; Combat service support MOS training	780th Ordnance Bn	

Designation	Dates Active	Remarks	Other Designations	Nickname
5th Brigade, 80th Div	1996-present	USAR; Wilmington, DE; Health services training		
6th Brigade, 80th Div	1996-present	USAR; Fort Belvoir, VA; Professional development training		
7th Brigade, 80th Div	1996-present	USAR; Salem, VA; Training support	80th Committee Group (1968-1978) 80th Training Command (1978-1984)	
8th Brigade, 80th Div	1996-present	USAR; SROTC; Provisional unit		
1st Brigade, 81st ID	1963-1965	USAR; Atlanta, GA	HQS Co, 81st ID	
2d Brigade, 81st ID	1963-1965	USAR; Athens, GA	161st Infantry Bde (1917-1942)	

Designation	Dates Active	Remarks	Other Designations	Nickname
3d Brigade, 81st ID	1963-1965	USAR; Nashville, TN	162d Infantry Bde (1917-1942)	
1st Brigade, 82d AB Div	1964-present	Fort Bragg, NC; Deployed to Dominican Republic 1965. Panama 1989-1990, SWA 1990-1991; Operation IRAQI FREEDOM 2004	Command and Control Bn, 82d AB D (1957-1964)	
2d Brigade, 82d AB Div	1964-present	Fort Bragg, NC; Deployed to Dominican Republic 1965, Grenada 1983, Panama 1989-1990, SWA 1990-1991; Operation IRAQI FREEDOM 2003-2004	155th Infantry Bde, 78th ID (1917-1942)	
3d Brigade, 82d AB Div	1964-present	Fort Bragg, NC; Deployed to Dominican Republic 1965, Grenada 1983, Panama 1989-1990, SWA 1990-1991; Separate brigade in Vietnam 1968-1969; Afghanistan 2002-2003; Operation IRAQI FREEDOM 2004	156th Infantry Bde, 78th ID (1917-1942)	The Golden Brigade
4th Brigade, 82d AB Div	1968-1969	Fort Bragg, NC; Replacement for 3d Bde while it was in Vietnam		

Designation	Dates Active	Remarks	Other Designations	Nickname
1st Brigade, 83d ID	1963-1965	USAR; Akron, OH	HQS Co, 83d ID	
2d Brigade, 83d ID	1963-1965	USAR; Columbus, OH	165th Infantry Bde (1917-1942)	
3d Brigade, 83d ID	1963-1965	USAR; Cincinnati, OH	166th Infantry Bde (1917-1942)	
1st Brigade, 84th Div	1968-present	USAR; Milwaukee, WI 1968-1993; Fort Sheridan, IL 1993-1996; Livonia, MI 1996-present; Infantry One Station Unit Trng (OSUT)	HQS Co, 84th ID	
2d Brigade, 84th Div	1968-present	USAR; Beaver Dam, WI; Basic Combat Trng	909th FA Bn	

214

Designation	Dates Active	Remarks	Other Designations	Nickname
3d Brigade, 84th Div 	1968-1995 1996-present	USAR; Milwaukee, WI 1968-1993; Fort McCoy, WI 1993; St Louis, MO 1993-1995; Fort Snelling (St Paul), MN 1996-present; Combat support MOS training	309th Engineer Bn	Timberwolf Brigade
4th Brigade, 84th Div 	1968-1995 1996-present	USAR; Milwaukee, WI 1968-1995; Indianapolis, IN 1996-present; Combat service support MOS training	784th Ordnance Bn	
5th Brigade, 84th Div 	1996-present	USAR; Milwaukee, WI; Health services training		
6th Brigade, 84th Div 	1996-present	USAR; Waukegan, IL; Professional development training		
7th Brigade, 84th Div 	1996-present	USAR; Milwaukee, WI; Training support	84th Committee Group (1968-1978) 84th Training Command (1978-1984)	

215

Designation	Dates Active	Remarks	Other Designations	Nickname
8th Brigade, 84th Div	2000-present	USAR; Milwaukee, WI; SROTC support; Provisional unit		
1st Brigade, 85th Div	1968-present	USAR; Waukegan, IL 1968-1992; Fort Sheridan, IL 1992-present; Simulations training	HQS Co, 85th ID	
2d Brigade, 85th Div	1968-present	USAR/AC; St Louis, MO 1968-1993; Fort McCoy, WI 1993-present; Exercise training support	910th FA Bn (12th Support Bde)	
3d Brigade, 85th Div	1968-present	USAR/AC; Des Plaines, IL 1968-1972; Arlington Heights, IL 1972-1992; Selfridge ANGB, MI 1992-present; Exercise training support	310th Engineer Bn	The Bayonet Brigade
4th Brigade, 85th Div	1968-1973 1993-present	USAR/AC; Chicago, Il 1968-1973; Fort Sheridan, Il 1993-present; Exercise training support	785th Ordnance Bn	

216

Designation	Dates Active	Remarks	Other Designations	Nickname
5th Brigade, 85th Div	1993-1999	USAR; Fort Snelling, MN; Exercise training	85th Committee Group (1968-1978) 85th Training Command (1978-1984)	
6th Brigade, 85th Div	1993-1999	USAR; Fort Benjamin Harrison, IN; Exercise training		
1st Brigade, 87th Div	1993-present	USAR; Birmingham, AL; Simulations training		
2d Brigade, 87th Div	1993-present	USAR/AC; Louisville, KY 1993-1999; Patrick AFB, FL 1999-present; Exercise training support	(158th Infantry Bde)	
3d Brigade, 87th Div	1993-present	USAR/AC; Jackson, MS 1993-1999; Camp Shelby, MS 1999-present; Exercise training support	(177th Armored Bde)	

Designation	Dates Active	Remarks	Other Designations	Nickname
4th Brigade, 87th Div	1993-present	USAR/AC; Fort Gillem, GA 1993-1999; Fort Stewart, GA 1999-present; Exercise training support	(188th Infantry Bde)	
5th Brigade, 87th Div	1999-present	USAR/AC; Fort Jackson, SC; Training support	(157th Infantry Bde)	
6th Brigade, 87th Div	1993-1999	USAR; Fort Buchanan, PR; Exercise training		
1st Brigade, 89th Div	1968-1975	Wichita, KS; Training	HQS Co, 89th ID	
2d Brigade, 89th Div	1968-1975	USAR; Denver, CO; Training	914th FA Bn	

Designation	Dates Active	Remarks	Other Designations	Nickname
3d Brigade, 89th Div	1968-1975	USAR; Lincoln, NE.; Training	314th Engineer Bn	

Designation	Dates Active	Remarks	Other Designations	Nickname
4th Brigade, 89th Div	1968-1975	USAR; Kansas City, KS; Training	789th Ordnance Bn	

Designation	Dates Active	Remarks	Other Designations	Nickname
1st Brigade, 90th ID	1963-1965	San Antonio, TX	179th Infantry Bde (1917-1942)	

Designation	Dates Active	Remarks	Other Designations	Nickname
2d Brigade, 90th ID	1963-1965	San Antonio, TX	180th Infantry Bde (1917-1942)	

Designation	Dates Active	Remarks	Other Designations	Nickname
3d Brigade, 90th ID	1963-1965	Dallas, TX	915th FA Bn	

219

Designation	Dates Active	Remarks	Other Designations	Nickname
1st Brigade, 91st Div	1968-present	USAR; Sacramento, CA 1968-1993; Camp Parks, Dublin, CA 1993-present; Simulations training	HQS Co, 91st ID	
2d Brigade, 91st Div	1968-present	USAR/AC; Hamilton AFB, CA 1968-1992; Norco, CA 1992-1999; Fort Carson, CO 1999-present; Exercise and training support	916th FA Bn	
3d Brigade, 91st Div	1968-1973 1984-present	USAR/AC; San Jose, CA 1968-1973; Marina, CA 1984-1992; Dublin, CA 1992-1999; Travis AFB, CA 1999-present; Exercise and training support	316th Engineer Bn (21st Support Bde)	
4th Brigade, 91st Div	1968-present	USAR/AC; Fort Cronkhite, CA 1968-1978; Presidio of SF 1978-1992; Tumwater, CA 1992-1996; Fort Lewis, WA 1996-present; Exercise training	791st Ordnance Bn	
5th Brigade, 91st Div	1996-192000	USAR; Salt Lake City, UT; Exercise training	91st Committee Group (1968-1978) 91st Training Command (1978-1984)	

220

Designation	Dates Active	Remarks	Other Designations	Nickname
6th Brigade, 91st Div	1996-2000	USAR; Denver, CO; Exercise training		
1st Brigade, 95th Div	1967-1995 1996-present	USAR; Tulsa, Ok 1967-1995; Lawton, OK 1996-present; Field Artillery One Station Unit Trng		
2d Brigade, 95th Div	1967-present	USAR; Lawton, OK 1967-1984; Norman, OK 1984-1997; Oklahoma City, OK 1997-present; Basic Combat Trng	920th FA Bn	
3d Brigade, 95th Div	1967-1995 1996-present	USAR; Oklahoma City, OK 1967-1975; Stillwater, OK 1975-1995; Broken Arrow OK, 1996-present; Combat support training	320th Engineer Bn	
4th Brigade, 95th Div	1967-present	USAR; Shreveport, LA 1967-1975; Bossier City, LA 1975-1995; Lafayette, LA 1995-1996; Dallas, TX, 1996-present; Combat service support training	795th Ordnance Bn	

221

Designation	Dates Active	Remarks	Other Designations	Nickname
5th Brigade, 95th Div	1996-present	USAR; San Antonio, TX; Health services training		
6th Brigade, 95th Div	1996-present	USAR; Topeka, KS; Professional development training		
7th Brigade, 95th Div	1996-present	USAR; North Little Rock, AR; Training support- basic combat training and engineer MOS training	95th Committee Group (1968-1978) 95th Training Command (1978-1984)	
8th Brigade, 95th Div	2000-present	USAR; Stillwater, OK; SROTC support; Provisional unit		
1st Brigade, 98th Div	1968-1995 1996-present	USAR; Schenectady, NY 1968-1995; Providence, RI 1996-present; Replaced 76th Division units 1996	HQS Co, 98th Div	

Designation	Dates Active	Remarks	Other Designations	Nickname
2d Brigade, 98th Div	1968-present	USAR; Buffalo, NY; Basic combat training support	923d FA Bn	
3d Brigade, 98th Div	1968-present	USAR; Ithaca, NY 1968-1993; Mattydale, NY 1993-1997 Bronx, NY 1997-present; Combat support MOS training	323d Engineer Bn	
4th Brigade, 98th Div	1968-1995 1996-present	USAR; Swornville, NY 1968-1970; Buffalo, NY 1970-1995; West Hartford, CT 1996-present; Replaced 1037th USARF School (Ft Devens); Combat service support MOS training	798th Ordnance Bn	
5th Brigade, 98th Div	1996-present	USAR; Fort Hamilton, NY; Health services training		
6th Brigade, 98th Div	1996-present	USAR; Mattydale, NY; Professional development training		

Designation	Dates Active	Remarks	Other Designations	Nickname
7th Brigade, 98th Div	1996-present	USAR; Rochester, NY; Training support- basic combat training and engineer MOS qualification	98th Committee Group (1968-1978) 98th Training command (1978-1984)	
8th Brigade, 98th Div	2000-present	USAR; West Hartford, CT; SROTC support; Provisional unit		
1st Brigade, 100th Div	1968-1995 1996-present	USAR; Lexington, KY; Mobilized 1991; Current mission: armor basic combat training	HQS Co, 100th ID	
2d Brigade, 100th Div	1968-present	USAR; Owensboro, Kentucky; Current mission: cavalry training	925th FA Bn	
3d Brigade, 100th Div	1968-1996 1996-present	USAR; Lexington, KY 1968-1996; Huntsville, AL 1996-present; Current mission: Cbt Spt training	325th Engineer Bn	

Designation	Dates Active	Remarks	Other Designations	Nickname
4th Brigade, 100th Div	1968-1973 1996-present	USAR; Louisville, KY 1968-1973; Montgomery, AL 1996-present; Current mission CSS training	800th Ordnance Bn	
5th Brigade, 100th Div	1996-present	USAR; Memphis, TN (1996-1997); Millington, TN (1997-present); Current mission health services training		
6th Brigade, 100th Div	1996-present	USAR; Louisville, KY; Current mission professional development training		
7th Brigade, 100th Div	1996-2000	USAR; Fort Knox, KY; Exercise brigade inactivated upon division's reorganization as a training support division	100th Committee Group (1968-1978) 100th Training command (1978-1984)	
1st Brigade, 101st AB Div	1964-present	Fort Campbell, KY 1964-1965; Vietnam 1965-1972; Separate brigade in Vietnam 1965-1967; Fort Campbell, KY 1972- present; air assault bde since 1968 (called airmobile until 1974); SWA 1990-1991; Haiti, 1995-1996; Operation IRAQI FREEDOM 2003-2004	HHC, Command and Control Bn, 101st AB D (1959-1964)	

Designation	Dates Active	Remarks	Other Designations	Nickname
2d Brigade, 101st AB Div	1964-present	Fort Campbell, KY 1964-1967; Vietnam 1967-1972; Fort Campbell, KY 1991-present; Fort Campbell, KY 1972- present; air assault bde since 1968 (called airmobile until 1974); SWA 1990-1991; Operation IRAQI FREEDOM 2003-2004	159th Infantry Bde (80th Div) (1917-1942)	
3d Brigade, 101st AB Div	1964-present	Fort Campbell, KY 1964-1967; Vietnam 1967-1972; Fort Campbell, KY 1972- present; replaced 173d AB Bde 1972; parachutist qualified 1972-1974; air assault bde since 1968 (called airmobile until 1974); SWA 1990-1991; Afghanistan 2002: Operation IRAQI FREEDOM 2003-2004	160th Infantry Bde (80th Div) (1917-1942)	
1st Brigade, 102d ID	1963-1965	USAR; St. Louis, MO	HQS Co, 102d ID (to 1959)	
2d Brigade, 102d ID	1963-1965	USAR; Quincy, IL	203d Infantry Bde (1921-1942)	
3d Brigade, 102d ID	1963-1965	USAR; Urbana, IL	204th Infantry Bde (1921-1942)	

226

Designation	Dates Active	Remarks	Other Designations	Nickname
1st Brigade, 104th Div	1968-present	USAR; Vancouver Barracks, WA; Current mission: basic combat training	HQS Co, 104th ID (before 1959)	
2d Brigade, 104th Div	1968-1995	USAR; Pasco, WA	929th FA Bn (before 1968)	
3d Brigade, 104th Div	1968-1995 1996-present	USAR; Fort Lawton, WA 1968-1989; Bothell, WA 1989-1993; Fort Lewis, WA 1993-1995; Vancouver Barracks, WA 1996-present; Current mission: combat support training	329th Engineer Bn (before 1968)	
4th Brigade, 104th Div	1968-present	USAR; Fort Lawton, WA 1968-1982; Fort Lewis, WA 1982-1993; Sacramento, CA 1993-1996; Camp Parks (Dublin), CA 1996-present; Current mission: combat service support training	804th Ordnance Bn (before 1968)	
5th Brigade, 104th Div	1996-present	USAR; Fort Douglas, UT; Health services training		

Designation	Dates Active	Remarks	Other Designations	Nickname
6th Brigade, 104th Div	1996-present	USAR; Aurora, CO; Current mission: USAR professional development (CGSC, CAS3); Replaced 5046th United States Army Reserves Forces School		
7th Brigade, 104th Div	1996-present	USAR: Fort Lewis, WA; Training support brigade	104th Committee Group (1968-1978) 108th Training Command (1978-1984)	
8th Brigade, 104th Div	2000-present	USAR; Fort Lewis, WA; SROTC support; Provisional unit		
4690th Brigade, 104th Div	1999-present	USAR; Fort Shafter, HI; Multifunctional training; Provisional unit	4690th USAR Forces School	
1st Brigade, 108th Div	1968-present	USAR; Clemson, SC (1968-1995); Spartanburg, SC (1995-present); Current mission: basic combat training	HQS Co, 108th ID (1946-1959)	

228

Designation	Dates Active	Remarks	Other Designations	Nickname
2d Brigade, 108th Div	1968-1995 1996-present	USAR; Hickory, NC (1968-1995); Garner, NC (1996-present); Current mission: basic combat training	507th FA Bn (before 1968)	
3d Brigade, 108th Div	1968-1995 1996-present	USAR; Charlotte, NC 1968-1980; Winston-Salem, NC 1980-1995; Fort Jackson, SC 1996-present; Current mission:combat support training	235th Engineer Bn (before 1967)	
4th Brigade, 108th Div	1968-1996 1996-present	USAR: Raleigh, NC 1968-1978; Garner, NC 1978-1996; Decatur, GA 1996-present; Current mission: combat service support training		
5th Brigade, 108th Div	1996-present	USAR; Jacksonville, FL; Health Services training		
6th Brigade, 108th Div	1996-present	USAR; Charlotte, NC (1996); Concord, NC (2002); Officer Educational System/ NCO Educational System support		

Designation	Dates Active	Remarks	Other Designations	Nickname
7th Brigade, 108th Div	1996-present	USAR; Fort Jackson, SC; Training support	108th Committee Group (1967-1978) 108th Training Command (1978-1984)	

Designation	Dates Active	Remarks	Other Designations	Nickname
8th Brigade, 108th Div	2000-present	USAR; Puerto Rico; Multifunctional training		

Designation	Dates Active	Remarks	Other Designations	Nickname
9th Brigade, 108th Div	2000-present	USAR; SROTC support; Provisional unit		

Designation	Dates Active	Remarks	Other Designations	Nickname
Separate Brigades				
Berlin Brigade	1961-1994	TDA [i.e. administrative] unit 1961-1983; West Berlin, Germany		
1st Infantry Brigade	1958-1962	Fort Benning, GA; Replaced by 197th Infantry Bde	See 1st Bde, 1st ID	
2d Infantry Brigade	1958-1962	Fort Devens, MA; Replaced by 2d Bde, 5th ID	See 2d Bde, 1st ID	
5th Brigade (Training)	1975-1994	USAR armor training brigade in Lincoln, Nebraska; Converted from former 5th Armor Group (1954-1956), descended from 5th ACR (1951-1954) and 5th Tank Destroyer Group (1942-1945)		
6th Cavalry Brigade (Air Combat)	1975-present	Air cavalry attack brigade created as a separate brigade from assets of the 1st Cavalry Division (TRICAP)'s 2d Brigade; Transferred from Fort Hood to Korea in 1996		

Designation	Dates Active	Remarks	Other Designations	Nickname
11th Infantry Brigade (Light)	1966-1971	Activated in Hawaii with number of old 6th ID brigade as the 6th was projected to be activated next; Sent to Vietnam (1967) and became part of American Division.	1st Bde, 6th ID (current)	
21st Cavalry Brigade (Air Combat)	1984-present	Fort Hood, TX	AH-1964 Task Force HQs, 6th Cavalry Bde (1984-1985) Apache Training Bde (1985-1991) US Army Combat Aviation Training Bde (1992-1996)	
26th Infantry Brigade	1993-1995	CT/MA ARNG; see 26th Bde, 29th ID (L); Springfield, MA; designated after former 26th ID	26th Infantry Div 3d Bde, 26th ID 26th Bde, 29th ID (L) (1995-present)	Yankee
27th Infantry Brigade	1986-present	NY ARNG; former 27th ID (NY ARNG); Roundout brigade for 10th Mountain Div (1986-1992); Enhanced brigade 1996; designated after former 27th ID/AD; slated to lose enhanced status in 2006	27th Infantry Div (1917-1955) 27th Armored Div (1955-1968) 27th Bde, 50th AD (1968-1975) 27th Bde, 42d ID (1975-1986)	Empire
29th Infantry Brigade	1959-present	HI ARNG/USAR; Organized as a Pentomic brigade; Reorganized as a ROAD brigade 1963; Mobilized 1968-1969; Roundout for 25th ID 1973-1985; Enhanced brigade 1996; Honolulu, HI		
30th Armored Brigade	1973-1997	TN ARNG; Became 230th Spt Gp; designated after former 30th AD; Jackson, TN	3d Bde, 30th AD HQs, 30th ID (Tenn part) (before 1973)	Volunteers

Designation	Dates Active	Remarks	Other Designations	Nickname
30th Infantry Brigade (Mech)	1973-present	NC ARNG; Enhanced brigade 1996; Under 24th ID (M) headquarters 1999; designated after former 30th ID; Clinton, NC; Operation IRAQI FREEDOM 2004 (attached to 1st ID (M))	HQs, 30th ID (NC part) (before 1973)	Old Hickory
31st Armored Brigade	1973-2001	AL ARNG; Became 31st Chemical Bde; Tuscaloosa, AL 1973-1979; Northport, AL 1979-2001; designated after former 31st ID	31st Infantry Div (1917-1968) 31st Bde, 30th Armored Div (1968-1973)	Dixie
32d Infantry Brigade	1967-1997 2001-present	WI ARNG; Became mechanized in 1971; designated after former 32d ID; Milwaukee, WI; slated to gain enhanced status in 2006	32d Infantry Div 32d Bde, 34th ID (1997-present)	Red Arrow
36th Infantry Brigade	1968-1980	TX ARNG; Disbanded 1980; Reconstituted as a divisional element 1988; patch with star was authorized 1968-1973, but never worn (authorized for 36th Bde but unit was called 71st then); Houston, TX	36th Infantry Div (1917-1968) 71st Airborne Bde (1968-1973) 36th Airborne Bde (1973-1980) 36th Bde, 50th Armored Div (1988-1992) 36th Bde, 49th Armored Div (1992-present)	Arrowhead
39th Infantry Brigade	1967-present	AR ARNG; Enhanced brigade 1996; Under 7th ID headquarters 1999; Little Rock, AR; Operation IRAQI FREEDOM 2004 (attached to 1st CD)	39th Infantry Div (1917-1967) 39th ID Artillery (Arkansas part] (1946-1967)	Arkansas Brigade

Designation	Dates Active	Remarks	Other Designations	Nickname
40th Armored Brigade	1968-1974	CA ARNG; Los Angeles, CA	40th Infantry Div (1917-1954; 1974-present) 40th Armored Div (1954-1968)	
40th Infantry Brigade	1968-1974	CA ARNG; Became elements of the 40th ID;		
41st Infantry Brigade	1968-present	OR ARNG; Roundout 7th ID 1977-1984; Enhanced brigade 1996; Under 7th ID headquarters 1999; Portland, OR	41st Infantry Div (1917-1968)	
45th Infantry Brigade	1968-present	OK ARNG; Enhanced brigade 1996; Under 7th ID headquarters 1999; Edmond, Ok 1969-1996; Oklahoma City, OK 1996-present	45th Infantry Div (1920-1968)	Thunderbird
48th Infantry Brigade (Mech)	1968-present	GA ARNG; Roundout 24th ID (M) 1975-1992; Mobilized 1990-191; Enhanced brigade 1996; Under 24th ID (M) headquarters, 1999; Macon, GA	59th Infantry Bde, 30th ID (1922-1942) 121st Infantry, 48th ID (1946-1955) CCB, 48th Armored Div (1955-1963) 1st Bde, 48th Armd Div (1963-1968)	Gray Bonnets

Designation	Dates Active	Remarks	Other Designations	Nickname
49th Armored Brigade	1971-1973	TX ARNG; Fort Worth, TX	CCA, 49th Armored Div (1946-1961) 49th Armor Group (1968-1971) 2d Bde, 49th Armored Div (1961-1968; 1973-present)	
53d Infantry Brigade	1968-present	FL ARNG; Enhanced brigade 1996; Tampa, FL; Operation IRAQI FREEDOM 2003-2004	HQs, 51st ID (Florida part) (1946-1963) 53d Armored Bde (1964-1968)	
58th Infantry Bde	1975-1985	MD ARNG; Baltimore, MD	3d Bde, 29th ID (1963-1968) 3d Bde, 28th ID (1968-1971) 58th Bde, 28th ID (1971-1975) 3d Bde, 29th ID (L) (1985-present)	
69th Infantry Bde	1963-1984	KS ARNG; Mobilized and attached to 5th ID (M), Fort Polk, LA, 1968-1969, replacing the division's 1st Bde, stationed in Vietnam; Replaced by 4th Bde, 5th ID Dec 69; Converted to HQs, 35th ID 1984; Topeka, KS		
72d Infantry Bde (Mech)	1968-1973	TX ARNG; Dallas, TX	3d Bde, 49th Armored Div (1963-1968; after 1973)	

Designation	Dates Active	Remarks	Other Designations	Nickname
76th Infantry Brigade (Light)	1994-present	IN ARNG; Enhanced brigade 1996; Indianapolis, IN; Bosnia 2001: Operation IRAQI FREEDOM 2003-2004	1st Bde, 38th ID (1963-1994) 76th Bde, 38th ID (1965-1994)	
81st Infantry Brigade (Mech)	1968-present	WA ARNG; Roundout to the 9th ID (1988-1991); Enhanced brigade 1996; Seattle, WA; Operation IRAQI FREEDOM 2004	HQS, 41st ID (Washington part) (1917-1968)	
86th Armored Brigade	1964-1968	VT ARNG; Montpelier, VT	86th Infantry Bde (1963-194) 86th Bde, 50th Armored Div (1968-1988) 86th Bde, 26th ID (1988-1993) 86th Bde, 42d ID (1993-present)	Vermont Brigade
92d Infantry Brigade	1959-present	PR ARNG; Pentomic 1959-1963; San Juan, PR		
116th Cavalry Brigade	1989-present	ID ARNG; Enhanced brigade 1996; designation from 116th Cavalry Regiment (ID ARNG); Actually a mechanized infantry brigade in organization; Boise, ID; Roundout 4th ID 1989-1996; Operation IRAQI FREEDOM 2004-2005		

Designation	Dates Active	Remarks	Other Designations	Nickname
116th Infantry Brigade	1975-1985	VA ARNG; Staunton, VA; designation comes from old 116th Infantry regimental headquarters	2d Bde, 29th ID (1963-1968) 116th Bde, 28th ID (1971-1975) 1st Bde, 29th ID (L) (1986-present)	Stonewall Brigade
149th Armored Brigade	1980-1984	KY ARNG; Bowling Green,/Louisville, KY; Became part of 35th ID; designation comes from former 149th Infantry		
155th Armored Brigade	1973-present	MS ARNG; Roundout brigade 1st Cavalry Div 1984-1991; Mobilized 1990-1991; Enhanced brigade 1996; Tupelo, MS	108th ACR 1st Bde, 30th AD (1968-1973)	
157th Infantry Brigade (Mech)	1963-1995	USAR brigade in Pennsylvania; designation from former 79th Division Bde; Created from excess USAR personnel after inact of 79th ID (USAR); Upper Darby, PA 1963-1968; Horsham, PA 1968-1995		
171st Infantry Brigade	1963-1972	Stationed in Alaska; Designation from former 86th Division Bde		

Designation	Dates Active	Remarks	Other Designations	Nickname
172d Infantry Brigade 	1963-1986 1998-present	Stationed in Alaska; Replaced by 6th ID (L) 1986; designation from former 86th ID Bde; Replaced 1st Bde, 6th ID; Stryker Bde 2000		
173d Airborne Brigade 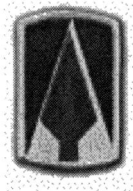	1963-1972 2002-present	Activated in Okinawa and deployed to Vietnam (1965-1971); Inactivated at Fort Campbell, 1972; Reactivated in northern Italy 2000; 2d maneuver battalion added 2002; designation from former 87th ID bde; Operation IRAQI FREEDOM 2003-2004		
177th Armored Brigade 	1991-1994	OPFOR brigade, Fort Irwin; designation from former 89th ID bde; Replaced by 11th ACR; designation briefly used by USAR/AC training support brigade in 1999		
187th Infantry Brigade	1963-1994	USAR brigade in New England; designation from former 94th ID bde; Created from excess USAR personnel after inactivation of 94th ID (USAR); Boston, MA 1963-1971; Wollaston, MA 1971-1976; Fort Devens, MA 1976-1994		
191st Infantry Brigade	1963-1968	USAR bde in Montana, Arizona; designation from former 96th Division Bde; Created from excess USAR personnel after inact of 96th ID (USAR); Helena, MT		

Designation	Dates Active	Remarks	Other Designations	Nickname
193d Infantry Brigade	1962-1994	Panama; designation from former 97th Division bde; Reorg as light infantry 1985		
194th Armored Brigade	1962-1995	Fort Knox; designation from former 97th Division bde		
196th Infantry Brigade (Light)	1965-1972 1998-present	Replaced 2d Bde, 5th ID at Fort Devens; Originally designated to deploy to Dominican Republic, instead went to Vietnam (1966) and attached to American Division; Separate again 1971-1972; designation from former 98th Division Bde; Reactivated 1998 to serve as AC/RC training support element for Hawaii, Alaska and the Pacific area		
197th Infantry Brigade	1962-1991	Replaced 1st Infantry Bde at Fort Benning; Converted to mechanized 1984; Attached to 24th ID (M) for DESERT STORM; 1991; Inactivated 1991 and replaced by new 3d Bde, 24th ID; designation from former 99th Division Bde		
198th Infantry Brigade	1967-1971	Activated at Fort Hood and deployed to Vietnam (1967), where attached to American Div; designation from former 99th Division Bde		

Designation	Dates Active	Remarks	Other Designations	Nickname
199th Infantry Brigade	1966-1970 1991-1992	Activated at Fort Benning; Deployed to Vietnam (1966); designation from former 100th Division Bde; Reactivated at Fort Lewis to replace 3d Brigade, 9th ID; Transferred to Fort Polk, LA, and replaced by 2d ACR		
205th Infantry Brigade	1963-1994	USAR brigade in Minnesota and Iowa; designation from former 103d Division Bde; Created from personnel of inact 103d ID (USAR); Roundout unit to 6th ID (L) 1985-1994; Fort Snelling, MN		
218th Infantry Brigade (Mech)	1974-present	SC ARNG; former 2d Bde, 30th ID; Roundout brigade for 1st ID (M) 1991-1996; Enhanced brigade 1996; Under 24th ID (M) headquarters, 1999; Newberry, SC	2d Bde, 30th ID (1968-1974)	
256th Infantry Brigade	1967-present	LA ARNG; Roundout brigade for 5th ID (M) 1975-1992; Converted to mechanized 1977; Mobilized 1990-1991; Roundout 2d AD 1992-1996; Enhanced brigade 1996; Lafayette, LA	1st Bde, 39th ID (1961-1967)	Louisiana Brigade
402d Brigade (Training)	1985-1996	USAR Artillery training brigade at Fort Sill; Part of 95th Div (Trng)		

Lightning Source UK Ltd.
Milton Keynes UK
UKOW012337170512

192729UK00009B/14/P